Essays on Politics and Literature

By the same author

The American Science of Politics
In Defence of Politics
The Reform of Parliament
Basic Forms of Government: A Sketch and a Model
Political Theory and Practice
Crime, Rape and Gin: Reflections on Contemporary Attitudes
to Violence, Pornography and Addiction
With Derek Heater: Essays on Political Education
With Alex Porter: Political Education and Political Literacy
George Orwell: A Life
Socialist Values and Time
With David Blunkett: Labour's Values: An Unofficial Statement
With Tom Crick: What is Politics?
Socialism

Essays on
Politics and Literature

BERNARD CRICK

EDINBURGH UNIVERSITY PRESS

P N
3352
P6
C74
1989

© Bernard Crick 1989
Edinburgh University Press
22 George Square, Edinburgh

Set in Itek Times Roman
by Waverley Graphics,
Edinburgh, and
printed in Great Britain by
Redwood Press Limited,
Trowbridge, Wilts

British Library Cataloguing
   in Publication Data
Crick, Bernard *1929*
Essays on politics and
   literature.
1. English literature, to 1988.
   Special themes.
Politics. Critical studies
I. Title
820.8'0358

ISBN 0 85224 621 8
ISBN 0 7486 0105 8 pbk

Contents

Preface

One feels that a volume of mixed essays needs some excuse. Nowadays it is most often monographs or novels or nothing. But I enjoy both occasional writing and more considered essays, and try to put a lot of thought into both. Contrary to the advice I used to give students, about thinking it all out before beginning to write an essay, I usually can only think in the act of writing—but then there is always re-writing. Good political writing is no different from any other creative and critical writing in that respect. Also thought itself is often better represented and runs more freely in speculative essays than in heavily constructed or even hedged conclusions. Critical argument deserves a wider public than the purely academic, or rather academics should try to reach out as well as in: and when one tries to reach out, disciplinary boundaries become hard to observe even if one attached much respect to them in the first place. I am afraid I never have. I always had a sense of being or of wanting to be in a university community more than a department. That is why I respected LSE, who first employed me, but never liked it as much as University College London where I was an undergraduate with friends all over the shop. And that is why I enjoyed writing about Orwell so much and about theatre when a cynical or sensible editor of the *Times Higher Education Supplement*, Mr Brian MacCarthy (not the present serious fellow), asked me 'to write', primarily, I soon gathered, to fill a big page and was surprised but tolerant when I chose to do so on my real love, theatre. I can answer the question 'if you had your life over again . . .?'

I could confess to a *slight* boredom with the academic study of politics by which I earned my bread for many years, and this partly led to me early retirement; but the boredom was decently concealed and to elaborate now might damage a companion volume shortly to follow this, *Political Thoughts and Polemics*. So I prefer to say that the essays here are those in which I found the

mantle of 'Professor of Politics' too restrictive. But if Pol. Sci. can
be narrow, so too can academic Eng. Lit., to judge by a few who
reacted to my *George Orwell: a Life* by not merely hinting but *saying*
that I was a 'political scientist' and therefore, they implied, ill-
equipped, incompetent, insensitive, crass, and wickedly perverse
to cross a sanctified line of craft demarcation. To be honest, I
found some of them just as politically literate as they stereotyped
political scientists as culturally illiterate, say 'philistine'. They
seemed not to have heard of 'Politics' in the Aristotelean sense of
free speculation and analysis about the conflicts of interests and
values inherent in the human condition, but only of politics as
either instrumental immediate commitments or the empirical
study of elections. American academic reviewers were generally
much more generous. Most of these plainly thought of themselves
as 'general intellectuals' ('by analogy to "General Domestics",' as
Isaiah Berlin once put it) rather than subject specialists and
academic *Grenzpolizei* (border-guards). That is part cause and part
effect of the wider liberal education that good American
universities give compared to our obsessive specialisation. The
joke is that *real* political scientists would not welcome my being
called such without severe reservations. My first book was, in fact,
an attack on the idea that politics should and can be studied
scientifically. But we political philosophers are a much misunderstood and forgotten tribe today: sincere opinion rules, psychological assertion rather than philosophical reasoning and judgement. But most of us political thinkers are literate, work with texts
and some of us are aware that thoughtful people more often
encounter political ideas both as speculation and as analysis
(more interesting than polemic, however sincere and theatrical) in
novels and plays than in disciplinary monographs.

BRC
Edinburgh, April 1988

Acknowledgements

For permission to reproduce here material that has previously appeared in their journals, I thank the editors of *Biography, The Critical Quarterly, Granta, The Listener, The New Review, The Partisan Review, The Political Quarterly* and *The Times Higher Education Supplement;* and I similarly thank BBC Publications, the Cambridge University Press, the University of Georgia Press, Macmillan, Robson Books and the National Theatre.

In compiling many of these essays and reviews I was helped greatly while at Birkbeck College by Audrey Coppard.

I would not so much dedicate this book to my son, Oliver—that sounds so formal—as hope that, as an actor, entertainer and mime, he will enjoy it.

Foreword

What attracts me most in Bernard Crick's essays is the speaking voice. In an age when academics write more and more for fellow-specialists in a de-natured professional jargon, it is refreshing to find an academic (even a retired one) using the English language with unostentatious elegance to discuss, present, argue or meditate. These essays show a combination of humane intelligence, wide-ranging curiosity and precise knowledge in a variety of fields. They also show wit and humour and a rather appealing kind of wry egotism which manages to parade the self without glorifying it. And most of all, they show an ability to cross the boundaries set artificially by the rigidities of our academic structure. (I might add, in the Crickean vein of personal interpolation, that we invented a new curriculum-structure at the University of Sussex in 1961 precisely in order to remove those rigidities and make this kind of discourse more possible.)

Professor Crick is of course known as the biographer of George Orwell, and his sympathetic understanding of that remarkable writer shows through in much of his writing on other subjects as well as in the five illuminating essays on Orwell that form a central part of this book. He shares Orwell's feeling for unpretentious lucidity in his use of English as well as his general approach to politics and society. But the tone of reasoned argument is his own. One can disagree with some of the points he makes—as indeed I do—without feeling outraged or bullied, for this is a man voicing considered but sometimes tentative views in a conversational manner, almost tempting us to reply (as F.R. Leavis said one critic's reply to another ought to be, though it was something he never put into practice himself) with a 'Yes, but—'.

The intelligent general reader, if such a person is not an invention of reviewers, will relish this book. It entertains as well as informs (and provokes). This surely is a primary function of the essay, a literary form which is here given new life.

DAVID DAICHES

One

Literature and Politics

Originally in *The Critical Quarterly*, vol. 22, no. 2, (Summer 1980) and a revised version was given as the Hannah Arendt Memorial Lecture at the University of Southampton 1983.

If one set a group of good students an essay with this title, one might anticipate any or all of these interpretations: (i) the antipathy of the two concepts; (ii) their necessary interdependence; (iii) the duty of writers to commit themselves; (iv) the duty of writers not to commit themselves; (v) the influence of politics in writers; (vi) the influence of writers on politics; (vii) the clash of censorship and free expression; (viii) the control and use of writers by the state in other countries than our own; (ix) examples of good and bad political writing; (x) a case for the privatisation of public libraries; (xi) a demand for subsidies for unsuccessful writers; and (xii) a demonstration (granted certain theoretical premises) that Literature is a bourgeois concept and that the novel has a special role in maintaining the class system. There could be other angles. There are more than seven types of ambiguity. And as is said of the Irish problem, every time a solution is offered the question is changed. But Professor Flowers comes to help us all; he is general editor of a recent series of short books with the general title 'Writers and Politics': J.A. Morris, *Writers and Politics in Modern Britain.* C.E. Williams, *Writers and Politics in Modern Germany.* J.E. Flower, *Writers and Politics in Modern France.* John Gatt-Rutter, *Writers and Politics in Modern Italy.* Janet Mawby, *Writers and Politics in Modern Scandanavia.* J. Butt, *Writers and Politics in Modern Spain,* all published by Hodder and Stoughton, 1977-9.

What the series is not about is at least clear. It is not about the sociology of literature, which is a welcome change. Long before the *Frankfurt Schule* and the epochal birth of the Hungarian trimmer, George Lukacs, even before the coming of Raymond Williams to Cambridge, German students of Shakespeare in the 1900s used to learn all about the social composition of the audience at the Globe, who looked after the horses and when oranges were first sold in English theatres, long before they came to read the texts for themselves, still less to deconstruct them.

1

There is thus both an empiricist and a theoretical version of the sociology of literature. So much of it happens to be badly written, in itself an odd tribute to literature: full of neologisms, long-winded, psuedo-technical and with a monstrous proportion of fat to lean. Now it is perfectly proper and sometimes quite fruitful to study the degree to which forms of expression or ideas of any kind are *conditioned* by circumstances, particularly those associated with the economy or social class. But it is foolish to think that works of art and ideas are *caused* by objective or external factors alone, can thus be explained, indeed usually explained away.

The *Writers and Politics* series is concerned with literary values and only incidentally, Professor Flowers makes clear, 'with an examination of political ideas *per se* in various works of literature, or with an assessment of the ways in which parties and movements have controlled and used to the best advantage writers and intellectuals who claim political allegiance.' But not all his authors have chosen to or been able to avoid this second question, one which involves both matters of fact and of political theory. For Nazi Germany, as in Russia at least before *Glasnost,* the questions of the control of writers inevitably dominates both the subject matter and the form of literature. And the temptation is obvious to over-value as literature the writings of men and women who cannot be praised too highly for their courage and love of liberty in writing freely at all in face of persecution. Even in climates less cold, say in Britain, France and the U.S.A. of the 1930s, it was possible for the passion and sincerity of committed writers to have gained them an exaggerated reputation for literary merit, and without much compensatory originality in either political influence or original political thinking. The philistinism of so many politicians and, alas, social scientists can at least be matched by the political illiteracy of so many famous writers (or should I say naivete, ignorance and wilfulness?). As David Caute has shown explicitly in his study *The Fellow Travellers* and as emerges implicitly in Valentine Cunningham's monumental *British Writers of the Thirties,* famous names were used by party hardmen, but the owners of the names had no demonstrable influence over them. And the same was true for Picasso and Sartre in France, let alone minor figures like Spender and C. Day Lewis in Britain.

Yet Professor Flower's attempt to exclude 'political ideas *per se*' from critical consideration is more debatable and, if not impossible in principle, certainly self-defeating in any cultural critique. Is not political thinking as distinctive a part of our culture as the novel or drama? Is not freedom itself basic to any kind of true scholarship and critical inquiry? And while poets may not be, in Shelley's words, 'the unacknowledged legislators of the world', nor yet have any bardic insight into esoteric knowledge or Gnostic mysteries, if indeed poetry is mainly and happily for 'contemplation and delight' (as Michael Oakeshott argued in his *The Voice of Poetry in the Conversation of Mankind*), yet both the intellectual historian and the political philosopher have a proper interest in the political concepts used by any good writer. Such studies may or may not detract from appreciation of literary writings 'as works of art'; it depends how well and sensitively they are done. Political philosophers in the British tradition are now a days nearly all analytical and discriminatory, but literary critics often coarsely confuse them with sociologists whose approach to literature is all too often generalising and reductionist. Spontaneous reactive defence of disciplinary territory is both unnecessary and uncharitable (anyway, very academic and unintellectual). Need it be said that all academics are not intellectuals, and that no discipline has a monopoly of intellectualism? That Thomas Hobbes' masterpiece of baroque prose *Leviathan* is not in the canon of English Literature, never appears as a set book, is as odd as that Conrad's *Nostromo,* Koestler's *Darkness at Noon* and Orwell's *Nineteen Eighty-Four* seldom appear as set books for political theory. Some contemporary political theory happens to have literary merit. Cries of 'rude poacher' or 'insensitive intruder' are not raised when Sir Isaiah Berlin leaps from Hegel to Tolstoy, or from Vico to Pushkin, nor if he were to link George Eliot with Jeremy Bentham.

The troubles of contemporary political philosophers are of a contrary nature, not bad writing and lack of literary sensibility but an excessive internalisation of debate, the temptations and pressures to write only for each other; and the consequent decline, which Hannah Arendt bewailed, of the great Western tradition of political thinking as a cultural and public activity (what some have called 'public philosophy'), the critique and explication of political concepts wherever they occur: in parliaments and in the Press as well as in learned journals and monographs. Certainly some poets too seek only to reach other poets, novelists novelists and philosophers philosophers; but the dangers are of too much introvertion, certainly of a cult of introvertion, and lack of progeny and lack of public influence precisely from those who have something unusual and usually unpopular to say. Culturally it is always a matter of balance. Some political philosophers still try to address themselves to public questions and real problems, others are still preoccupied with the very possibility and meaningfulness of political philosophy and write only about each others' work.

And some critics of literature write only theories of criticism and about other critics, rarely if ever about actual works of literature.

Both tribes neglect the necessary mainstay of our civilisation, the general educated reader. Literary critics in the Press are viewed in as dim a light by critics of literature in the Academy as are political journalists by political thinkers. Often, of course, they deserve disparagements: but not necessarily so. Each academic vocation, however, needs the intelligent and honest publicist as well as the pure scholar. (Best of all, we each need to be both). Too rarely do students of politics offer a serious critique of the political concepts found in literature, or (more surprisingly) even of the general concepts used by practical politicians in their habitual rhetoric (self-deceiving ever that they are purely practical persons and not stuffed to the ears with unexamined abstractions like 'sovereignty', 'community' and 'national security'—what R.G. Collingwood called 'presuppositions' and Oliver Wendell Holmes 'inarticulate major premises'). And only a few students of literature have risked studying politics as discourse. The best writing of any kind about the human condition can make our contemporary university disciplines look petty-minded, obsessed with territorial imperatives, boundary disputes and kinship taboos. Too many academics write as if drawing distinctions precludes reaching conclusions. 'Only connect', said E.M. Forster; indeed.

Now I am well aware of that students of literature have had cause to be nervous of social scientists plundering the golden treasury, often for partisan purposes heavily disguised as science. But need they be as nervous of political philosophers moving from discussing Rawls on justice and Nozick on Rawls, and Barry on Nozick on Rawls, into, say, George Eliot's *Middlemarch*, Melville's *Billy Budd*, Dan Jacobsen's *The Rape of Tamar*, or William Golding's *Rites of Passage*, all of which novels contain subtle and profound discussions of the meanings and dilemmas of justice? Some novelists discuss little else than the nature of freedom and others endless debate justifications of violence, and so are especially tempting to interdisciplinary raiding parties. Be cautious but not nervous, remember that we political thinkers also earn our bread and butter in the academy by trying to teach the reading of complex texts. We too are professionally aware of the interdependence of form and content, of structure and meaning. Only in extreme cases can what a writer has put together be sundered by ink-stained scholars. Even Shakespeare is never quite destroyed by premature exposure to the Third and Fourth Forms. The French habit of printing commentaries *after* a text, not introductions *before*, seems to me an admirable if idealistic gesture, pointing to the right relationship between criticism and literature, especially for political writing. We do need to put the text in its context; but only when we have read the text.

No one, however, can talk about everything at once. So it is both salutary and sensible to find students of literature (as in this series under review) examining writers who are ordinarily seen as political writers for the effect that politics had on their writing. When social scientists try to do this, gross mistakes can, indeed, be made; taking one text as typical of a whole *oeuvre*, for instance. Conrad wrote other things than *Under Western Eyes* and *Nostromo*. I once encountered a whole class of students to whom Henry James was only *Princess Casamassima* and *The Bostonians*. And what do you know of Orwell who only *Nineteen Eighty-Four* know? Alien poachers often shoot the wrong sort of game. As Professor Flower says:

> It is fair to say that the majority of critics have concentrated more on *what* ideas are expressed than on *how* they have been. In addition therefore to attempting to define the concept of political literature more precisely and the exploring such issues as the suitability of imaginative literature as a vehicle for political ideas or the effect such literature can have on the public for example, one of the principle concerns of these essays is to attempt to examine ways in which an author's political sympathy or affiliation can be seen to affect or even dictate the way in which he writes.

Notice that his delimitation is a double one. There is the salutary stress on the 'how?' rather than the 'what?' question. But there is also the limitation of only studying political writers with 'political sympathy or affiliation', which in fact means, judging by the authors studies in these books, explicitly and self-consciously 'committed writers'. This is an unfortunate limitation, though one that the editor takes for granted, assumes without argument. But it is equally interesting to study how apparently non-political writers react to politics, either because it is thrust upon them or because they make political incidents or dilemmas part of the plot or tale of their novel or play. Flower's limitation leads to the paradoxical result that both Stendal (in his own volume) and Conrad (in D.J.A. Morris's) are not allowed onto the pitch. Nor, to give an extreme example, is there even a passing reference to to Proust's profound characterisation of the Dreyfus affair and of the parallels he draws, throughout almost the whole of one volume, between the political malaise of France and the pathology of his main characters. Now, of course, no one would dream of calling Proust a 'political novelist', nor Henry James neither—although with Stendal and Conrad the description is far from absurd. But they all had profound things to say not merely about contingent incidents but about the very nature of political life; yet because their writing is not politically motivated nor dominated by political 'sympathy or affiliation', out they go! This is to throw away the better half of the game: it is not merely to put an aesthetic fence around 'Literature' but is to label 'politics' as mainly a matter of sympathies, affiliations and, above all else, commitment. It actually debases politics by ignoring the speculative, reasoning, analytical tradition of Western political thinking—nowadays often found embedded in the apparently non-political novel, and more accessible there, hence possibly more influential, than in pamphlets, polemics, manifestoes and academic monographs.

The best understanding of politics rarely comes from committed writers. Political correspondents and columnists, for instance, may often know more about politics and have better political judgement than the politicians. Spectators do see more of the play than the players: critical judgement (as Kant argued) begins with empathy but must end with distancing. Similarly the sense of political dilemma, indeed the specifically Machiavelliam dilemma of doing evil for the sake of peace, law and order, is profound in John Arden's complex *Armstrong's Last Night* and lacking in his later, lively but simple-minded propaganda plays. (As I will argue in another essay, not merely does much drama that labels itself 'political', 'committed' or 'alternative' have a shallow and debassed view of politics, but it often misses what the uncommitted Shakespeare never missed, the essentially dramatic nature of true political dilemmas and real alternatives. What if the true heir (Richard/Hamlet) is less fit to rule than the usurping predator (Bolingbroke/Claudius)?

For though the one can lead to the other, political thinking and political activity are different things. Political thinking arose from Greek and Roman culture precisely because there was an awareness that not merely are actual states governed according to very different principles, but that in all complex societies different groups hold different values and interests. So each state could have alternative ways of attending to its political arrangements. In all societies, groups contest for hegemony. But hegemony is a relative term and a writer need not be a protagonist to make just such conflicts of right and wrong one of his or her major themes. Indeed Camus found himself torn by Algeria, as in a tragedy, between what he saw, when every other intellectual was taking sides, as the equal plausibility of two incompatible views of right:

that of the French *colons* and that of the Arab rebels. My own reaction to Nationalist and Unionist in Northern Ireland is similar; but who now would dare write about black and white in South Africa or Israel in Palestine in the manner of Camus on Algeria? It would take rare moral courage as well as great insight and dispassion. (Conor Cruise O'Brien tried, but his courage was only the conventional courage or pugnacity of taking sides strongly). Much political debate is close to the dynamic of much drama: the conflict of character and circumstance. The very nature of political debate, especially when conducted in assemblies, often takes on a public and a dramatic form. No wonder many writers have made use of political debate for the purposes of literature, leaving all questions of commitment aside. But if *Writers in Britain* had ranged through all space and time, Professor Flower's ground rules would have excluded Shakespeare. Not enough for him to have laid bare profound and basic problems of political obligation in the Histories, the Roman plays and in *Hamlet*. He would have to have shown his credentials as a committed activist to the selection committee.

As a political writer I've got a short fuse when it is suggested by literary critics that politics is little more than the 'world of telegrams and anger', of sympathies, allegiances, affiliations and commitments; or of valueing things, as Lionel Trilling showed, simply because they are widely and democratically believed in, are 'sincere' or are, finally and awfully, 'authentic'—rather than because, say, they are true, humane or sensible. It is surpassing odd for scholars to elevate authenticity over reason.

Dr Morris speaks well for England though he clips his wings with the scissors of Professor Flower's editorial proscription. He distinguishes between a kind of political writing which simply uses politics as a background, 'as other works might include sport or farming or travel', and to him the more interesting 'hard-core political literature' devoted to persuasion, to trying to change in some ways the political understanding and convictions of the reader. Yet he then admits that some writers, like Shaw, Wells, Wyndham Lewis and Orwell, have 'been quite capable of veering first to one end and then to the other' of that spectrum. His book happens to be the longest in the series and the most interesting, perhaps in part because, as he says, 'Britain has a less clear tradition of politically committed literature than most other European countries.' He has more problems to tackle, even if his formal definition of 'politically committed writing' appears to render problematical a good deal of the famous British tradition of great and clear political writing: Hobbes, Defoe, Swift, Hume,

Burke, Paine, Bentham (who admittedly only wrote well when in polemical mood), Cobbett, Hazlitt, Coleridge, Mill, Carlyle, Morris, Shaw, Wells, Russell, Tawney and Orwell. I call the roll only of those who can be read with pleasure for their prose quite apart from their politics. If there are no contemporary worthies of quite that stature, there are many novelists and playwrights who see themselves, or are seen as, in part at least, political writers. However, Dr Morris happily does not in practice beg the question by rejecting some political writers as not wholly 'committed'. He worries away at the problem and reopens it, especially in an admirable discussion of Shaw.

Dr Morris, unlike the authors of the German and the Spanish books, can take background more or less for granted and concentrate on explication and criticism of his committed writers. Dr Williams, however, has an almost impossible task within a hundred pages to try to convey both the great and explicit intellectual debate of German writers about artistic *versus* political commitment and the complex historical factors that created this passionate if false antithesis, this almost universal belief that there was no middle ground. No wonder he gives up at 1945 saying, rather implausibly, that this old Weimar debate is simply repeated in the post-war German scene. Thus he excludes the debate in the post-war generation about war-guilt and national identity, and does not consider the argument of writers like Gunter Grass and Heinrich Boll that their language itself, or rather the old way of using German, must carry some of the burden of guilt. In Britain only Orwell (whose style was influential among young post-war writers in the Federal Republic) attempted to argue that the plain style and humanitarian progressive politics had some necessary connection, even if his version of progressive politics was, like that of Grass, Boll and Camus, more open-ended and tolerant than that of Sarte and of (if one judges them by what they chose to say rather than by how they chose to live) the French literary Left in general.

Morris remarks that while our political literature has been compared unfavourably to that of France, Germany and Russia for lack of great passion and total commitment, 'yet those virtues or vices of compromise, phlegm and a sense of tradition', which permeate even our most committed writers would certainly be called *political* at Westminster. Political indeed they are, even if liberal rather than revolutionary. Morris's commonsense, in other words, survives the starters' orders of the series which would seem to ban good horses like Burkean Prudence and Bourgeois Compromise from the course at all and leave Total Commitment

and Powerful Authenticity as joint favourites. The wider definition
of politics I propose would have made the task of selection more
difficult, but why reduce politics in this silly liberal way to
passionate *intrusions* into both art and life, rather than see it as a
normal part of our Western cultural tradition? Indeed Arendt in
her *The Human Condition* said that politics was the greatest part,
whether in it's Burkean conservative or in its republican mode.

Morris understands but also sees through the inwardness of old
Chesterton, the anti-socialist, thundering about Shaw, 'The best
plays were written by a man trying to preach socialism. All the art
of all the artists looked tiny and tedious beside the art which was a
by-product of propaganda.' This is less a tribute to Chesterton's
tolerance than to his fanaticism. 'Such writing is for him akin to, or
a substitute for, religious literature', says Morris, '. . . we find the
assertion that political propaganda can produce good, even great,
art and indeed there is the implication that in a time of pessimism
or loss of religious faith such writing can produce *the only* true
literature.' And Morris nicely remarks that Chesterton was
therefore 'less than fair' to Wilde. Indeed. It would be sensible, I
would argue, to say that Shaw was both a great writer (some of the
time) and a great propagandist (much of the time); and that there
is no reason why these two attributes should not sometimes run
happily in harness, but no guarantee either that they may not
sometimes pull apart. The test of whether they can run together
lies in the quality of the writing not in the vigour or content of the
argument. Orwell in his essay 'Why I Write' wrote sensibly about
the need both to have something to say and to keep one's integrity
as a writer when arguing a case. But he never said that a writer
could not be a party man, only that he could not be "a loyal
member of a political party". The distinction is important.

The realistic novel is an obvious form for political and social
criticism. Such novels can be good or bad. Dr Morris defends the
form against a misplaced general attack.

Orwell, Koestler and Rex Warner were all to suffer from the
faint praise of critics who found their works deficient by the
rise of arbitrary criteria that derive from the novels of a quite
different and irrelevant kind. It cannot be said too often that
literature that anticipates or reflects rapidly changing social
or political conditions will appear increasingly varied and
thus demand an unprecedented critical response.

There is, indeed, a sociological as well as a psychological
imagination. The worst novels of Henry James cannot be used to
condemn the best of H.G. Wells. Anti-utopian novels, as Morris
remarks, have 'an intellectual coherence and an historical

justification' quite apart from their inferiority if compared to
psychological novels of character. In his chapter, 'Despair of
Systems', his argument moves away from examining political
writing as passionate commitment into considering some that was
aggressively sceptical of all 'systems'. Some ' "Political" literature
had indeed become, generally, *anti*-political and certainly uncommitted to any national or international party: its concerns
were increasingly moral and aesthetic.' Even in the 1930s some
Right-wing authors made this just their stance. They saw
themselves as driven into support for strong government, social
order and hierarchy to prevent the constant intrusion, uncertainty
and meddling of 'politics' or of an unleashed 'anarchy', as Yeats
cried out. Many writers and artists sympathetic to Facism used
images of 'the machine', specifically of fast war-planes, as the
symbol of 'the New Era'; the Left had no monopoly on futurism
and on visions of science replacing politics. Yet to make such a
sharp distinction between the political and the anti-political,
certainly to see the political simply in terms of party allegiance,
must once again raise the worry that the concept is defined too
narrowly. Not all anti-politics was totalitarian; most of it, in fact,
was a Right-wing protest at "bad" or liberal politics, not a rejection
of all politics.

☆   ☆   ☆

The idea of a vast and perennial intellectual conflict between
the 'aethetic and the political', 'spirit and power' or 'right and
might' are mighty themes that agitate German thought from
Napoleonic times, even before the era of unification. Wagner
heroically put his money on both horses. But philosophers,
professors and writers had all too often been, as Marx had gibed in
The German Ideology, dependent creatures, first on Court patronage
and then on State appointments. German writers were expected to
defend authority in general, or if they rebelled, then to speak out
against all authority. They had this public role well before the
Kaiserreich or the days of Weimar, and it was more institutionalised
than even in France. Any non-political tendencies seemed to call
for the most elaborate theoretical justifications and could not, as
for most British men of letters in the Victorian and Edwardian
eras, simply be taken for granted. Yet *'politik'* could be taken, was
usually taken in fact, to be something base and low, *Kuhhandlung*
virtually, not lofty *Staatswissenschaft*. Many intellectuals along the
way saw politicians and political parties as enemies of the State:
'politicians exist to perpetuate differences', said the hero of
Goebbel's youthful novel, *Michael*, 'We exist to solve them'. Dr
William's does well in a short space to explain the nature of the

great manly *Bruderschlacht*, the brothers' war of Left-wing, Francophile Heinrich and Right-wing, traditionalist Thomas, Mann. The latter's polemical *Betrachtungen eines Unpolitischen* ('The Testament of an Unpolitical Man') was fiercely anti-liberal, anti-modernist and anti-cosmopolitan, defending both the traditional State and the individualistic cult of psychological inwardness against the social and republican ideals of fraternity and citizenship espousel by his brother.

Nothing in the history of writers and politics is more interesting than the contrast between the conservative Thomas Mann of the First World War and the liberal Thomas Mann of the Nazi period. Faced with totalitarianism, not simply old autocracy, he reverted to and reasserted the Germany of Kant and of Goethe. But Dr Williams, in a brilliant analysis fo Mann's famous short story or parable of Fascism, "Mario and the Magician", points to the guilt of complicity in the fictional narrator's position. He says it would be 'egregious to identify Mann with the narrator. Perhaps, but Mann's narrator muses:

> It has often been pointed out, can hardly be missed, that the hypnotist Cipolla's victims lack any positive view of life to resist his degredation, but it has seldom been said that the narrator is fully aware that you do not just stand watching, photographing a drowning man, as it were, unless you too feel like drowning. That the sin of ommission can be as great as the sin of commission does not, I would guess, lie in the nature of a man or his mode of writing, but in the extremity of the circumstances. [H.T. Lowe-Porter's translation]

In traditional autocracies a writer can always feel that somebody else more politically competent will take up the cudgels, but under a totalitarian system nobody can be sure that anyone else will move; so the choice is between complete silence and desperate and probably futile protest—as Solzhenitsyn found. Hannah Arendt in her *Eichmann in Jerusalem* even argued that hopeless resistance is a human duty. One must testify to human freedom and political action. When divorced from all hope, free actions become primal ends in themselves. We should act with Burkean prudence and Aristolelean rationality, but if we were utterly prevented from so doing, if we are to remain human we must still act somehow. Hence true politics, the Greek pride in action and debate, can even be seen as having a moral and an aethetic justification. The wheel can turn full circle. As in Yeat's poem, *Grandfather on the Gallows:* 'And he kicked before he died, He did it out of pride.'

Dr Williams argues that, in *Doctor Faustus* 'Mann remains tragically enmeshed' in the very tradition of aetheticism he finally

wishes to condemn. Leverkuhn's oratorio 'The Lamentation of
Faustus', to write which he sold his soul, repudiates Goethe and
Beethoven, everything that Mann sees as rational and good in
the German tradition; but the oratorio is portrayed as a supreme
aesthetic achievement, a sublime masterpiece. But Mann himself,
if not his fictive narrator, is surely aware of this 'enmeshment', is it?
or is it necessary ambivalence, even a creative tension? He is fully
conscious of the clash of political and artistic values at their
absolute extremes. This is part of the book's almost agonising
impact. The contradiction does not destroy it. The contradiction
may be in the nature of things and there is no glib resolution.
Synthesis may be for metaphysics or religion, but in Orwell's
commonsense terms there is no contradiction between a critic
saying 'great music' and 'diabolical composer'. Orwell could
calmly picture Ezra Pound as an evil man but as a considerable
poet. Why not? This duality is not uncommon in much intense
creative writing. It is not necessarily 'tragic' for Mann to have
thrived on this contradiction or tension, simply perceptive of him
as a writer, even if, as it were, he devours his own torn flesh. He
happened to live in an era of crises in which any great artistic
achievement involved a painful use of the writer's own experience,
the risk of public obloquy and (if lucky) exile, and a perpetual
burden of guilt. Such a writer would always feel that, quite apart
from what he wrote, he should have misused earlier the authority
of his reputation as a famous writer to protest against barbarism as
a human being or citizen.

Professor Flower recalls the quite extraordinary prominence
that French writers once held as public figures. To the envy of New
York intellectuals today, their opinions were sought by the Press
on just about everything. Flower laments that 'in an age that is
becoming increasingly reliant on mass Media it seems unlikely
that the writer will ever again be placed in such a responsible and
potentially influential position.' But the use made of their position
was not always happy. Perhaps literary writers today who want to
pontificate on politics, finding that they have less authority, have
to think more carefully what they say. A word about authority. It is
not a bad thing, as such, if some people have some skill or craft
that others need, recognise and admire. What makes authority
authoritarian is precisely when someone who has real authority in
one prestigious field uses it to lay down the law in others. So many
able French and British writers in the 1930s were simply
fashionable, silly or extreme in their political opinions. To say that
is not to draw the moral that writers should stick to pure writing
(whatever that may be), but simply and boringly to urge more

caution: there is content as well as form, and what someone says should be looked at critically, not appreciated or sanctified because of where it comes from or how it is said. One thinks again of those critics and poets who simply will not admit that Pound was a foul anti-semite and a true Fascist, who claim in the teeth of the evidence that his wartime broadcasts from Rome are not authentic, simply because he was, indeed, a great poet. Poets are as free as any of us to say anything but what they say has no special privilege or moral authority, only how they say it. And perhaps there are some things that cannot be said in any manner that should attract serious attention.

Flower praises Stendhal for his 'justness of opinions' and ability 'to strike a balance' when writing about politics, but astonishingly uses this as a reason for *not* considering him a political writer! The concept is explicitly limited to 'committed' writers. Within this serious limitation, the book is subtle and rewarding and he tackles the interesting but essentially sociological questions of the effect on the *lives* of writers of their political activities, rather than, as he promises, the effect on their *writings*, their form and formal values. Thus Camus, too complex, serious, dispassionate and sane to be a political writer in Flower's sense, is quoted as a commentator on political writing but not studied as a major political writer himself. Dr Morris sidelines Orwell similarly. Even if this paradoxical conclusion did not induce them to reconsider their basic definition, one would have thought that they would recognise that Orwell and Camus produced both political writing, in their sense, and critical writing about politics.

This failure of perception may arise from a formal reason as well as from the restrictive definition. Political writing as a *genre* more often takes the form of the essay, the short polemic and the occasional piece than of the integral book. Dr Flower and his team, like examination boards, seem only to want to consider whole texts of, as publishers' contracts say, 'normal book length'. But many of Orwell's essays, for instance, are far better writing, richer and more complex in almost every way, both in form and content, than all but two of his books. His lasting greatness is likely to be seen as an essayist. Indeed the essay, since the time of Montaigne and his translator, Florio, has been a noted French and English literary speciality. The book length specification also underestimates such writers as Camus and Orwell as themselves critics, indeed some of the their book reviews are not to be ignored as literature. 'A text which is committed to the critical elucidation of political issues and which manages to remain aesthetically interesting', remarks Dr Williams, 'is relatively rare in the

literature we have examined.' Well, it depends what one means by
a text, otherwise his judgement is foolish if extended to post-war
German writing. Many 'aethetically interesting' essays, articles
and books have been written on the themes of German identity
and responsibility: consider the non-fiction of Boll and Grass or
an historian like Golo Mann or a professor of politics like Kurt
Sontheimer. Orwell does not even figure in the useful general
bibliography to the whole series because, presumably, he did not
write a full-blown book on political writing: only three truly
seminal major essays on politics and literature, propaganda and
language.

Even essays, one discovers with alarm, are too formal for
contemporary Swedish intellectuals; or so Janet Mawby tells us in
a short study of Scandinavia. Even though she largely limits her
account to the effects of the Second World War on Swedish
literature and its politicisation in the 1960s, it is difficult to judge
how selective she has been. She tells us that 'almost all literature of
any significance with political intent has been produced by the
Left', an assertion which begs many questions. Mawby pictures
the writers of the 1960s as being drawn by a concern with the
Vietnam War and with apartheid in South Africa into a general
critique of the malaise of Western capitalist society. And this
critique apparently led to questioning 'the basic assumptions of
creative literature'. Novelists like Jane Myrdal have virtually
abandoned the novel for polemical journalism, that is for 'critical
writing' (in its special modern Marxist sense) in newspapers.
Writers, we are told in tones of envious awe, have come to see 'the
writer as a parasite in a parasitic society'. God knows, she may be
right. Perhaps there are no calm, reflective voices left in Sweden
who can articulate traditional ideas about politics as a mediation
of differing values. The acceptance of any differences may be
instantly denounced as sexist, racist, ageing or classist. Perhaps
there are no contrary voices raised against this wind of (when I
read 'newspapers' I suspect) Radical Chic. Documentary writing
can aspire to literature, Orwell proves that, but it cannot swallow it.
She *could* be right about the forms of Swedish writing, but the
snippets of content she quotes, and presumably she quotes the
best, all sound politically simplistic. Actual Swedish politics are
enviably sensible, so perhaps they have simply learned how to get
on without political writers.

☆　☆　☆

Dr Butt makes Spain political writing sound both simpler and
more congruent to the nominal concern of the series with the *how*
rather than the *what*. His thesis is that there was a literary

stagnation in the 1950s and 1960s which owed less to the repressive politics of the Franco regime, already lapsing into a senile tolerance, than to a uniquely Spanish identification of literary modernism with the reactionary and stridently elitist writers of the 1920s and 1930s. This perception was not entirely true. For every Fascist Futurist a revolutionary Modernist can be found; but there were enough of the former to taint the latter. In the poisoned atmosphere of Franco's Spain, the idea grew up that modernism was at best escapism and at the worst militant individualist elitism. What was then needed was 'realistic' writing. Long sociological novels came into fashion. They avoided explicit politics but were grimly descriptive of the constraints and boredom of ordinary rural and urban life. Stalin' censors had demanded positive heroic proletarian virtues, but Franco's stupidly skimmed the pages seeking only to remove explicit socialism, atheism, freemasonry and liberalism.

> For ten years Spanish literature was engulfed by a wave of curiously flat and underwritten prose narrative designed to mobilize readers against the Franco regime ... excessive (though understandable) concern with the political effect of literature halted the growth of what was promising, by the early 1930s, to be a major European literature and caused writers to throw out the very critical premises on which the promise was based.

Things can, indeed, go too far. The allegedly political effect (whether reactionary or progressive) of a literary form is too dubious a ground on which, like the alledged effect of pornographic books, to base any proscriptions. Ridicule, satire and contempt, where appropriate, are better than law based on pretend measurements of the immeasureable. But, as Dr Butt wrily remarks, 'it often happens that when it rains in Europe, it pours in Spain, and arguments which bear on the life of the whole continent are pushed to clarifying extremes across the Pyrenees.'

Dr Morris's last words might save us even from clarifying extremes.

> Certainly some politically committed works are of great artistic merit, but whether they are as effective politically as lesser, more propagandist works, is a question to be decided by other means than concern us here but which are the province of social scientists. What we can say is this: political literature that succeeds as literature does so, not despite its political content or commitment, but because of an aethetic potency unassessable and unjustifiable in political science.

I say 'might save us' because the old question still remains, what

is 'aethetic potency' is great political nonsense (as in much of
w or Chesterton) or great political evil (as in much of Pound or
nnunzio)? The aesthetic judgement need not be false, but is it
sufficient? Does the literary critic judge one way and the political
commentator another? Do two separate people judge the same
thing differently, or does each whole man or woman make two
separate judgements simultaneously? Is a person not less of a
whole human being if they apply one mode of judgement alone?
Dr Morris tries to draw boundaries by saying that the *effect* of
political ideas can be measured by social scientists. Leave aside
that while I respect his confidence, I do not share it: there have
been no statistical studies of whether art or propaganda is more
effective politically, nor are there likely to be (at best one could
only measure opinions about what is thought to be the case, not
what is the case). But what if this 'aesthetic potency' is the carrier of
ideas potentially destructive of freedom? That would be no case for
banning them, but it is a case for anyone (including the literary
critic) to criticise them. I don't want to ban pornography, for
instance, but I want it disparaged as almost always bad art and
restrictive sexuality. Both political writers and their critics, literary
or not, cannot avoid moral judgements. Perhaps the real reason
for this series treating 'political writing' as simply political
commitment is so that they can remain professional and treat all
commitments as equal. But if all values are equal some are more
equal than others. And it is perverse to make confident aethetic
judgements and yet shun moral judgements.

We have to recognise that we live in a dualistic world.
Externality and internality are both as real as each other,
objectivity and subjectivity are both as necessary and as unavoid-
able. Form and content are only speculatively, hypothetically
separable. Certainly we make some judgements weightily as
scholars and others more lightly in everyday life as ordinary
human beings. But when we make important moral judgements
we must think as a complete person. We should at least grant that
the real Karl Marx was right, as was Schiller before him, to protest
that excessive or unnatural divisions of labour (such as Dr Morris
judging aethetic potency and Dr Crick considering truth and
measuring political effect) are alienating.

☆ ☆ ☆

How odd and unexpected, by reviewing this brave but flawed
series, to have discovered literary scholars adhering to a concept of
politics as unreflective sincere activity, one so much at odds with
the great tradition of European political writing as a reflective and
judgemental dialogue. The ideal remains clear, however much

actual politics and politicians fall short. Perhaps we all find it hard to see clearly what is under our noses: the political significance of that uniquely modern literary form, the novel. It is, indeed, a bourgeois literary form, as Lukacs argued; and it's main subject matter is, indeed, as Trilling argued, the interplay of individual psychologies and social class. Bourgeois indeed, but bourgeois at its historical best, exemplifying most of the bourgeois virtues in its very form, such as individual inventiveness, adaptability and a comprehensive viewpoint, and famously capable within its concept of exploring and exposing the vices of the bourgeoise or ruling classes—as, say, court poetry or the official epic never could. The novel is not a necessary instrument of class relationships but can comprehend them. Both Lukacs' and Trilling's critical theories are highly political, but Lukacs' Marxism narrows relevancies whereas Trilling's liberal imagination extends them.

The very form of the novel arises from and embraces conflicts of character, values, interests, circumstances and classes. And the form that only seems to work well, as Sartre pointed out in his *What is Literature?*, when the author has at least an implicit commitment to freedom and can empathise with and portray plausibly social diversity. Where, he asked, is there a great totalitarian novel? That was not just a contradiction in terms but a psychological impossibility. The purely didactic novel lacks, indeed, variety and complexity, shuts out not opens up alternative experiences. In trying to show that things can only work in one way and move in one direction, the official novel is invariably boreing and repetitious. Fine lyric poetry, expressing more briefly the intense inwardness of a personal vision, has come from enemies of freedom, like Ezra Pound or Stefan George, or from writers hostile to civic humanism like T.S. Eliot or, in a less consistent way, W.B. Yeats; but the novel is a unique carrier of ideas of freedom and of a republican or political culture. If political philosophy in its academic mode remains esoteric, even to the educated reader and citizen, and has lost its public role, the novel often carries this tradition of speculation about types of justice and the nature and limits of freedom. Where else can one look to for graphic portrayals of moral dilemmas in general and of conflicts of ethical principle and political prudence, or of the individual and conscience against the State? Sometimes this occurs in the theatre, but only rarely and fleetingly, alas, in the popular media. This is, indeed, the message.

In academic terms I have tried to make a protest against a particular disciplinary fracturing of our culture—which is, when at its best, a political culture in the finest sense. We believe in settling disputes by public debate. Thus political writing (which should be both good politics and good writing) is too important to be left to craft-conscious academic disciplines, and when it is so left, as we have seen, a restrictive view of the political emerges. Political philosophers should talk less to themselves and more to the public using examples from what is left of our common literary culture. These works must, of course, be respected as whole texts: meaning cannot be extracted from them out of context, but the novel has always been a form in which argument and much miscellaneous information can be carried in the artistic structure. (Truth to tell, many of us first read novels 'to find out about life and the world', and that is still part even of the adult motivation). The novel, like the late medieval cathedral, can be a supreme aesthetic structure with a unified design, but under the one roof an extraordinary range of secular and profane activities took place, not merely spiritual. Nonetheless, the form and structure of works of art are as much a part of their meaning as is the content of any part that can be torn, for other purposes, from the whole text. The truth of a fiction ultimately lies in the psychological plausability of a coherent imaginary world. The actual cases we political philosophers or political writers examine are necessarily selective and somewhat arbitrary, but we need to choose texts which have a richness and complexity, not a single or simple mindedness, however sincere or 'authentic', in relation to great themes like justice, authority, obligation, order, equality, toleration and liberty. Only after considering many actual literary texts is it sensible to consider academic critical writings about the general relationship of politics to literature.

These reflections may help to hold some humanistic middle ground between an aestheticism or an academicism which would exclude from literature all political and even moral considerations always, and that sociological materialism that would reduce (debase indeed) all imaginative literature to distorted reflections of social structures, historical contexts and alleged economic and political necessities. 'The seeming needs of this fool driven land', said Yeats. But a land is only 'fool driven' when it is thought by the State that there is only one set of 'seeming needs' worth satisfying. Yeats himself wrote notable poems about 'seeming needs', but fortunately (not merely for his poetry) these needs seemed highly changeable. But he also, of course, wrote many poems that are completely non-political, and a powerful few raged against the incursion of politics into decent life. His genius was in giving voice to all this, not for one mode and mood alone or in finding (as once he sought) some esoteric synthesis. He even wrote some reflective poems about inevitable conflicts of public and private life. His expressive genius as a poet and his many changes of political stance show why (*pace* Professor Flower and his colleagues) it is foolish to characterise political writing as simply passionate sincerity. Unbridled and uncritical polemic always makes for bad politics and, without the lyric genius of Yeats, too often bad art.

Two

The Political in Britain's Two National Theatres

From James Redmond, editor, *Drama and Society* (Cambridge University Press, 1981).

The Royal Shakespeare Company, in its theatres at London and Stratford, meets the obligations of a National Theatre as comprehensively as does that national theatre on the South Bank of the Thames. These obligations were formulated in the National Theatre Committee Handbook of 1909:

    (i)   to keep the plays of Shakespeare in repertoire

    (ii) to revive whatever else is vital in English classical drama

   (iii) to prevent recent plays of great merit from falling into oblivion

   (iv) to produce new plays and to further the development of modern drama

    (v) to produce translations of representative works of foreign drama, ancient and modern

   (vi) to stimulate the art of acting through the varied opportunities which it will offer to members of the company.

In considering the intricate relationships between drama and society in Britain in the 1970s, we will naturally regard with special interest the ways in which these heavily subsidised national institutions treat political issues.

I write as a political philosopher who happens to be an addicted theatregoer. I have reviewed some of the plays discussed here, but in conditions of relative leisure.[1] Unlike newspaper reviewers, therefore, I have always been able to read the text or acting script (after the performance, on principle and also to preserve the basic dramatic joy of surprise). And unlike most literary critics, I shall limit myself here to a discussion of specific productions. The choice of plays may therefore seem rather random, but the procedure has some advantages. It should reveal how our national companies perceive politics in plays in general, rather than in the specifically 'political' theatre, or in drama of 'commitment'. One of

20

my main points is that politics is important in plays which do not invite those labels.

Literary critics sometimes worry that drama is debased or simplified by intense political commitments. While this is not necessarily so, I share their worry, since political sincerity is no excuse for bad drama. Indeed I add to it a concern of my own craft: that dramatising politics in some contemporary ways can debase politics. A strident, wholly partisan view of politics expressed in one-sided dialectic is essentially undramatic. The perennial is reduced to the topical, the transitory and the arbitrary. I invoke what I conceive to be the tradition of Aristotle, Machiavelli (of *The Discourse*), Montesquieu, J.S. Mill, Tocqueville, and Hannah Arendt—a tradition that sees politics as a way of mediating between conflicts of values and interests: ideally, the mediation elevates (Hegel), but if that is not to be, at least a practical, humane compromise can be struck (Burke). Elsewhere I have defined politics as the creative conciliation of naturally differing interests and ideals.[2] I would add that I expect there to be politics even in the classless society. We will never be rid of it: it is a perennial human activity that reflects our freedom (whether as gift or curse) to choose different preferences and values. We can choose better or worse, but the manner of our choosing should be *political:* that is, through public discussion, recognition of alternatives and other people's perspectives, and acceptance of reasonable procedures, not through command based on a single view of authority enforced by power.

The inference is clear. Politics, in this sense, has many similarities with drama. Both involve contrast, clash or conflict of differing viewpoints, values or characters, often in changing or differing circumstances. Both of them may find or seek some resolution, but the manner of reaching that resolution is what makes a decision political rather than autocratic or arbitrary, or play a political drama rather than propaganda, or 'triumph', or *tableaux vivants*. Most dramas, indeed, have some politics in them, in this sense, however, small or incidental.

The image conjured up by 'political theatre' is all too often the converse both of what I mean by 'political' and of what I mean by 'drama'. 'Committed theatre' is, indeed, a better phrase; for politicians or *le temperament humain et politique* are often the prime target of the committed playwright. For him, all important questions have already been decided: it remains only to dramatise the answers so that people (the theatregoing public? the streets?) can understand them better, be proselytised by them or, if the audience are the converted already, kept on heat. I am far from saying that 'committed theatre' cannot on occasion make good drama. The ends may be pre-judged, but the means may be open to debate, permissible objects for play. For example, the RSC production of David Edgar's *Destiny* (1976). Having heard that it dealt with the rise of fascism in the West Midlands, I felt sure it would be awful; but it turned out to be what I had often imagined but never expected to see: a strongly committed left-wing play able to understand and empathise with different types of fascism in conflict with one another, each well embedded in rich and diverse characters. Or consider Shaw. His deliberate propaganda can lead to good drama because he allows his devils so many good lines, and gives them memorable characters, indeed considerable intellectual dignity. They may sometimes be caricatures, but they are caricatures of plausible ideas, not simply of class interest and class malice, as are the cardboard figures of 'them' in agit-prop theatre. On the one hand, there is Brecht's profound and dramatic *Galileo*; on the other, the shallow claptrap of *The Days of the Commune*. On the one hand, there are the genuine political dilemmas, necessity of state against character and loyalty, of John Arden's *Armstrong's Last Goodnight;* but on the other, the strident, stereotyped rant of *The Ballygombeen Bequest.*

So to look at our two national companies is to allow a chance, for once, to see how well political themes are handled in the best plays, classical or modern, whether politics is a main themes or only incidental. So much good drama already contains good politics. I mean, of course, a good understanding of politics. For politics is concerned with dilemmas and alternatives, with the clash of values and interests, and with uncertainties as to which is which. Nothing is more dramatic than politics. But whereas the *theatricality* of politics is understood all too well, very many 'political' playwrights and producers mistake commitment for politics, or the end of an argument for the beginning. Drama thrives on moral dilemmas. If we think that there should be no moral dilemmas, or no 'problematic' after the revolution, then indeed we *ought* to chase out the poets and the playwrights or turn them simply into official foghorns.

One further justification for only considering the RSC and the National Theatre Company: here we can observe the effect of political material on a very general audience, not a politically selected gathering (as in the fringe, or Unity Theatre of yore). We should never forget a simple difference between drama and other art forms–which accounts for so much of the peculiar and perennial tension between the State and the Stage—that a play must be performed in public, usually to an unrestricted audience.

We sit and we see how our fellow-citizens react, and reactions are hard to control, not simply when political satire is overt, but also, say, when the RSC Feste is played as a professional comic, desperate to keep his job—a little jab of reality which visibly disturbed and stirred many of the audience. We should never forget that a performance involves not just the audience watching the actors and the actors reacting to the audience but also the audience—as in any *polis*—anxiously watching each other.

Feudal Power

Whether politics is seen as of perennial or only of topical problems, is well revealed in productions of Shakespeare's histories. Directors in our national companies have, on the whole, shown considerable political sense. The politics is there in the text—is it not? What a bore it used to be thought. But Hall, Barton, Hands and Nunn have, with their respect for the text and for language, not for partisan reasons, brought it back to life. In rescuing so many of the minor parts and the minor lines from the neglect of the bad old star system, they have necessarily repoliticised plays that used to be seen as simply dramas of noble characters, flawed, floored or overawed. The RSC's Roman plays of 1973-4 were a fine example, particularly *Julius Caesar* and *Antony and Cleopatra*. Trevor Nunn gave them a political unity: political firstly in the sense that he saw them as plays primarily about politics, even in their original intention (so much Elizabethan political thought used or was possessed by the many sided image of Rome) and, secondly, as ways for the contemporary theatre to discuss the perennial issue of politics.

Nunn did not try to twist Shakespeare into being topical, as did Jonathan Miller, or actually abuse him for not being topical, as does Charles Marowitz: he simply brought out perennial issues of justice versus reason of state. Having heard that they were 'political', I began to attend with my usual prejudices. I feared at the worst that it would be all 'production', and that the politics of the Romans would simply be those of the director's personal affirmation: the telling us what to think, or the feedback mirror of trendy sentiments, such as the great rubbish of the RSC's *US* Vietnam pantomime of 1966, which was all burning Buddhist monks, butterflies and wicked Yankees. At the best, I feared the more subtle mistake of John Barton in the *Wars of the Roses* or 'the matter of England' plays, that politics is simply a struggle for power, one noble beast tearing another down, in a purely Hobbesian world of 'life is a restless search of power after power that ceaseth only in death'. Sometimes Barton missed the level of political ideas: the feudal preconception of loyalty expected and loyalty betrayed, of honour upheld and honour sacrificed for interest.

In the Romans, however, I saw, and kept on going back to see, Shakespearian theatre and thought about Shaekespeare of a very high order indeed: productions poised between bringing out all that he meant and pointing up certain things that should peculiarly worry us.

Only in *Julius Caesar* did the politics go wrong. Today we are very unsubtle in our perceptions of different types of autocracy. We are such good democrats, that we hump together crudely all types of autocracy. A feudal nobility is one thing, the Roman senatorial class another; but both had in common a political situation in which no man, not even a feudal king, not even a Roman consul could become dictator (a constitutional office) and assume absolute authority without gaining the support of powerful fellows. There was no army to be commanded as one: feudal levies and Roman legions followed their local commanders who had to woo them and give them constant success and rewards.

What we feared partly happened, Caesar was a fascist. He was surrounded by guards dressed in black leather who drilled with Prussian precision, not with feudal or Roman practicality. The programme notes got it half right by stressing the enormity of 'dictator for life', but then they betrayed their misunderstandings of autocratic senatorial or oligarchic politics by including photographs of Mussolini and (to show no fear or favour) of Mobutu—quite the wrong images. This instantly weakens the play, the tyrannicide is now prejustified and the retribution only follows because of the impure motives of Cassius (envy) and Brutus (pride). But surely the act itself must be at least questionable for the play to work well? The political reflection upon a Roman or a feudal notable who has become Protector and who may seek to become king (so close to the Bolingbroke theme) is coarsened if the director suggests that there is no doubt at all that Caesar got what was justly coming to him. The text shows Caesar dedicated to the good of Rome, proud and wilful certainly, perhaps in danger of being a tyrant, very likely to be so if he listened to Antony too much, but far from certainly so. Also, as his perceptive remarks on Cassius show, he is no fool. That he is a lesser man than the role he plays only makes him like Richard II or Henry IV, conscious of the politician's need to act: it does not, in a modern radical sense, 'unmask' or expose him as unequivocally a tyrant.

The temptation of contemporaneity was, however, too great.

Caesar becomes a fascist, so that the moral dilemma of to kill or not to kill almost vanishes, and Cassius and Brutus merely coincide: the issue between them and Antony–Octavius is simply settled by force of arms, the strongest winning. As in *Henry VI*, politics is then simply portrayed as a struggle for coercive power. And psychological interest in the play has then to be sustained by a wholly eccentric reading of the stoic Brutus as an overeducated neurotic and youth-of-our-times who loses his cool in a most un-Roman way.

In spite of these flaws in the actual content of political thought, no one could mistake from the production that Shakespeare expected his audience to discuss seriously the ethics of tyrannicide and to see analogies with their own politics in the republican versus oligarchical debate. It argues considerable political sophistication that *Julius Caesar* could be written and played in Elizabethan London (just as it does for President Nyerere personally to have translated the play into Swahili).

A proper sense of topicality was uncovered by the very speed of the production. It marched at a remorseless and frightening pace, as of events beyond control and men struggling vainly to contain them or catch up. And Antony is established in his turn, for if Caesar is a fascist then Antony is a pure opportunist; whereas surely Antony is, for all his faults, a loyal man and, perhaps because of his self-indulgence, a more humane man than the ice-cold operator Octavius—there is even a suggestion, perhaps, that he is more humane than Brutus. His repeated 'honourable men' is not just an unworthy sneer at Brutus's alleged hypocrisy, but is a genuine lament for the dying feudal world of honour, loyalty and friendship, here violated by the killing of one's master, that world which Falstaff blows away in his speech on honour.

Despite this, *Julius Caesar* could be made to follow from *Coriolanus* because everywhere the republican symbols were stressed—SPQR indeed. Proud trumpets accompany the assassination of Caesar which became a Delacroix-like tableau of tyrannicide, *'sic semper tyrannis'*, as even Lincoln's assassin cried. They repeated the assassination scene in slow motion, once in triumph, and then yet again as a nightmare to haunt with its moral ambiguity both actors and audience. Here Trevor Nunn was morally so right: realising the necessity of violence, but never revelling in it. In both plays, the power, the sheer physical power, of the people, is never far from the stage, whether for good or ill, spontaneous or arranged.

Antony and Cleopatra is also political all through, even though now the people are absent as a force. Common soldiers speak clear political common sense right at the beginning, and these lines were emphasised massively:

> *Philo.* Nay, but this dotage of our general's
> O'erflows the measure . . .
>   His captain's heart
>   . . . reneges all temper,
> And is become the bellows and the fan
> To cool a gipsy's lust. Look where they come!
> Take but good note, and you shall see in him
> The triple pillar of the world transform'd
> Into a strumpet's fool. Behold and see.
>
>   (I, i, 1ff.)[3]

And see we did, the most marvellously political Cleopatra with an 'infinite variety' indeed of charms and lusts. 'The old ruffian' Antony could not keep up with her and she hardly seemed to know in her own mind whether she was coming out of policy or going out of passion. 'Know you not me?' she cries when he thinks she is betraying him to Octavius. But she cannot answer that herself, neither Janet Suzman as Cleopatra nor, I suspect, the closest student of the play. For the gipsy is a very mixed up young middle-aged woman indeed, and was rightly played as such. The only trouble is that then one got carried away by all the imperial symbols (not republican now) of the production, as well as by the fast pace of the finely pointed political dialogue in all the minor characters, so that one sat there nearly shouting: 'Go home, you fool, mend your fences. Rome needs you! pay attention to politics!' One sides with his unfortunate loyal soldiers, but it can hardly be a tragedy simply of personal sloth and political ineptitude.

Since it cannot really be shown, as there was some hint at doing, that Cleopatra is as clear-headed as Octavius in wanting the whole world for herself and is simply using Antony, then the gipsy must also have majesty, must be played as something of a female Henry VIII, so that her fall and death are even more terrible than Antony's. An invented pageant of their crowning in gold as gods is inserted before the first words of the play, presumably to build up the 'majesty and mystery' of kingship of charismatic authority lacking in the actual acting of the part. And they must have between them—Shakespeare did know about it—a real love, indeed a mysticism of love.

How odd now to remember that Olivier and Vivien Leigh in 1951 could simply do the play as a love duet, if in Roman rather than Illyrian dress, and that most of the bit parts were then either cut or grabbled through. But now, as often, in restoring it as a play with so many great small parts and complex cross-currents, the director has allowed the balance to swing too far. Surely much of the play is about the rival claim of politics and love, of the public and the private; it is not *just* about the neglect of politics for sexual passion. Is this not also a message for our time?

But again, despite some uncertainties, possibly weakness in the principals, the play was made magnificent by that quite admirable team-playing which is the hallmark of the RSC. Every small part was given its full value and the play emancipated from the stars of all sorts of good ways which reveal Shakespearian thoughts too often lost, particularly political thoughts. One example is the first scene of act III. Antony's captains have won a battle in Syria, and Silius urges Ventidius to press on to Mesopotamia.

> Oh, Silius, Silius!
> I have done enough. A lower place, note well,
> May make too great an act, for learn this, Silius:
> Better to leave undone than by our deed
> Acquire too high a fame when him we serve's away.

And there is the common soldier who speaks out of turn but who is so right about not fighting at sea. Again, on the eve of Agincourt, the common soldier sees the odds more clearly: the king has got them into such a mess that only heroism will save them. No blame is attached to Ventidius and the others for deserting Antony when his cause is lost—as if Shakespeare anticipates Thomas Hobbes in suggesting that 'honour' and 'loyalty' have been the great killers of men, so that obedience should rationally go to him who can effectively enforce the peace—even the cold and nasty Octavius. But there are feudal distinctions there too: the close personal follower, the member of a noble household, is in a different position, as even Hobbes recognises. Enobarbus is not just a 'captain', he is a companion. Rationally, like a good bourgeois utilitarian, he deserts when all is lost. But unlike all the others he suffers, he is torn; the old ethic of feudal loyalty has him in its deadly grip; so that when Antony forgives him 'nobly', he kills himself miserably, not even quickly and cleanly.

Images and customs of autocracy are, thus, as peculiar and varied as those of democracy. They cannot be lumped together, as they were in *Julius Caesar*. Caesar as *princeps* was top dog, but top dog among champions. Obviously these absurd fascist *squadristi* of the Stratford stage could not accompany him into the Senate House. He could not be well-guarded, for he was a politician in enforced and sweaty intimacy with fellows. But he was thinking of going too far. If I had wanted a topical image for the programme, I would not have been so seeming-daring as to have a photo of poor old Musso, the dictator, but I would have been really daring and more accurate by showing Nixon, Wilson, Heath, or even De Gaulle—bad and arrogant politicians, but politicians nonetheless.

Tudor Power

The question of whether to adopt a political approach or an a-political approach to many classical plays is a false question. The real task is to discover what kind of political assumptions motivate the play, always having in mind the difficulty of a modern audience who will probably assume that feudal kingship was autocracy and not immediately grasp (without the director's help) the sharpness of conflict between the different political ethics of honour, loyalty and reason of state when the three coexist in the same dramatic situation. Or we will comfortably and liberally think of all 'reason of state' as wicked, rather than—as Shakespeare and his audience critically assumed—often a path towards peace, justice and order against the feudal anarchy of honour and dynastic or personal loyalties. (They were connoisseurs of the doctrine of 'the lesser evil', while we are so often hypocrites, enjoying its benefits and denouncing or denying its claims). These issues can be brought to life by a relatively straightforward playing of the *Henry IV* plays and a particular reading of *Henry V*. Indeed, the plays, as produced by Terry Hands at the RSC in 1975-6, stressed a general modern dilemma: whether to follow an ethic of honour and loyalty or one of utility.

I would like to have offered him for the programme notes (which can be so helpful, or not) a passage from Hobbes to follow that speech of Falstaff's:

> *Falstaff.* . . . honour pricks me on. Yea, but how if honour pricks me off when I come on? How then? . . . Who hath it? He that died o'Wednesday . . . Therefore I'll none of it. Honour is a mere scutcheon. And so ends my catechism.
>
> (*I Henry IV*, v. 1. 139 ff.)

Honour consisteth onely in the opinion of Power. Therefore the ancient Heathen did not thinke that Dishonoured but greatly Honoured the Gods, when they introduced them to their Poems, committing Rapes, Thefts and other great but unjust or unclean acts . . . Scutcheons, and Coats of Arms hæreditary, where they have any eminent Priviledges, are Honourable; otherwise not: for their power consisteth either in such Priviledges, or in Riches, or some such thing as is equally honoured in other men. This kind of Honour

commonly called Gentry, has been derived from the Antient
Germans.   (Thomas Hobbes, *Leviathan*)[4]

One suspects that old Thomas Hobbes may have had Falstaff's
speech in mind when he turned his mockery against honour, the
conceptual lynch-pin of the feudal ethic. 'Brutus *was* an honourable
man', while 'Yours in the ranks of death' was what traditional
apologies for political obligation had worked towards; reasons
and beliefs that would lead men to follow their lord and master, or
at least the oath-bound cause, to death or glory and not to count
the cost to themselves. But Falstaff in Shakespeare's bounding
imagination and Hobbes in his philosophical treatise were among
the first to popularise and to justify a purely prudential utilitarian
obligation.

To Hobbes the only aim of civil society is to preserve peace and
individual life. 'When armies fight', he disarmingly observed,
'there is on one side or both, a running away; yet when they do it
not out of treachery but fear, they are not esteemed to do it unjustly
but dishonourably.' Jack Falstaff was never traitor, only coward. I
have a fancy that the turncoat Stanley must have been very close
to the hearts of Hobbes, Shakespeare and of Shakespeare's
audience. Stanley it was who sat on his horse waiting at Bosworth
Field until he could bring peace at last by changing sides; by
deserting his declining King, he made what had been a probable
victory for Henry Tudor certain, total, and lastingly decisive.
Having been obsessed for some time with Sir John Falstaff's
anticipation of the philosophy of Hobbes, I was happy to hear
Terry Hands remark that they kept the character of Henry VII in
mind throughout rehearsals and they tried to imagine what kind
of relationships an Elizabethan audience would have seen
between Bolingbroke and Hal, the progress from *Henry IV* to
Henry V.

The plays got the now familiar RSC treatment in producing the
historical sequences in Shakespeare: (1) unity of design; (2) an
overall conception linking the plays and treating them as a larger
unity; (3) a sense of politics and a stress on contemporary
relevance; (4) a great quickness of pace; (5) clear speaking and
faith in the text; and, above all else, (6) much care and thought for
each minor part and scene in ensemble playing of the highest
possible order.

The key lay in the treatment of the character of Henry IV
himself. He was played by a character actor, Emrys James, which
in itself was a useful shock. Traditionally the part has usually been
played as epitomised by Sir John Gielgud in Orson Well's film, *The*

Chimes at Midnight: the noble, tortured, sleepless, high-minded king, worried for the peace of England when he dies leaving such a son, and remorseful for some act of unsurpation, far in the past, by which Bolingbroke had gained the crown. The audience is so sympathetic to this good king that, while they think it very noble of him to worry about some slight skulduggery in the past (killing a king), they so readily see that the noble Henry IV is more of a king in character and ability than was Richard that they think all the better of him for crying over the spilt milk (royal blood). If it were not for the poetry, this reading of the part would invite a director to cut some of those sleepless scenes, since the audience might even become rather impatient at his going on so about those far-off days (a decade before).

Emrys James, however, portrayed him as politician Bolingbroke, boasting to his son of how well he played the king and courted the citizens compared to dead Richard; and still playing the king to keep his head and to ensure his clan's succession, which happened to be the best security for peace in the realm. We see him almost livid with jealousy at news of Hotspur's victories, but when Hotspur speaks his famous speech, 'When I was dry with rage and extreme toil/Breathless and faint, leaning upon my sword,' Bolingbroke first eyes him with malign cynical admiration (as if 'what fine acting, what a figure for a prince's part!'), but then openly scoffs, laughs in his face when he gives the heroic account of his brother-in-law Mortimer's fight with Glendower. 'This vile politician Bolingbroke' (Hotspur's words) can admire good resolute propaganda, but his old tummy turns with disgust to see that this roaring lad actually believes what he says. The King, after all, flatly says, 'He never did encounter with Glendower.' And provocatively adds, 'I tell thee, he durst as well have met the devil alone.' John Gielgud spoke all this remotely, as if the noble King had been given false reports traducing such men of honour and was repeating them in good faith. Emrys James said is as if it were true, and as if everyone there knew it to be, including Northumberland. The 'honour' of Hotspur is made to look sincere, indeed, but destructive, anachronistic and foolish. The audience is torn two ways, neither of them utterly nice—and that is politics. This is in the text. And this is the kind of political rather than heroic eye that the modern RSC directors have always had.

Now, of course, Emrys James did rather overdo it. To see him walking round the Northumberlands in circles cackling, was, at first, to think that he was still playing his mad King John. It took me a few minutes to see that he was over-registering the cynical politician, not the mad tyrant. But the dramatic limitation of the traditional reading of the part is that if the King has already reached (apart from insomnia) a substantial serenity and inner release from the sins of his youth, because of his hard work in the prime business of kingship, namely care for the peace of the realm, this contradicts the dramatic point that such release can only be achieved by his son, not by his Bolingbroke self at all. The kingship Hal knows he will have to assume is a very practical kingship, which needs the myths of honour and divine stewardship, but is political, prudential and bourgeois in spirit. Hal relaxes amid backstage company while waiting for his call to take the centre of the stage. He indulges Falstaff and is indulged by him.

Falstaff here personifies irresponsibility, perpetual childish naughtiness and adolescent indulgence (so comic in an old man). It was plainly necessary for England for Hal to cast the fat knight away; but the Prince was not corrupted by an evil Falstaff—that is only what his father said in family quarrels held in public. He was simply indulging himself in irresponsible company, acting irresponsibly between bouts of duty, before the institution closed in totally around the man, making it necessary for him to act the king twenty-four hours a day, even act an heroic king in the pattern of Hotspur if policy dictated transmuting civil into foreign strife.

If we assess the Stratford *Henrys* by the six features of production I have identified above, it will emerge how sensible (with one bad lapse) is their reading of the political relationships.

Firstly the unity of design, I put design before the intellectual conceptions because this is a director's theatre. One has the feeling that everying follows from the director having thought of certain key symbols or patterns. In the *Wars of the Roses*, it was steel: great hanging, square screens of grey and bronze metal and the frightening clash and echo of medieval two-handed swords with five- or six-foot steel blades. In the Romans, it was symbols of power, republican then imperial, the fasces, the banners with SPQR, but used economically, as ever, with a very few realistic objects on a long, bare stage. Now in the *Henrys*, the selective realism of dress stressed the propaganda and mythology of kingship, the putting on and taking off of rich, ceremonial, sometimes sacred garments, but work-a-day leisure gear, as it were, underneath (and sometimes battlegear): a great stress on actors acting actors. Something like all those shows or pageants of power put on by or for the great Queen, to mask a more precarious reality. In *Henry V* this was carried to an extreme. The first scene at the English court was played in modern rehearsal dress-track suits and sweaters. Only the Ambassador is in medieval magnificence. But as war is decided upon, the nobility of England don their costumes. And parts of the King's 'costume' are his speeches reverting back to feudal 'honour', donned for necessity of national war. The common soldiers are portrayed as the Old Contemptibles, although clad half-way between battledress of the 1940s and the padded jackets of Brecht's own definitive production of *Mother Courage;* and they talk all too realistically about the odds and the motives. This worked well. Chorus's appeal to our imagination works when we are aware of the props. The Chorus himself remained in modern dress throughout. And it is Emrys James— the actor who played Henry—again. So 'Henry IV' introduces his son's triumph, his seeming eradication of the curse on Bolinbroke and his issue, just as in the first part of *Henry IV,* the King, after his opening scene, actually stays on stage, still and shadowy, to watch sadly his son wake Falstaff in the tavern and plan the Gad's Hill Massacre.

Secondly, an overall conception seemed to be there, because of the overall design, but was in fact harder to sustain. The play of *King Herry V* does, after all, have almost as little relationship to the *Henry IVs* as any of the comedies do to each other. And the two parts of *Henry IV* really are two different and self-contained plays. The prince's reconciliation to the tasks of kingship is fully resolved in Part One and even the rejection of Falstaff is clearly implicit. Part Two does have some marvellous scenes, but it is episodic and repetitive. The temptation to treat the scenes as separate set pieces is greater. As a result, there was too much comic business between Shallow and Silence, so that the humour and sadness of Sir John's affable Hal-like condescension to these clowns, under the shadow of his own impending overthrow, gets lost or muted. But a play is a play and takes place in a stage, not in the mind of a scholar. The two plays of *Henry IV* can be played as if one, and in the theatre they can gain by such treatment.

Thirdly, a sense of politics, even down into the lesser parts, and a stress on contemporary relevance were there unmistakably. Northumberland and Worcester, for once, were three-dimensional, power-hungry men: Worcester resolute, Northumberland fearful, no mere attendant lords. The full test of the conspiracy scene at Southampton was given which, though hardly Shakespeare's finest hour, shows both the *politique* needed to export domestic quarrels to France and the risks involved. And having seen war-like Douglas in *Henry IV Part One,* one was inclined to listen seriously to the arguments in council against not going abroad at all with Scotland still unsubdued.

Fourthly, the great quickness of pace, sustained by the bare stage, and the familiar RSC convention of one group of actors coming on stage before the others are off; and now, beyond that, sometimes lingering and listening throughout the next scene. They not merely had a Brecht-like alienation effect, but were also, when seen in character, threatening. The thrust and rake of the stage (a gradient of 1 in 12) sustained both the pace and the sense of proximity without any of those overworked gimmicks of galloping through the audience. This was marvellous theatre: the sense of events hustling men.

Fifth, clear speech and faith in the text were never sacrificed to business, action, 'production': there was none of those signs that actors and directors are convinced the audience does not want to listen, and should therefore be given something to watch. I still look back with anger to all the naked bottoms and bongo drums with which the National Theatre in 1973 successfully destroyed the words and meanings of the *Bacchae*. In the *Henrys* we were given an almost complete text of the plays; and when there were difficult words or concepts, they were not smothered in stage business. On the contrary, for a moment the swift pace slowed and the lines were pointed. Indeed, even all those long political speeches of Henry IV, that long exposition of the Law Salic of the Bishop of Ely, were not cut but were delivered clearly and intensely. We were made to feel what follows from such logic. Actions will follow, but later. It was unforgivable of Olivier (as Robert Speaight has said), all those years ago but still on celluloid, to guy the Bishop of Ely. For this just turns Henry V into a patriotic predator, rather than someone with as good a dynastic claim as any to the old French lands of the Plantagenet, Angevin, Anglo-French dynasty.

Sixth and lastly, there was great care for every minor part and scene. As in the Romans, much of the most telling political commentary is found in minor scenes and parts which used to be so much in the shadows when the great stars shone too brightly. The Northumberland scenes were all excellent: he appeared so much more calm and powerful than Bolingbroke himself, but was in fact crippled in his pursuit of power for his family by his fear for his own life. Hobbes's individualism does not work well for dynastic, feudal loyalties.

Only in the scene of Henry's renunciation of Falstaff did their political sense falter, in a lapse back to the unsubtle view of autocracy. For the King appears not just in the splendour of coronation robes, but transfigured in a huge and impersonal golden suit of armour. The director has said that it was meant to show the machine taking over the man; but I saw the gold as others did, as a symbol of divine transfiguration. They made just such a mistake in a recent production of *Richard II;* as if Shakespeare had the mid-seventeenth-century theory of the divine right of kings in mind. This anachronism is a bad misreading of Shakespeare's politics. The divinity that hedges a king is not to his person, as Stuarts and Bourbons claimed, but to the dynastic principle of descent. To break that is to strike at the heart of the feudal system of obligation and honour to superiors and to family loyalties; but in the name–and hence the dilemma–of better governance.

Granted, the Tudors tried to have it both ways. But the rejection of Falstaff by a man (the son of Bolingbroke) acting the part of king is made inevitable, not free and thus tragic, if the coronation is seen as divinisation. We are meant to feel the heavy need for 'reason of state', for 'the matter of England', for Hal to become Henry and cast off Jack Falstaff, not because of any sacerdotal necessity. The doctrine of the divine right of kings is one of those precise concepts that often get misapplied, through secular ignorance, to almost anything in the past involving kings and religions.

Politicisation too far

I shall stay with Shakespeare a little longer, for production of the classics in some fresh manner is the great test of modern directors. And they have been lucky, for a 'fresh manner' can be achieved simply by going back to the text, a fuller text, and to the minor parts (the famous 1946 season of the Old Vic was the beginning of an attempt at ensemble playing, but only the beginning: all my memories are of Richardson and Olivier themselves).

The National Theatre directors have avoided extravagances like Jonathan Miller's *Merchant of Venice*, with Shylock as a frockcoated nineteenth-century banker. But applying a sense of politics of our times to the histories is one thing, elsewhere it is more problematic. Consider recent productions of *Twelfth Night, Hamlet* and *King Lear.*

The RSC's *Twelfth Night* of 1974-5 could not, at first glance, have been less political. It was marvellously lyrical: a celebration of one night of misrule in an artificial kingdom of self-love. The director had, for once, absolute faith in the script-writer. Peter Gill gave us a straightforward production, with no great tricks or reinterpretations, no sign that he was obsessional in any way, only many marks of thought, bringing out things not often noticed and playing down things over-noticed. (I have seen swings, saws, custard pies, coloured bladders, weak bladders, pails of water, and God knows what else besides, swing into action as heavy comics and directors have shown their lack of trust in the lines as written—as the kitchen upstages the court.) The simple strength of this production was that it had confidence in the comedy of Viola, Olivia and Orsino: it got the social relationships right. High life is high comedy (social ambiguities), and low life is low comedy (drunkenness and lust). Is this a banality? But I have seen so many productions in which Sir Toby and his crew are the comedy and Viola and Olivia are simply romantic. *A Midsummer Night's Dream*, too, is often damaged in this way, by Bottom upstaging the comedy of Puck and the courtly lovers.

Here from the start it was clear that Orsino was fooling himself, acting extravagantly, not to be taken seriously in his passion for Olivia. He is not guyed as a person: on the contrary, the cult of hopeless love is guyed. And Olivia, in an important new reading, was no longer the stately, majestic, beauty. Mary Rutherford was very much like the merry tom-boy Hermia she played in Peter Brook's great production of the *Dream* (1970), and also fooling herself, like the Duke, by plunging into the game of an equally fashionable cult—that of extravagant mourning.

So Illyria is, at first glance, totally removed from the real world. Seen as a tract, it could only be an anti-Puritan tract against the folly of earnestness. There is nothing to do but amuse oneself. But the production suddenly shows us that amusing others is harder graft. Traditionally the most artificial of the characters, Feste is in this production pulled down to earth: he is not the sweet fool we have come to expect, the gentle, witty zany, someone to fit easily in a great lady's entourage, more like a naughty domestic animal, a Christopher Smart's cat or John Skelton's parrot, than a wilful human servant. No, Ron Pember was a hard-bitten, professional comic, working all the time, watching the audience's reaction, fearing that the fashion for him will pass and that he will prove boring, but equally fearing that he will one day go too far. One mistake, one gag mistimed, one insolence too close to the bone, and the next job might be as porter with Macbeth in cold Scotland. (And so it was.)

He speaks with the accent of a Petticoat Lane salesman, or the last stand of the dregs of the music hall. Far from powdered and pretty, he is perpetually in need of a shave. His voice has a rough, sardonic, cutting edge. He is the most un-Illyrian, a reminder of the outside world, of servitude and even death. He sings 'Then come kiss me, sweet and twenty,/Youth's a stuff will not endure' harshly, almost mockingly, a profane version of the Duke's idyll of true love thwarted; not an erotic encouragement, but a reminder of old mortality. He is closer to Rahere than to Touchstone.

The reality of Feste jarred at first, but then actually accentuated the deliberate artifice of the high-life comedy, which otherwise seems 'just a play'. Certainly it makes Viola's lines on Feste become not just a condescending compliment to a servant, but a rather more profound and melancholy reflection on the human condition:

> This fellow is wise enough to play the fool;
> And to do that well craves a kind of wit.
> He must observe their mood on whom he jests,
> The quality of persons, and the time;
> And, like the haggard, check at every feather
> That comes before his eye. This is practice
> As full of labour as a wise man's art;
> For folly that he wisely shows a fit;
> But wise men, folly-fall'n, quite taint their wit.

(III, i, 57-65)

For there is this dying fall within the play, as in Feste's own last song. And at the end another pardonable liberty, the director gave us Antonio standing with his back to the audience, like Feste also left alone, for he had loved Sebastian (why not?). Yet the high life on its own is too artificial for us to feel sadness amid laughter, so the little political touch, Feste's whiff of cold reality, was more than pardonable, it was profound.

Such a directorial liberty shows a sense of political and social reality, but does not seek to politicise the whole play. One could fearfully imagine lame beggars and hungry poor being intrude on the stage to watch the fruits of exploitation, as was done recently to politicise (yes) *King Lear*. But that enormity in a moment. First, *Hamlet*.

Peter Hall's 1976 National Theatre production of *Hamlet* got a bad press. Few critics seemed bold enough simply to say that Albert Finney ranted, that Fortinbras had played the Prince prematurely. Most blamed the production as being astonishingly and deliberately static and old-fashioned. I blame both. But the reason why the production was so immobile, stagey and undramatic seems to have been missed: it was a failure in political thought.

Hall put the production firmly in a political context. The stage was made deliberately shallow by a wall right across it with a single central door, so that all characters and extras, more extraneous than I had seen for twenty-five years (ten players, twelve rioters, eight councillors with grey beards) all lined up in a shallow semi-circle around the throne and watched the great ones, reacting but little. Hierarchy was stressed. The court was made the context. The issue was the succession to the throne of Denmark.

The uncut text, with all the politics about Old Norway and young Fortinbras in it, so seldom heard, and a very powerful reading of Claudius by Denis Quilley, strengthened this interpretation. Claudius was every inch the 'new prince', almost deadpan, even if the lower lip would tremble for the nonce; but who asks too nicely how a man came to power, if he can keep the realm at peace? And who better: Claudius or Hamlet? Well, in the end the guilt of Claudius is too great a primordial curse; but so are the instability and incompetence of Hamlet. Fortinbras from a neighbouring kingdom it has to be; and Horatio speaks for Denmark in its hour of need. Good government must come first.

Now all this is in the text, and is often supressed or not noticed. I remember the Hamlets of Olivier and Guinness and do not suspect that Gielgud's was very political. But the political issue, a powerful peripheral theme, is not the storm centre of the play. Hamlet himself is, of course, more important. The tragedy, certainly, is not just that Hamlet does not get his rights, but that he is not *fit* to be king; and yet the play does centre on the man, not on the realm of Denmark. It is not one of English histories, where the context matters and the story so often dominates the characters, nor is it like the Roman plays, with their deep analogies with English history and specifically with Elizabethan politics. If the minor parts *should* be politicised, Polonius, for example, given back his dignity, the Prince must still o'er tower them.

The RSC did much better with the late Buzz Goodbody's small-theatre, modern-dress production of *Hamlet* for a cast of fourteen. There were deft political touches. The lines, for instance, where Polonius instructs Reynaldo to spy upon Laertes are usually got through quickly.

> *Polonius.* You shall do marvellous wisely, good Reynaldo,
> Before you visit him, to make inquire
> Of his behaviour.
> *Reynaldo.* My Lord, I did intend it.

(II, i, 3-5)

But in the RSC production, the actor gave it with a deprecatory, cocky little half-sneer, as if to say, 'Don't tell me how to suck eggs. I've learned all I can from you about the business. Why don't you retire and let me take over?'. He was thrusting, junior executive, an arrogant company creep. Of course it is there: what other meaning can the scene have? The big fish eat the little fish, but every dog must have his day. Polonius, like Caesar, was no fool: rather he had been the embodiment of 'politique' wisdom, Cecil or Burleigh-like, but now on his way out. Ambition sours and destroys every human relationship at court.

The modern dress neither distracted nor seemed a gimmick. The King, George Baker, wore a marvellously over-well-cut chairman of the board suit, perhaps a little bit like Prince Rainier; just as Gertrude was, bless my soul, got up like Mrs Simpson. He is so rational and commanding that if the state of Denmark is to avoid inflation and industrial anarchy, it must be him at the helm, however he got there. Whereas Hamlet is the non-political humanist and intellectual, so intelligent, so much more civilised and profound; but could a man of such volatility and indecisiveness, a bit manic-depressive even, be king, be trusted with the care of the state?

Ben Kingsley played the Prince as feigning mad, which is too dangerous a game for Hamlet, for playing at it drives him into madness, able to recover but each time with diminishing coherence; and if his energy grows throughout the play, it loses any rational sense of direction. Ben Kingsley was hardly the Prince, more a humanist–courtier, unsure (like Horatio) about what he is doing there at all; but Hamlet the man lets us hear every word of his soliloquies, every word being thought over, as if thought really is decisive. 'To be or not to be.' We really wonder what conclusion he (and we) finally will reach. But when he warns Ophelia off him, 'I'm very proud, revengeful and *ambitious;*, that is his sane side, as when he complains that Claudius stood 'between the election and my hopes'. Part of him would rather be back with Horatio in the seminars of Wittenberg, but part is indeed ambitious, caught up in the court, quite apart from motives of filial vengeance and dynastic justice. This was a great reading in a great production, precisely because it was the complementary relationships between the dramatic and the political, the heroic and the social; unlike Peter Hall's production which could have had as subtitle, 'The Business of Good Government'.

With the 1977 Stratford production of *King Lear*, it was, however, the RSC's turn to go over the top. The curtain rises to reveal Kent and Gloucester in frockcoats, and as the court assembles we find the three sisters in turn-of-the-century court dress, glistening, sharp bare shoulders; and then the King appears in cream imperial Franz Joseph costume, medals and sashes and all, in high top boots which jut up ludicrously when he sits on his throne, almost reaching his chin, making him appear both puppet and petulant autocrat. The use of such a precise historical or imaginative locale shows us instantly what the production is supposed to be about: tyranny, or more precisely the whimsicality and arbitrariness of absolute power. Lear is not a feudal monarch.

He does not have to conciliate his fellow-nobles. Unlike in the histories, there appears to be no rival military powers before his abdication. So he can banish Kent as quickly and with as little dispute as he can divide his kingdom. Lear is a new monarch, *rex absolutus*. Regan and Goneril are on the edge of their nerves; with this old man anything could happen, whatever has been said beforehand. They push their advantage and luck ruthlessly and speedily; they are frightened and tense, but they are true daughters of their father's will and wilfulness.

The directors, Nunn and Barton, plainly thought they had found a contemporary political inwardness to render the strange old story plausible to us, some real motivation for launching old Lear out on the blasted heath to howl against humanity. Great pains were taken to show that Lear, even more than Antony or Hamlet, is not fit to govern. The production had Lear embodying the folly of arbitrary will, the bloody consequences for inhabitants that follow from giving kingdoms away as if they were personal gifts. And the interpretation worked very well at the beginning. Donald Sinden, who played Lear, had played Henry VIII five years before, so the face and presence of the wilful, childish, petulant, but also majestic and powerful autocrat were right. It is almost as if Henry VIII when he was old had three daughters and he decided to divide the kingdom between Mary, Anne and Elizabeth, none of whom lived happily for a moment afterwards. 'Better had thou not been born than not to have pleased me better', says Lear to Cordelia. '*Quod principi placuit legis habet vigorem*', Thomas Cromwell had reminded King Henry that the late Roman law so spake (what pleases the king has the force of law). He sits on the dragon throne and stamps his boot impatiently for the daughters' flattery to begin. Regan actually stammers with fear, though her vicious intent is clear-cut within.

Even into Goneril's house the reinterpretation works well. The ugly sisters do, quite frankly, have quite a lot to put up with. Lear and his knights burst into the house like a Romanov hunting party (or perhaps the Hapsburgs in the Carpathians), dressed like peasants, stinking like peasants, drunk as lords and firing off their guns with rowdy extravagance. The two sisters are needlessly cruel to the half-senile old man, but god he is a handful, all whim and will and neither reason nor policy. Even the court of Denmark was far bettered ordered.

The costuming in this production did present some difficulties. Lear on the heath stripped down to his woollen combinations is downright silly, and a French army in capes and kepis distracts our attention, as does Cordelia reappearing in long khaki skirt and tunic, a military tailoring half fit for the Countess of Athlone inspecting her regiment leaving for Flanders, and half for Fanny's First Fight with the Fascists. Alas, it distorts as well as distracts. For to cry on their reunion:

> Oh my dear father! Restoration hang
> Thy medicine upon my lips, and let this kiss
> Repair those violent harms that my two sisters
> Have in thy reverence made.

(iv, vii, 26-9)

while all kitted out with Sam Browne and bullet pouches is to create a quite meaningless paradox. She does what she has to do against the grain of her gentle nature, she does not find a new, true nature in political crisis and battle. She is not the devil's discipline. And a group of wretched poor are twice interpolated between scenes at the beginning, singing a non-textual ballad about what a rotten lot it is to be poor—an arbitrary and crude piece of Brechtian routine.

Doubts about the design are, however, only preliminary to a graver doubt. The design in itself could have been amended. The directors need not have been so consistent with time and place. In *Henry V's* last campaign they began in actors' rehearsal gear, moved into medieval finery but ended aptly in drab trench clothes. Similarly with *King Lear*, what the directors needed at the outset to establish the politics of autocracy or absolute monarchy, need not by itself have dictated the costuming of later scenes. But integral to the production was a resolute determination to give the play a time and place, to stop Lear himself rising out of the play to comment too freely and terribly on the eternal human condition.

They seem to have treated *King Lear* as if it were one of the histories, a part of the 'matter of England'. It is about a quarrel in a noble house, the tearing of a country to shreds by fratricide and patricide, so strong and terrible is the *libido dominandi,* the lust for power, generating other lusts, not rising from them. It was a kind of trial run for the 1977-8 *Henry VI* cycle and an echo of Barton's *Wars of the Roses*. The playing of Goneril and Regan made this initially very plausible. Their behaviour is almost to be respected, considering what life at Lear's court must have been like. Royal folly and cruel caprice lead to downfall, but humanity, in the shape of Cordelia returned and Lear briefly reborn, is asserted, however temporarily and precariously, at the end. The death of Lear and his favourite daughter is disaster but not utter defeat for the human spirit: they were reconciled, they became themselves again without the royal robes. Indeed in his long smock and flowing beard he seems transfigured from Czar into Tolstoy.

But Lear also faced the storm. And so far I have said nothing of the scenes on the heath, the mad scenes. Making the play a history almost forces a playing down of these scenes, if not to nothing at least to very little, only to a rather odd happening which holds up the action. We are to feel that the King says such dreadful things because he is mad (and serve the old tyrant right), not because in madness he gains a terrible insight (however speculatively the playwright may have meant it) into the empty, transitory loneliness of the human condition. It is one thing—and always to the RSC's credit—to have escaped from the old-fashioned star system, but it is another deliberately to mute Lear and to play down or simply to mismanage the dark and strident middle scenes. There is a political element, certainly; but it is only a small one. Schiller firmly labelled his *Don Carlos* 'a domestic drama in a Royal House'; and this *Lear* almost came down to that, as if domestic rivalry produced the savage condition of England, not the extremities of natural man. How much more moved one was at the traditional but almost unbearably intense Lear of Tony Church in Buzz Goodbody's 1972 Other Place production when a few characters stood in a Beckett-like metaphysical abstraction, exposing tortured human nature, not products of some Brechtian time and social condition.

The tight sense of time and place imposed on *Lear* is at odds with the language. And the driving sense of event piling upon event, beyond the control of the royal actors, the directors' style and the message in the history plays, seems oddly eccentric in this most episodic and loosely structured of the tragedies—a drama more expressionistic and metaphysical than narrative and political.

So determined are they to politicise it and to tie it down in time and space (and a time, moreover, very close to us) that when the Fool in the storm on that 'brave night to cool a courtesan' utters his ironic prophecy:

When every case in law is right;
No squire in debt, nor no poor knight;
When slanders do not live in tongues;
Nor cutpurses come not to throngs;
When usurers tell their gold i' th' field,
And bawds and whores do churches build—
Then shall the realm of Albion
Come to great confusion.
Then comes the time, who lives to see't
That going shall be us'd with feet.

(III, ii, 85-94)

and adds: 'This probably shall Merlin make for I live before his time', they deal with this foolish anachronism on the Bard's part by the simple and economic means of cutting it. Yet this absurd anachronism is important. Shakespeare himself prevents any attempt to anchor the play in history. And it is so often remarked what pains he took (compared, say, to *Macbeth*) to take all references to Christianity out of the play and even, as far as possible, most Christian presuppositions: part of the matter, at least, is speculation about what happens to man's mind and reason when isolated in extreme situations of both cruelty and of compassion, or in nature without society. The world is a prison, he seems to say, and we are Fools indeed to think that dream of better kings and of social justice will take away the doom of tragedy and grief from man's mortal and perhaps salvationless lot.

Why should the directors have done it this way? Perhaps extraneous extras furnish a clue, as does also a haunting double page photograph in the programme of Victorian poor children in flithy overalls, three rows of them, but here endlessly repeated, forming a human pyramid of repetitive poverty-stricken faces– under which is quoted:

> Poor naked wretches, wheresoe'er you are,
> That bride the pelting of this pitiless storm,
> How shall your housless heads and unfed sides,
> Your loop'd and window's raggedness, defend you
> From seasons such as these? O, I have ta'en
> Too little care of this! Take physic, pomp;
> Expose thyself to feel what wretches feel,
> That thou mayst shake the superflux to them,
> And show the heavens more just.

(III, iv, 28-36)

So we are to read this as a kind of prophecy of the welfare state (more incredible than Merlin's), rather than sympathy for what any Jacobean, Shakespeare almost certainly, could only see as part of the inevitable suffering of humanity.

As this theme of social injustice has no warrant at all the text of the play and does not follow from the well-perceived but overdone political dimension of Lear as autocrat rather than feudal monarch, where did they get it from? In Bertolt Brecht's key essay *Uber experimentelles Theatre* of 1939, he asks:

> What is alienation? To alienate an action or a character first of all simply means to deprive that action of character of anything matter of course, well known or obvious and to arouse amazement and curiosity about it. Let us once again take the example of Lear's rage at his daughter's ingratitude.

By means of empathetic technique the actor can present this rage in such a way that the spectator would regard it as the most natural thing in the world, so that he'd be incapable of imagining that Lear could not be angry, so that he has full solidarity with Lear, identifies with him, entirely, and grows angry himself.

By means of the alienation technique, on the other hand, the actor represents Lear's anger in such a way that the spectator can be amazed at it, that he can imagine different possible reactions of Lear's than simply one of anger. Lear's attitude is alienated, that is it is represented as peculiar, striking, remarkable, as a social phenomenon that need not be taken for granted. This rage is human but not general for all humans, there are people who do not feel it. The experiences that Lear has do not rouse rage in all people at all times. Rage may be an eternally possible reaction of human beings, but this rage, the rage that expresses itself in this way and has this cause, is conditioned by its time. Thus to alienate means to historicise. It means to represent actions and persons as historical and hence as transient . . .

What is gained by this? The gain is that the spectator no longer sees the people on the stage as utterly unchangeable, beyond influence and helplessly delivered up to their fate. He sees that this man is as he is because the conditions are as they are. And the conditions are what they are, because the man is what he is . . . and man is received in the theatre as the great changer who is able to take a hand in natural processes and social processes, and no longer simply accepts the world, but masters it.[5]

Might one of the directors have read this and seen it as the final challenge to their school of modern, politically conscious production, to historicise even *Lear*? All very well for some types of play, but surely not for *Lear*? Brecht himself never, in fact, produced *Lear*. An historical *Lear* can be, as this is, a perfectly coherent and enjoyable production. But at such a low level. So much is lost. I was not harrowed, only interested. And this, presumably, was the narrowing, Brechtian rationalising effect intended. But on the lower level, as a student of politics, I must hint at certain well-known dangers to that very freedom that Brecht thought he was talking about if one tries to politicise everything. Everything can be made politically relevant, but a world in which everything must be politically relevant would be a world of unfreedom, not the realisation of true politics. How much I have enjoyed and praised the Hall-Barton-Nunn style of producing the histories and their rediscovery of the political elements in the complex compounds of *Hamlet* and *Antony*. But everything tragic is not history and politics. Will thoughts such as Lear expresses simply not occur *ex hypothesi* in the classless society? We might be happier, but we would certainly be poorer if so.

Modern Politics

There are plays whose main concerns are the dilemmas of politics, or the differing values of the public and the private life. The National has done very well for some of them, not over-politicising them. Buchner's *Danton's Death*, of course, almost defies ideological simplification: it is both the tragedy of Danton the man and of the inflexibility, and ultimate cruelty, of Roberpierre's principles. There is a sympathety with *La Revolution* which the conservatives must dislike, but a sense of tragedy that is hardly 'the noble example' or the clear-cut enemy sought for in revolutionary theatre. Their production of Beaumarchais' *Marriage of Figaro,* while a simpler play, was exactly what a national theatre should do, a surprise for most of us, something we all had heard of, but few seen—or we may have *thought* we had seen it, for Da Ponte had taken the political guts out of Beaumarchais for Mozart. What we now saw had something to do with the bourgeois, French revolution (as the literary histories have told us), not just the chastening of aristocratic arrogance and excess by the humane and sentimental values of the opera.

Satire can pose difficulties. *The Captain of Kopenick* mocks the idiocies of a very specific society, so if the audience cannot be trusted to have some sense of what the old Kaiserreich was like (*nothing* like Nazism) and if the (much wasted) programme notes cannot be used sensibly, refuge has to be taken, alas, in over-playing the broad comedy. Indeed, Paul Schofield had similarly over-done the main role in the RSC's *Government Inspector* of a few years before. Shades of autocracy cause difficulties for modern directors habituated to stark images of twentieth-century totalitarianism. Some satire, while grotesque, should evoke the wry smile of recognising a fitness, not the guffaws of harmless catastrophe. After seeing Tom Stoppard's highly political *Travesties* done by the RSC (political in the sense that it was a double swipe at Dadaist irresponsibility and at the Leninist social theory of art), I suspect that his earlier *Jumpers* was meant to be more political. Perhaps we were meant to be generally worried about the future under the rule of the rational-seeming 'Radical Democratic Party', not merely to sympathise with a solitary moral philosopher holding out. But that one part—either as written or as played—was too farcical and rich.

Best of all modern political plays has been, I think, John Arden's *Armstrong's Last Goodnight.* Here is the explicit theme of the good man and, indeed, the poet, Sir David Lindsay, the king's herald, trying privately by 'polite guile', 'Machiavel's art' and 'through craft and through humanity' to overcome without bloodshed the disturber of the peace of the border, Johnny Armstrong. He fails. His misplayed strategies lead to the death of his friend. In the end, he has to don his herald's clothes again, to betray his office 'for necessities of state' by luring Armstrong to ambush and a sudden hanging. A dishonourable act will, none the less, maintain peace between the kingdoms and save many a life. Our sympathies are divided. This was Arden the realist. His later plays, in collaboration wit Margaretta D'Arcy, and all *engage* and either shallow or, as in *The Island of the Mighty,* a vast cauldron of strange, incompatible and unmeasured ingredients. He has moved from having a profound sense of politics into being a propagandist. And, as a person, why not? My only point is still, however, that drama thrives on dilemma and on conflict, not even on the best resolutions.

A movement in the other direction is shown by Trevor Griffith, a committed dramatist taken up by both the national companies. They have responsibilities to new playwrights, certainly; but they can also be dangerous to new playwrights, particularly when these great institutions ape the fringe. Griffith had his *Occupations* very well presented by the RSC at The Place, a small and intimate theatre, good for small audiences, minority plays, tryouts and informality. *Occupations* was about Gramsci and Lenin—well, a Lenin-like figure, anyway, and certainly the historical Gramsci. The play never moves outside the assumptions of Marxism. But there develops a deep and genuine clash both of personality and of doctrine between Gramsci and Kabak, the Soviet agent, sent either to stiffen socialist militancy in the Fiat strike of 1920 or, if the strike failed, to conclude a trade deal with Fiat, which he does. The harsh Leninist Marxism confronts the humanistic Marxism of Gramsci, to which a dash of anarcho-syndicalism is added by the author. The drama works psychologically, the protagonists are full characters as well as ideological types, and they work upon each other.

Then, however, he wrote *The Party* for the National Theatre's main stage. It was a good idea, a trendy left-wing television producer holding a party to bring together (irreconcilable) elements of the advanced Left, while they watch on television the Paris students' uprising. But the characters relevant to the action were cardboard figures: a lot of fashionable over-production crept in, bedroom scenes with mirrors, nothing to do with the main theme. There has to be a lot of lecturing at the audience, since 'the National crowd' would need much more explanation than the students at The Place. The programme read like discussion notes for a seminar at the Workers' Education Association, and a drunken wise-fool of a playwright, whose main role is to expose the shallowness of the trendy television producer, has to be wrenched out of character at the end to prophesy revolution by popular spontaneity rather than by the tactics of any party. It was bad. I did not see a version that subsequently toured student unions, but many say that it was better: the over-production was out and the audiences more fitting and responsive.

Griffith, however, came back to the National with a Nottingham Playhouse production of *Comedians*, a truly rich and complex image of the war between consumerism, art and political commitment. An evening class for comics sees its decent old teacher defending the traditional craft, fit for the family, against both the calculating, smutty debaser ('give 'em what they really want') and the zany revolutionary ('shock the bastards into thinking'). They both let him down and go their own way at the audition. Parliamentary politics is doomed: fascism and anarchism will be left to fight it out. I do not share the author's catastrophic view. But the play is the richer for being open-ended and for having, in the traditional masks of comedy and the art of teaching about art, found rich metaphors for debasement, doomed tradition and the hope of transformation.

Two superficially similar young left-wing playwrights, David Edgar and Howard Barker, have been taken up by the RSC, and divide rather like the two souls of Mr Griffith: the tortured enthusiast (who can dramatise) and the conceited demagogue (who can only preach in theatrical images). As I have said already, David Edgar's announced theme of the fortunes of fascism in the West Midlands (in *Destiny*) did not warm my blood like wine, at least the everyday blood I use for understanding and delight, rather than that saved to be spilt in the last flight. But, despite a conventional ending, of capitalists hiring fascists to fight trade unionists (as dramatically simple-minded as it is historically silly), the main body of the play was about types of fascism and nationalism in conflict with each other, together with sub-plots of different kinds of compromise made by 'decent' or ordinary politicians. And each idea was well embedded in plausible characters who are rarely seen on the stage. Howard Barker, in the other hand, in *That Good Between Us* has a number of unrelieved and largely undifferentiated bastards *all* grinding down the workers and their friends, when a social democratic government, in a slightly future Clockwork Orange Britain, takes off the kid gloves and reveals itself for the oppressive, violent class force it really is. The author achieves remarkable dramatic images: the first naked gang rape on the stage (to my knowledge), beatings, bicycles, punts, burials, striptease, and groaning beds. A series of scenes succeeded each other at great pace, as only the RSC directors can achieve, as if the stage were screaming to be cinema; and, in the end, to make a really partisan point, the result was as full of technically and psychologically shocking images as much modern cinema, and as pointless, mindless and undramatic. We didn't know what was going to happen next, but we knew exactly what was happening all the boring time. Even in adolescent religious days I was bored by sermons, however bizarre their quotations from the Old Testament, and rationally puzzled about why all this incitement to a change of life should be aimed at those already converted.

Political theatre is at its worst when it sees politics simply in terms of violence by undifferentiated oppressors against equally undifferentiated oppressed. Politics is, indeed, about conflict: but conflict by all means available, violence, fear, propaganda, and (perhaps most of all) by argument, persuasion and example. Every tyrant, even, has to persuade someone, or he would not be able to sleep at night. Political theatre is at its best when it makes us aware of the price to be paid, always, for progress, or at best the plausibility and equal authenticity of differing ideas. Such is drama. All good drama has some political element in it, some choice between real alternatives. If choice is lacking, as in a Maoist text, or if it is made clear that Caesar *must* die, Falstaff *must* be forsaken, Hamlet *clearly* is or is not fit to be king, or if the play is a mere history lesson with a known result and fixed course (as equally Robert Bolt's recent *The State of Revolution* or Brecht's *The Day of the Commune*), then both drama and politics are diminished.

NOTES
1. I have used materials from reviews contributed to *The Times Higher Education Supplement* and *The New Review*. I thank the editors for permission.
2. Bernard Crick, *In Defence of Politics* (Harmondsworth: Pelican, 1964).
3. Quotations from Shakespeare are from *The Complete Works*, ed. Peter Alexander (London: Collins, 1951).
4. Thomas Hobbes, *Leviathan,* introd. A. D. Lindsay, Everyman's Library (London: Dent, 1914), part I, chapter 10, p. 47.

Three

Young Writers of the Thirties

From *The New Review,* July 1976

The MacSpaunday family album has been opened to the public at the National Portrait Gallery. The actual title of the exhibition is 'Young Writers of the Thirties'. It's an important exhibition, but it is in fact much narrower and more personal than the title suggests. The director writes in a Foreword to the catalogue:

> The last great writers to be celebrated in exhibitions at the National Portrait Gallery were Pepys and Boswell. Both these exhibitions were on a rather larger scale and offered the visitor a panorama of the life of their respective periods. Our objective on this occasion is quite different, and is more an extension of our aims in the permanent display: to show a number of great writers in relation to each other, and in the context of their literary achievements . . . We have chosen five writers from that extraordinary generation, four of them poets, and all of them men who had the most profound effect in their contempraries: Auden, Day Lewis, Isherwood, MacNeice and Spender. The varied way in which these five writers–who knew each other well but were no sense a group–responded to the problems of their age, and the effect of their particular preoccupations on the development of their work, is the subject of this exhibition.

As a political writer who is only a common reader of literature (a reversal of roles of most reviewers of this exhibition or of Samual Hynes's recent book, *The Auden Generation: Literature and Politics in the 1930s*), I quote at such pedantic length to raise at once the main questions begged by the assumptions of the exhibition makers. If the five are all 'great writers', not just distinguished and interesting writers, then the case is ready-made for treating them as *the* young writers of the thirties, or 'as representatives' (says the catalogue) of all the rest,. Even so, however, is part of their greatness having had a 'profound effect' on their contemporaries? Or in reflecting so well some of the concerns of what Stephen

48

Spender later called 'the Divided Generation'? The attribute of 'greatness' that justifies reducing so many other good writers to a kind of *salon des refuses* (that should be set up outside on the Charing Cross Road) is clearly possessed only by Auden; and Auden, though the pace-setter at the time (the title of Professor Samuel Hynes's book is, he persuades one, far less misleading than that of this exhibition), was also the first deliberate deserter from this myth of the committed thirties. Indeed, he became a rewriter of his own past, soon even a positive antagonist to it and perhaps was never as fully committed in all his work of the period to the myth of necessary political commitment and of special poetic relevance as has been suggested.

If 'they were in no sense a group' and 'sometimes had to fight off such labelling from other critics', says the catalogue, why perpetuate the myth that they were? 'Alice Prochaska . . . has been responsible for the administration and research', we are told, and her name appear on the title page, but also in the Foreword: 'We have been privileged that Humphrey Spender, who shares the ideals of his brother and his friend, agreed to design the exhibition for us.' Indeed Humphrey Spender's own photographs of the period are an important part of the exhibition and he appears photographed with Isherwood; so it is perhaps difficult to expect the usual objectivity and critical distance of an exhibition maker, though it could be argued that we get something more expressive—if a lot less accurate—instead. Perhaps such exhibitions always tend to take a purely celebratory rather than an appreciatively critical stance.

This exhibition, however, has it both ways about being and not being a group. It is an odd phrase, indeed, that blames 'labelling from other critics'. 'Labelling' is present-day jargon and yet 'critics' at that time none of them were, if 'literary critics' is meant and not 'social critics'. Someone, probably Stephen Spender, is still getting his past and his present a bit confused: back then he wrote considerable poetry, but not since: nowadays he is a considerable critic, but not then.

As Hynes makes clear, they were in a sense a group, they liked each other's work and responded to it, even if they never all met together at one time or regularly. (C. Day Lewis said in his autobiography, *The Buried Day:* 'Though Auden, Spender, MacNeice and I have known each other personally since the mid-thirties, each of us had not even met all three others till after the publication of *New Signatures* in 1932, while it was only in 1947 that Auden, Spender and I found ourselves together in one room'.) Only if an intimate group, however, does the elevation of Isherwood

among the four poets make any sense (there were, after all, other
and better novelists); and this test fails for Louis MacNeice and C.
Day Lewis—both of whom seem to grow in stature, incidentally, the
more one looks at them. They were all partly a group because,
indeed, others lumped them together, notably T. E. Lawrence, and
they played up to it; and they played up to the imposed reputation
of all the time being, of struggling with being, and not-being,
politically committed. But their literary talents and developments
were highly individual. So why perpetuate a mythological view of
five horsemen against the world as being the literary-political
essence of *the* 1930s?

Perhaps I suffer from an excess of commonsense and good
humour. The editor should perhaps not have sent such a political
philosopher along. For while I am vitally interested in the function
of myth in society, yet also and always there is the nagging
question of truth. But I perhaps am wrong to confuse the National
Portrait Gallery with the British Museum or the Public Record
Office. Why should not a portrait gallery simply produce a
portrait, in the style that Stephen and Humphrey Spender wish to
be remembered, and in what was their creative period? Two
possible arguments against this *l'art pour l'art* attitude to mounting
an exhibition are (i) that Auden, MacNeice and C. Day Lewis
would probably not have been quite as happy, had they been alive,
as Stephen Spender with the perpetuation of this myth, for much
of their best work was done later; and (ii) that the young and
innocent visitor may swallow it whole, and swallowing it whole
will lead him (a) to undervalue the non-political poetry of that
time; (b) to undervalue also the achievement of others actually
more committed than the five on exhibit; and (c) not to question,
which concerns me very much, this sadly crude view of political
thought which sees it as concerned with whether or not to commit
oneself to some existing system, hook, line and sinker, and not
with weighing the odds between rival systems and, indeed, rival
patterns of scepticism; appreciating the different plausibilities
and acting, but then acting sensibly and with discrimination; not
avoiding issues, but never believing that any one system can
answer all problems. Some men of literature have a view of politics
as crude as any philistine ward-healer might have of poetry. There
can be a very special political illiteracy among the literary
literate.

The question of period also arises. Of course, one has to start
somewhere. I am not going to argue for another pseudo-precision
to replace that under review—such as a reasonable view that 'the
1930s', as a style both of literature and popular politics, ran from

1926 to 1944. The point is rather a simple historical one. What is 'the context of their literary achievements' of which the preface speaks? Is context all those fine but familiar photographs of the Nazis and the Fascists marching, or isn't it also and more so the writers of the *previous* decade, particularly the literature of disillusion with war—Robert Graves's *Goodbye to All That,* etc. etc.? And poetically, does 'young' mean anything other than the biological age of the five when Eliot, Pound, Graves and Yeats are relegated to the shadows? They were all writing in the thirties and influenced nearly everyone else who wrote at that time. It is characteristic of modernity in general for each generation to believe that it is unique. If there was interaction as never before and a sense of time pressing as rarely before, then it covers all writers of the *entre deux guerres* period, not just an arbitrary half of the genuine period. Perhaps if Janet Adam Smith's account in the *TLS* (18 June, 1976) had been available earlier of how Eliot commissioned from her husband, Michael Roberts, *The Faber Book of Modern Verse* (1936), they could have used that as a centre-piece of a far more comprehensive exhibition of the poetry of the whole post-war, with hindsight 'between the wars', generation.

The claim is even made that these five were sociologically distinct. One of the first of the visual displays to face one as one goes down the exhibition's indivated tunnel of time says:

> They developed unconventional attitudes and ways of life which set them apart from most of their upper middle-class contemporaries. To be somewhat apart became a point of honour.

Read that twice, and if you don't see the unconscious humour of it, I must try to convince you. 'Somewhat apart' is what made me giggle, I mean smile with a wise sadness. Don't we all, who have come from such backgrounds or gone through such schools and have read, perhaps written, real books, have 'unconventional attitudes'? That is not to claim very much, indeed in their cases little more than a middle-class bohemianism. I don't want to put the stakes too high. What is at issue is not their failure really to pass over among or to be wholly and effectively on the side of the workers (not even Orwell did this), but the failure of most of them to be consistently serious even in what they did do. 'To be somewhat apart became a point of honour.' I once read a letter of the 1790s recommending a *bas bleu* lady as tutor to Coke of Norfolk's family: 'She is such a good Whig', enthused the referee, 'as to be almost a *republican.*'

Actually, to be fair, the passage I have quoted seems itself to see part of the difficulty and perhaps really doesn't claim too much:

'ways of life', it says. This rather unusual plural is used presumably because Alice Prochaska and Humphrey Spender realise that their five are politically and socially in many ways significantly different: no common 'way of life' existed or emerged, such as, for instance, Middleton Murry at that time was always trying, in one way and then another, to impose on his hopeful and bewildered followers. Good. But, we go round in a circle; for in that case why, once again, lump them together as 'the thirties' to the exclusion of so many other far from unknown warriors?

Perhaps I am plunging in too fast and being ungenerous. For pictorially the exhibition is a marvellous one: photographs, manuscripts and books all splendidly presented; and a final room of darkness in which slides are shown and an entaped Professor R. D. Smith endlessly intones a good fifteen-minute commentary (a good deal more balanced and cautious, incidentally, than many of the claims of the official catalogue).

The photographs are of two kinds, of the five themselves and those associated with them (with a few delicate anonymities), and of the background. Those of the five themselves include few studio or even professional portraits, most are from family or personal albums, many taken by themselves: some very beautiful, merry, and revealing. The exhibition is worth it for these alone. The background photographs, however, while excellently chosen— Nazis and Fascists marching, Berlin, Spain, unemployment and poverty (including some of Humprey Spender's own best work for Mass Observation)—yet reinforce my general worry about the impression given by the whole exhibition. What precisely had all this marching and counter-marching to do with them? It could provide the background for almost any group of writers in the 1930s. Indeed I have seen *Jackdaws* or similar illustrated kits for schools use much the same material to illustrate the rise and fall of Baldwin and Chamberlain. They could be used as backdrop to an exhibition on Osbert Sitwell to imply that he didn't respond to them or to Noel Coward that he did—in his own inimitable way. The claim isn't made that the five had any great effect on all this; but the risk is that to the politically innocent such an implication may appear to be there. Nor can the precise effect it had on them be made clear; but the implication of the photographs is obvious (and, I think, false) that this type of 'background' had more effect on how they reacted politically than the preconceptions they had from the writers of the immediate post-war decade whom they would have read at school and at university, and who were mostly still writing and by no means all literary men, either. We can forget the obvious, that Shaw and Wells were still writing and read; and, more mundanely, that some purely political writers were widely read by intellectuals, such as H. N. Brailsford, G. D. H. Cole, Harold Laski and R. H. Tawney, each of whom spanned the twenties and thirties with little essential change (they are worth photographic recall); and who were all active in the WEA and other workers' education movements to which the committed poets aspired or descended (lecturing was, in fact, often their main form of commitment). For it is crude to see the poets' politics simply as an immediate reaction to Fascism. They surely reacted to Fascism as they did because of the political viewpoints they had formed from the great anti-war literature of the 1920s and from the popular pamphlets of the Labour movement, particularly as taken up by those intellectuals who identified with, even after the event, the General Strike, the unemployed and with those who saw Ramsey Macdonald as a traitor. '1926' and '1931' were the shibboleths of commitment; and the difficulty that official Labour writers had with pronouncing on them adequately drove many intellectuals towards the Communist Party, even if more rarely into it, or into it for long. What is fair, however, about the international backdrop is the precise point that Auden, Isherwood, and Spender were not of the Francophile literary set. They knew German well, went to Germany and understood something of the terrible novelty of Nazism—that it was not just old nationalism writ large.

The books they wrote figure largely in the exhibition, a feast of first editions. My only disappointment is that the blurbs on the inside or on the back of the dustjackets were not either displayed or transcribed. For where one can see them, as when Faber's put quite a long text right across the front of Auden's second book, *The Orators* of 1932, one can see the myth in the making. Even then a unique and mainly political commitment for poetry was stressed.

Letters abound, mostly shown as if holy relics, but some are important to scholars of the literature of this period and have never been seen before. There is no consistency, however, in whether or not they are transcribed. Some are hard to read through the glass—one wonders if such serious viewers are really wanted (a 'small exhibition', some critic said, but not if you pause to read what you can). A letter of T. S. Eliot to Louis MacNeice on 7 February, 1939 praises his *Autumn Journal* highly, but asks him to think again (which he jolly well didn't) about the stanza on the Oxford by-election:

> . . . regretting that you simplify the issues so much in suggesting that the supporters of Quintin Hogg are a pack of

scoundrels. I think it is poor tactics to attribute motives, and one is likely to over-reach oneself in so doing.

But unlike his famous letter to Orwell of only five years later rejecting *Animal Farm* for reasons of state, he promises speedy publication notwithstanding.

A very important letter, which Professor Hynes could have used to good effect, is from Auden to his old teacher and friend (also MacNeice's) Professor E. R. Dodds, the classicist:

8 Dec. 1936

I've decided to go out in the New Year, as soon as the book is finished, to join the International Brigade in Spain. I so dislike everyday political activities that I won't do them, but here is something I can do as a citizen and not as a writer, and as I have no dependants I feel I ought to go; but O I do hope there are not too many surrealists there. Please don't tell anyone about this. I shan't break it to my parent until after Christmas.

Well, he finished that book and he went, to be an ambulance driver; but somehow he didn't: even the patient Professor Hynes cannot find out what happened, it seems that the Spanish Government wanted him instead to go into broadcasting, but he wandered around a bit, something disillusioning must have happened, or he realised that it just wasn't for him, and he came home.

Two other even more revealing letters to E. R. Dodds, of 16 January and 11 March 1940, try to explain, in answer to a series of searching, blunt and direct questions, why he won't come home to fight now that the war against Fascism had become general. Auden no longer uses the 'what I can do as a citizen' argument; rather he insists that, on the contrary, he would only return if he could find something special to do for the war effort as a writer. It is, I am sorry to say, a very shoddy and muddled argument, there is no pretending otherwise. Later, he changed his mind again (the war over) and wrote movingly in 'Squares and Oblongs' that while the state may well conscript a poet, if the state is in danger, it cannot conscript his poetry.

No wonder Orwell is relegated in the exhibition (though not at all in Hynes's book) to a single photograph on a wall of about a dozen other considerable thirties writers, otherwise ignored. I don't conjure up Orwell's nagging shade because he fought, simply, directly and nearly fatally in Spain, nor because he clamoured to fight in 1939; nor yet because *Homage to Catalonia* is one of the most important books of this period and yet is totally ignored in the exhibition—as is Orwell's poetically rather obtuse but morally rather just attack on Auden's poem, 'Spain'. No, Orwell is relevant because he saw clearly that the responsibilities of an artist and of a citizen are different things, but just that we must carry them together in one frame even thought neither can be used as an absolute excuse for the conduct of the other. P. G. Wodehouse was silly, no more than silly, pardonably silly, Orwell was to say, in making broadcasts from Germany; but that doesn't affect the peculiar merit of his writings. Pound was a Fascist and a detestable anti-Semite, said Orwell, and is not to be pardoned as a person; but that doesn't affect the greatness of his writings either, nor even should it be a reason not to give him a literary prize. Auden's letter on going to Spain is politically naive ('surrealists', indeed!) and strengthens Orwell's view of him as a political schoolboy, ideologically amateur and muddled. He held the same view of Spender, but it didn't stop him liking him personally when they eventually met; nor did it destroy his appreciation of Auden's poetry, even if perhaps it led him, like so many others, to exaggerate its political content as a proportion, at any time or period, of a much more complex, posturing, profound and tentative—all these at once—whole.

Spain, however, even with the uncomfortable Orwell excluded, does pose a problem for the exhibition. So an honourable solution is a special case containing poems, books, photographs and associated material of Julian Bell, Christopher Caudwell, John Cornford and Ralph Fox, who all made that 'Journey to the Frontier', of which Abrahams and Stansky wrote so well, and did not return. The heart is torn to look into that box.

Penultimately, by the side of twelve or so familiar faces who are also expendable in this personal myth, including Orwell, Connolly, Empson, Rosamond Lehmann, Edith Sitwell, is a delightful sign which suddenly introduces a whole new concept of exhibitions as an art form, a do-it-yourself or free-expression board.

There has been space to represent only a few of the writers, artists and musicians who were active in Britain in the Thirties. Visitors are invited to suggest others whom they would have liked to see included.

Now it happened that I went on the first afternoon and in the company of Frederick Grubb, the poet and critic, author of *A Vision of Reality: A Study of Liberalism in the Twentieth-century Verse* (Chatto and Windus, 1965). There were already a few good scribbles on this free-expression board, but Fred (very knowledge-able on the period) and I got to work in earnest to make additions so as to leave, by the scandalously early five o'clock closing time on the first day, a fairly comprehensive list of candidates for *le salon des refuses,* those excluded from the MacSpaunday family album: George Barker, Roy Campbell, Norman Cameron, David Gascoyne, Hugh MacDiarmid, Edwin Muir, Wyndham Lewis, William Plomer, Charles Madge, Herbert Read, Edgell Rickword, Bernard Spencer and (talking of commitment) A. S. J. Tessimond, with last but not least Dylan Thomas, who was well into his surrealist phase by 1936.

We limited our work to poets because, after all, the official exhibition was largely about poets—Isherwood is really only there as a friend of Auden and Spender, and we challenged the exhibition's assumptions that political and social concerns were more evident in the thirties than in the twenties, or rather we asserted the essential unity of dilemma of both or all the generations *entre deux guerres.* Even so, the list is large. Too large for an exhibition? Depends on how large an exhibition is. Not all of the same quality, certainly, prune it a little; and let the oldies cut out the oldies if they wish to preserve, so religiously and publicly, the memory of their youth. The official four are certainly the best of the new poets publishing after 1930 (if we limit Thomas to his strictly thirties work). But even if pruned and with such a hierarchy imposed, the point is surely clear: that there was a wealth of poetic talent in the 1930s (Eliot, Empson, Graves and Yeats too), far wider than the four and so diverse in interests as to make nonsense of the claim that the four are representative of their generation, and that the generation somehow broke from the 1920s as the 1920s had from the 1900s. Isn't there some responsibility to recall the better, lesser talents and not to carry on going round and round with the favoured few like an old horse in a pound?

If the free-expression board had allowed for corrigenda as well as addenda, we both felt that three editor writers, who did crop up in letters and photographs all through the exhibition, warranted a more individual and precise treatment themselves: Geoffrey Grigson, John Lehmann and Michael Roberts—who will be precisely those kind of 'important names', vaguely familiar names, which visitors will not as a rule be able quite to fix. T. S. Eliot and Leonard Woolf also appeared incidentally, but knowledge of who they were, both as writers and as publishers, may still, perhaps, just about be taken for granted.

Why, after all, were there such massive exclusions? Partly, I truly suspect, for the convenience of an exhibition as an art form in itself. This is a tendency very much to be guarded against. How marvellous that exhibitions are now so well presented compared with the old stick-it-in-the-case or hang-it-on-the-wall days. How marvellous also is much television camera work. But in both cases the danger is flagrant that the technique can dominate the matter. And in both cases the danger is greater when a didactic tone is adopted. We are teaching you something general about a genre or the period, but on the basis of an incredibly small, but ever so sincerely chosen, sample. Skilful simplicity.

Perhaps also some sensitivities enter in. Orwell was so rude to Auden and Spender and those he chose to call 'the nancy boys of literature', that perhaps they still don't want to include him. Edgell Rickword is an interesting case too, for in one of the key documents of the thirties myth, the 'Auden Double Number' of *New Verse* (November 1937), to which they all contribute, the rest of the five plus a dozen and a half solicited tributes, Rickwood, a true Communist and a poet, goes for Auden hard:

In his poem 'Spain' he says:
'Today the expending of powers
On the flat ephemeral pamphlet and the boring meeting'
which is an extraordinary example of what used to be
accepted as the aloofness proper to an intellectual . . .

And then Rickword goes for Auden more gently:

The lyric grace of Auden's later poems is achieved at the
expense of that sensuous consciousness of social change
which made his early poems such exciting discoveries. Auden
is too good a poet to fall back into the simple exploration of
individuality, after having originated a poetry of the social
type along the lines of which there are so many fertile
experiments to be made.

I don't share Rickword's perspective at all. Frankly, after seeing the exhibition, I think nothing of Auden as a political thinker, actually less of him as a moral person, but am not changed at all in thinking highly of him as a poet. Rickword, ever Orwell's point, must fuse and confuse the two judgments (it was called 'dialectic thinking' at the time). But he does bring out subtly how so many contemporaries saw the debate. He deserved a hearing.

Anyway, Auden did not speak for all. Not all Communists were so respectful in polemic against him as Rickword or perhaps as hopeful still to win Auden over (as C. Day Lewis was won over as a person, but never as a poet). A real 'social type' and 'fertile experimenter' let fly at him *et al.,* and again I think the exhibition a bit toffee-nosed or defensive in not quoting such a famous barbaric outburst:

Michael Roberts and All Angels! Auden, Spender, those
bhoyos,
All yellow twicers; not one of them

With a tithe of Carlile's courage and integrity.

Unlike these pseudos I am *of,* not *for,* the working class . . .
Only a very small part, alas, of Hugh MacDiarmid's 'Third Hymn
to Lenin'. But to be fair, C. Day Lewis certainly saw the dilemma.
We may smile at seeing in the catalogue the Visitors' Book kept by
Mr and Mrs C. Day Lewis in Cheltenham in the 1930s ('the entries
reflect Day Lewis's hospitality . . . to left wing and Communist
politicians', says the card), yet in his autobiography he writes
movingly of the pathos of his being made education officer of his
cell, as the intellectual, and having to take working men and
women in Cheltenham through Communist theory:

> . . . these men and women whose hearts were in the right place,
> never mind where their brains were; who gave up nearly all
> their small leisure time to dull, slogging Party work; who,
> although some of them no doubt had chips of their shoulders
> and axes to grind, had also an admirable devotion to a Cause
> they could get nothing from in the foreseeable future except
> victimisation.

If Auden's friend and contemprary, Edward Upward, is presented
in early letters and photographs, there is only a hint in the
exhibition (a letter of Isherwood's refers to Upward's 'humble
practical political work') that he was the one who took to *the* Party
and stuck to the Party, that it was probably he that Auden was
getting at in his dislike of 'the expending of powers' on 'the flat
ephemeral pamphlet and the boring meeting'—it all being so
personal. They could have quoted some of Upward's measured
criticisms of his old friend as he was eventually to write them in
'Remembering the Early Auden' in *Adam International Review*
(1973-74), or from the interview with him in *The Review* (No. 11-12),
'The Thirties—a Special Number'—which, not to praise the home
team, would have furnished a better guide to the people who
should be included in any thirties exhibition than that used by
Alice Prochaska and Humphrey Spender; and perhaps also a
gentle deflation of the exaggerated idea of Auden's poetic
commitment at that time even to political dilemmas—in Barbara
Hardy's 'The Reticence of Auden' (also in *the Review's* special
issue), which sees him as a poet of personal experience,
experiencing, it is true, the political, but among many other things
explicit but as often implicit.

What, indeed, was the commitment? It does not help very much
for the catalogue to quote and a board to display the famous June
1937 Paris Manifesto of Writers (which Auden signed):

> It is clear to many of us throughout the whole world that now,
> as certainly never before, we are determined, or compelled, to

take sides. The equivocal attitude, the Ivory Tower, the paradoxical, the ironic detachment, will no longer do.
For the sides were not drawn up with any obvious clarity: or even if Fascism was clearly to be fought, the question of how was not simple. Nor does the unequivocal and non-paradoxical become any clearer by being cleverly juxtaposed with an equally extreme contrary:

The escape into political or social propaganda is now the like of least resistance for young writers with sensitive consciences. It is to be hoped that the most talented of them will not succumb to so easy a seduction; for the fatal error, made by ever so many thinkers, from Plato to Wells, is to imagine that there is anything better to be than a poet.

(Edward Sackville-West, 1938)

There may, indeed, be nothing better to be than a poet. Certainly in poetry language reaches its highest intensity of meaning. Poets, for instance, both move me and make me think more than do philosophers and theologians, and more than novelists and most dramatists. To be a poet does not exclude political action, but neither does it imply political action, let alone of any particular *tendenz* (*pace* Eliot, Pound and Yeats). The myth of the thirties is that once upon a time people thought that the two must go together and go Left. For a short while they *did*, in fact, so go, contingently; but that's a different matter; and then only (the very variety of *les refuses* convinces me) if you pick and choose very carefully to sustain your thesis.

What is basically at fault, both in the exhibition and with thought of its subjects at that far-off time, is a literary intellectual's paradigm of politics as warm, excited and united action. To be committed to the Cause (Hope It's A Good One!). Very romantic— 'young', indeed, in the worst sense. A kind of substitute religion once again, one suspects. The genuine political thinker, in the tradition of Aristotle, Cicero, Machiavelli, Locke, J. S. Mill and Tocqueville, looks at politics as involving conflicts of values and interests. One set of general ideas may fit one circumstance, but they will never fit all (not even if one tries forcefully to make them fit). A principle, like Liberty, is a moral imperative, but so can be Equality, Fraternity, Tolerance, Love or the Preservation of Life. They may, indeed commonly do, conflict. We do the best we can with reason to steer between unattainable heights of altruism and ultimately untenable depths of self-interest. There are general principles, but no general formulae that can be automatically applied to practice. Moral and political life is like that. It calls for knowledge, skill, empathy and morality—sometimes patience and luck, as well as courage and endurance. Odd that, of all people, poets, who live off the ambiguities of languages and freedom of expression, should occasionally dream of a necessary and unambiguous practice—which they would call, at times, politics but which I call despotism.

Actually, Auden saw this, even before he abandoned his socialism. And he said it most clearly in a rather unexpected place, missed or ignored both in the exhibition and in Samuel Hynes's scholarly and sensible volume. The Left Book Club brought out an antholgy called *Poems of Freedom* in 1938, edited by John Mulgan, many of whose contributors more obviously hated oppression than they loved other people's liberties. Auden wrote a Preface, but it must have upset Gollancz, Laski and Strachey almost as much as Orwell's second part of *The Road to Wigan Pier*. In it Auden said:

> Great claims have been made for poets as a social force: they have been called the critics of life, the trumpets that sing men to battle, the acknowledged legisators of the world. On the other hand they have been accused of being introverted neurotics who find in infantile word-play an escape from the serious duties of adult life, the irresponsible fiddlers deserting a Rome in flames. Both opinions are bosh, but the second is the inevitable reaction from the first. Those who go to poetry expecting to find a complete guide to religion, or morals, or political action will very soon be disillusioned and condemn poets, though what they are really condemning is their own attitude towards poetry . . .
>
> The primary function of poetry, as of all the arts, is to make us more aware of ourselves and the world around us. I do not know if such increased awareness makes us more moral or more efficient: I hope not. I think it makes us more human and I am quite certain it makes us more difficult to deceive, which is why, perhaps, all totalitarian theories of the State from Plato's downwards, have deeply mistrusted the arts. They notice and they say too much, and the neighbours start talking:
>
> There's many a beast, then in a populous city
> And many a civil monster.

In fact Auden had been saying this in fragments from at least 1936, but it was part of the myth that Gollancz wouldn't listen to sensible doubts and would commission Auden, expecting a clarion call.

If Auden had sorted himself out, why should this exhibition try to revive the myth of a poetry wholly and necessarily committed?

Odd, but very, very interesting. Will everyone, however, see it for the nostalgia kick that it is? Some may think it to be true history. That it is not.

Most writers at the time reacted against Fascism not because of their reaction to day-to-day events in the newspapers and on the newsreels, but because of the lessons they thought had been drawn from the 1920s literature of denunciation of the First World War and from the war poets themselves. But the lesson was not usually seen as the need for simple but anti-reactionary commitment, nor for pacifism–though some espoused both contradictory alternatives. For most writers it was sadly apparent that you had to be prepared to be political to keep the political at arm's length: that the private can only be defended against the intrusion of the public by taking part in the social; and that the best of all worlds is one in which men and women can move freely, backwards and forwards if they choose, between the private and the public—emblematically between lyric poetry and official prose.

Four

Koestler's Koestler

A review of Koestlers *Bricks to Babel: an omnibus,* (Hutchinson, 1981) in *Partisan Review,* 1982 No. 2. It was written in his lifetime.

In 1942 George Orwell wrote about a new breed of writers who were specifically 'political writers', men whose best writing was to be found in that aesthetically unfavoured subject matter. Among them he numbered Malraux, Borkenau, Silone, and his new friend Arthur Koestler.

Koestler has been almost as difficult to come to terms with as Orwell, even though, born only two years later, in 1905, he is still very much alive and has written copiously about himself and his 'career'—he is fond of the word *career.* Admiration for both men is tinged with uncertainty as to quite what we are admiring; and some, whose wounds still ache from old cuts inflicted by one or the other of them, would deny their merit as writers at all, or call it grossly inflated. Part of the difficulty of appraising Koestler is that he has written so much and in a variety of forms on widely varying subjects, most of which stir strong reactions. A bibliography lists thirty published books.

Now Koestler seems to help us by providing a selection of his own writings. What is it in fact? 'An omnibus,' he says, which the *Concise Oxford* tells him 'is a volume containing several stories, plays, etc., by an author published at a low price to be within the reach of all.' That it is, a fine piece of publishing, incidentally, but in one respect it is a curious omnibus, for it is not 'the best of Koestler,' a selection of works as a whole, but rather heavily edited abridgements from all the thirty books. He has had to reduce 9000 pages to 700, so to seven and a half per cent of the total, he tells us with mock pedantry, obviously and understandably pleased with his own professional skill with the knife, even on himself.

This book must at least be his own view of his achievement, especially as at first glance it includes something of everything: Zionist, Communist, Anticommunist, philosopher, scientist, pamphleteer, deep pessimist, profound optimist, unsatisfied Yogi and frustrated commissar. Can we now judge whether he is a bourgeois hedgehog or a natural aristocrat of foxes? Whether he should be remembered and respected more for his philosophic and scientific speculation of later years or for his earlier political writings? And did he just have two good novels in him—which came out as *Darkness at Noon* and *Arrival and Departure*—or has his abandonment of the novel as a form in favour of scientific speculations about human nature and destiny both lost him an audience and diminished his art?

In some ways, however, this book makes general judgements more difficult, not less. For he tries to kill two very different birds with the same stone: the omnibus is both a remarkably fair selection from his published books (including those essays republished in book form) and a substitute autobiography. It is fair because the bulk of these books fall into his post-war scientific, post-political period; and yet if he values them more, he still gives half of this book to the political period, in professional deference, one suspects, to the majority of his readers. It is a substitute autobiography in that the extracts, whether from novels or non-fiction, are printed in chronological order, each with an interesting headnote explaining how and why each book came to be written. But the balance of extracts is only a careful editorial compromise. It must be wrong from one or another point of view: the demands of a truthful autobiography or the demands of a good selection of what he thinks to be his own best or most important work.

So Koestler has not done the critic's work for him, or even made a clear first bid. The claim he makes on our attention is still enigmatic. The character of the writings needs closer examination before we can accept or reject the younger Koestler or the older one, Orwell's 'political writer' or the scientific writer who is proud to insert a footnote on the third page of his preface to relate Sir Peter Medawar's conviction that reading Koestler led him to reconsider 'the conventional Darwinian explanation of evolution.' Indeed the alarming thought could occur, as some of Orwell's friends claimed of him, perhaps out of discomfort with the content of his writings, that it is actually the life of the man that is more memorable than the writings. To say this would obviously be to disparage Koestler's writings, but it is not a view to be dismissed out of hand. For his public life has been extraordinary. In 1925 he dropped out as a student of physics in Vienna, having lost his faith in determinism, and left for the Holy Land as already a member of a Zionist dueling fraternity and of Jabotinsky's League of Zionist Activists (the forerunner of Begin's Irgun). Life in a kibbutz was both too hard and too narrow, but with youthful effrontery and

skill, he began his journalism. He became Middle East correspondent for the Ullstein Press which in 1929 sent him to Paris,
and in 1930 he was recalled to Berlin and, at twenty-five, made
science editor of the group. He was the only journalist on the Graf
Zeppelin's flight to the North Pole, which brought his name into
prominence. Disenchanted with both pure science and Zionism,
Marxism was to be his next quest for certainty or 'search for
synthesis.' He joined the Communist Party, visited the USSR,
worked for the Party, was a war correspondent in Spain as an
undercover Communist, infiltrated onto the books of the British
liberal *News Chronicle.* Identified and imprisoned by the
Nationalists, he was saved from execution by a mistaken, popular
British campaign to save 'British journalists.' In a cell in Spain,
communism evaporated, and a knowing, wise and deadly anti-
communism succeeded it, first *Spanish Testament* of 1937, and then
the great achievement and fame of *Darkness at Noon* of 1941. By
this time he had escaped from a French concentration camp via
Portugal and reached Britain illegally, where he was at first
imprisoned as an illegal immigrant and then set to work in the
Pioneer Corps digging trenches and tank traps. As a connoisseur
of prison life, his praise of English prisons deserves remembering
at a time when the notorious 'H-Block' is in fact a veritable bed of
roses compared to grim, stone-flagged old Pentonville. All things
are, indeed, relative.

For a world view, he substitutes at first a passionate Englishness,
becomes the kind of central European emigre who becomes
almost more English than the English, displaying tolerance, love
of tradition, and good political manners, but an ultimate
scepticism about worthwhile political change. Personally kind
and helpful towards less fortunate fellow refugees as his own
fortunes repaired, yet he had little sympathy or interest in refugee
politics, all those dreams of a return. For a brief while he was like
that celebrated old lady of Boston: 'Why travel? I'm here.' Yet after
all that risk, pain, and suffering, three times he was rendered
destitute and many times close to violent death or long imprisonment, his individualism seems to have revolted at the bureaucracy,
drabness, and puritanical ideology of Attlee's Britain—to the
personal annoyance of Orwell who positively revelled in it and
who saw Koestler, perhaps unfairly, as a backslider from
democractic socialism (whereas Koestler would probably have
argued that he was a writer, simply moving on to different themes,
even grander and more complex). So although naturalized as a
British subject, from 1948 to 1952 he travelled restlessly, acclaimed
but unsettled, between 'Island Farm' in New Jersey and 'Verte Rive'

near Fontainebleau. Freedom was often his theme, but now equality was a threat to freedom and not, as in *The Gladiators*, its necessary condition. But then he finally settled in England, though with much intermittent world travelling on the lecture and conference circuit, albeit now a very critical admirer of his new homeland as shown in a brilliant and prescient series of essays in the early 1960s on national character and national decline (now extracted and retitled 'The Lion and the Ostrich'). And the self-consciously big books began: *The Trail of the Dinosaur* (1955), *The Sleepwalkers: A History of Man's Changing View of the Universe* (1959), *The Lotus and the Robot* (1961), *The Act of Creation* (1964), *The Ghost in the Machine* (1967), *The Case of the Midwife Toad* (1971), *The Roots of Coincidence* (1972), *The Thirteenth Tribe* (1976), and *Janus: A Summing Up* (1978). Why, then, has he not summed up in a full-scale autobiography, rather than this compromise volume? Or at least completed the series of the autobiographical books, *Dialogue With Death* (1941), *Scum of the Earth* (1941), *Arrow in the Blue* (1952), and *Invisible Writing* (1954)? He anticipates this obvious question, saying that despite the pressure of friends and publishers, his life ceased after 1940 to a 'typical (*sic*) case history of a central European member of the educated middle class born in the first years of our century,' and therefore ceased to be 'of any public interest.' The nonsequitur is startling! Even if we grant that the Anglicisation, indeed Atlanticisation, of such a typical central European bourgeois is of no public interest, the comment must be made that the professional writer slides from one sense of *public* to another, from his own former life as a public activist into what about him may be interesting to his reading public, personally interesting. This is a cross that great men have to bear. Before 1940 he was predominantly, but far from exclusively, interested in public, political affairs; and 'after 1940' (although most certainly he predates the change of emphasis), predominantly interested in strange, difficult, and important borderlands of psychology, physiology, biology, and philosophy. But his shift of emphasis was far from exclusive: witness 'The God That Failed' essay; his attempt in 1946-7 to found a 'League for Human Rights' with Gollancz, Orwell, Bertrand Russell, and others; his roles in PEN, UNESCO, and the Campaign for Cultural Freedom; his attacks on national and military misuse of atomic power; and his prominent role in the campaign in Great Britain for the abolition of capital punishment. Surely he cannot seriously mean that there is no public activity worth writing about after 1940, that the earlier connection between public life and private life (virtually forced on the prewar European intelligentsia) is severed by settling in

Britain? What he really means is that his private life comes to be more valuable to him than public, political activities, and that he finds the subject matter of his new books in contemplation, rather than in action, or in reading about science, not in recounting his own experiences, as in *Spanish Testament* and *Arrow in the Blue,* or even in imaginatively reshaping them, as in *The Gladiators* and *Darkness at Noon.* And also he is probably saying, with the decent reticence of a distinguished English man of letters living in Montpelier Square, SW7, that he simply does not want to write about his private life.

In some ways one sympathises. Not through Marx, not through Einstein, but through Freud, the reading public has grown naughty and demands more than Koestler would wish to offer or probably allow. Improper and irrelevant demands should, of course, be frustrated. The private life of some writers and most scientists, even many statesmen, may in fact have little relationship with the meaning of their published work; and even accounts of how and why they produce their work can be irrelevant if there are no ambiguities of meaning or intent to be clarified by accounts of antecedents. But these are hard conditions to meet, particularly for writers like Koestler and Orwell who have both become a legend in their lifetime and have, albeit on different occasions, and for specific purposes (not to help future biographers), written a lot about themselves, using their own legend, in some of their best works. To be fair, Koestler has allowed a biography of himself to be commissioned and is cooperating with it, although he does not mention this in his preface.

As someone who was careful to insist, before beginning work on *Orwell*, on a contractual right to see all papers and to publish anything, I would be fascinated to know what the conditions of the Koestler commission were. Certainly, a biography in anyone's lifetime is difficult—I go no further, for widows and heirs to copyright are not always easy either. Nonetheless, it is strange that, having written so much and so interestingly in an autobiographical vein in his 'Red' period, he has not done so in, as it were, his 'Blue' period; and has, as I've said, produced this fascinating but nonetheless compromised, commentated, chronological anthology. One sympathises if he has a distaste for doing a Bertie Russell and writing so frankly and egocentrically about his amours, marriages, and quarrels, as well as his ideas and activities, as if the feelings of others do not matter a damn is self-revelation is complete. But if so purely intellectual, why not an intellectual autobiography? Perhaps the difficulty is not one of either writing to conceal or needing to parade a private life, but a painful uncertainty about where his real achievement lies in his public life as a writer, a contradiction between his ideal image and his actual best work. A clue may be found in his editing of the anthology: he confines himself to books or essays republished in books, so practically nothing of his vast journalistic output appears. But for most of his life Koestler has been a journalist, in Zionist, Communist, and anti-Communist phases, still an occasional reviewer, since the middle 1940s able to choose his journals and write thoughtful feature articles rather than commissioned stories, but nonetheless a journalist, reporter, professional writer, in the best senses, through and through. This editing out of examples of early routine journalism may simply be because this anthology is, after all, meant to show his writing at its best. But then its chronological, quasi-autobiographic appearance is publicly misleading, perhaps even self-deceptive. I would like to see examples of how he did write as an Ullstein journalist and then as a party hack—not to demean him, but simply because his life was so interesting. Is he hiding something? And he may underestimate the reporter's craft, as if it diminished the thinker's status.

His pre-war books told in sturdy prose fascinating stories about his own adventures. When he comes to write in English, it is a workmanlike, even at times lively, prose, occasionally even florid, but certainly with little of the vivid feeling for a new language shown by Conrad or the sharp simplicity of Orwell's use of his native tongue. Personally, I don't find much difference between his own first writing in English and the earlier translations of his German or French (not Hungarian of course): it is almost as if he modelled his prose on his last translator. Before the war, then, he wrote well about his own experiences and matters arising from them—especially well about extreme psychological states; but he had also written, though no examples here, with some authority on scientific matters as the science correspondent of the biggest German newspaper chain in the 1920s. So when he returns to write about science, though now in books and on themes of his own choosing, he is speculative, most certainly, but not amateur or eccentric; and if he is selective in his use of evidence, he is a good reporter of what 'challenging' research and theories he reads: he can both understand and popularise scientific literature. Thus, there is both more continuity in his writing than first appears to be the case or than he is prepared to acknowledge.

Add to this the fact that his novels have all dealt well with the character and ideological contradictions of a central hero or anti-hero, as well as with extreme situations, but they have shown neither psychological depth nor complexity in the interrelations of the characters. Indeed, the minor characters are all ideological or social types, neither interacting upon nor modifying each other's characters: they break or burst each other, or some escape and others remain unchanged. Reflective and revealing auto- biography, then, beyond telling a good public tale of important and exciting public events, is not likely to be his strongest card as a writer. He may simply be well aware of this—no skeletons to hide, simply an old craftsman's dialectic awareness of his professional strengths and weaknesses. The one clear thread in all the variety of his themes, and linking closely his two periods, is that he has been a professional reporter of mighty themes, but always using his pen for his career, considering carefully his subject matter and his changing audiences.

This is perhaps why so many of us are still uneasy and uncertain about Koestler. His themes are great themes, but he is not a great writer, if in some sense great writing becomes, whether as political or scientific writing, an end in itself. He always demands our agreement or disagreement, not our appreciation—although we should appreciate very greatly the skill and cultural role of such writing, admitting that it is not great literature. I think of Koestler as one might think of Orwell if he had never written *Animal Farm* and *Nineteen Eighty-Four*. The claim for literary greatness could not be made, but he would still have been a figure—like Koestler— of extraordinary interest and importance.

What, however, if the content, if the message, is the thing? What emerges in his later, more difficult writings is both compelling and tantalising. What is compelling is his humanistic tone, even at times when journalistic cadences slip in. He sees the humour as well as the seriousness of life. Life is serious, not simply in how we react to each other, a purely humanistic position, but in how we must, he still believes, search for an overall synthesis or sense of purpose in humanity. He is an individualist who has come utterly to reject hedonism or utilitarianism in favour of a long-term responsibility for improving the human species.

In a paper of 1969, he identified 'four outstanding, pathological symptoms reflected in the disastrous history of our species.' They are (i) the 'ubiquitous ritual' of human sacrifice; (ii) that *'homo sapiens* is virtually unique in the animal kingdom in his lack of instinctive safeguards for his own species'; (iii) 'the chronic, quasi- schizophrenic split between reason and emotion, between man's rational faculty and his irrational, affect-bound beliefs'; and (v) 'the striking disparity between the growth curves of science and technology on the one hand and of ethical conduct on the other.' And in *The Ghost in the Machine*, he set out a physiological hypothesis about the differential evolution of the brain in support of the third and fourth points.

It could of course be objected that the species has survived and flourished despite all this; that 'disastrous history' is not a descriptive summary but an emotive prophecy; that 'ethics' is not something for which a 'growth curve' can be plotted, still less, extrapolated from; and that anthropological-physiological hypotheses are interesting as hypotheses, but virtually untestable, not established theories that could guide public policy and medical research. Koestler, I repeat, had real scientific training but, nonetheless, obvious tricks of the journalist creep in. He talks about 'conspecifics,' an easy piece of impressive jargon, though he immediately says in plain English, 'members of his own species.' This is a small and innocent example. I get more worried when he talks about 'neuro-physiological *evidence*' for a 'schizopsychology' in the human evolutionary process, without reminding his readers that such 'evidence' is only inference from untested and contentious hypotheses.

Yet one admires his courage and explicit determination to show that a genuine intellectual must take his stand in two cultures. How much more interesting he still is than C.P. Snow ever was. Reading Koestler never makes one snooze, though my schizopsychology comes out in an occasional desire to throw the book out of the window, but then to run down and pick it up again, hoping that nothing *disastrous* has happened to it, only some rich, disfiguring marks of human tragedy from which to fashion a significant anecdote. In other words, I prefer Koestler the sceptic, telling his tale of Malraux's suddenly saying at a Writers' Congress in Moscow, after hearing countless speeches promising universal happiness in a brave new world: ' "And what about a child run over by a tram-car?" There was a pained silence; then somebody said, amid general approbation: "in a perfect, planned socialist transport system, there will be no accidents".' This is better, to my taste, than the man who likes to be the H. G. Wells of the intellectual upper middle classes rather than of the self-taught lower middle classes.

So an assessment of Koestler's peculiar genius is difficult. Have any of us ever read all his books? And there is the journalism as well as the books. His own sense of achievement is shown clearly in the selection of this book. He probably disappoints his old readers or the young who read his old novels by calling fully half of *Bricks to Babel* his 'Search of Synthesis,' and presenting there mainly the scientific writings. But in terms of the sheer bulk of this scientific writing, the first half of the book, 'In Search of Utopia,' is in fact disproportionate. He would like to be remembered as a scientific thinker; but he is too good a professional writer not to realise where his greater effect and following still lie. So he presented his literary past fully and does not appear to rewrite. No Audenesque problems here.

The extracts from the novels fit in easily with the non-fiction works. The value of *Darkness at Noon* and *Arrival and Departure* is in their authenticity. Camus's *The Rebel* is a better philosophical analysis of the totalitarian mind, but it is too abstract for most readers, just as Arendt's *Origins of Totalitarianism* is too pedantic and monumental. Even Orwell's *Nineteen Eighty-Four*, impossible though it is to put down, can be brushed aside as a nightmare or diminished as an overdrawn satire on post-war Britain. Koestler knows what he was talking about and is hard to diminsh; he is easier to ignore or foolishly dismiss in New York as a nice 'cold war warrior' or in London as 'too clever by half.' The issue in the 1940s, as the Party hacks and the fellow travellers put it, was only whether he was a liar or not. And plainly he wasn't.

This very factualness is both the clue to and the continuity in his achievement. It is not an aesthetic achievement. We read his books for their matter and to learn something from them. This too links the old with the new Koestler. We should read the new scientific Koestler just as we read the earlier political novels: because he is talking about something we need to know, but all the time aware that it is a prince of journalists, a cosmic reporter, the doyen of conferenceurs, who is addressing us as an audience, mingling, like any good feature writer, personal angles with hard information. We open the quality press and we are informed, stimulated, but always on our guard. He writes columns as big and bustling as Babel, not monographs.

Whether or not Koestler himself believes that he has philo-sophical or scientific originality (as did Wells, alas) is irrelevant. I hope he doesn't, but it really doesn't matter. He is one of the greatest intellectual popularizers of our time, the interpreter for one set of intellectuals of the concepts of another. And his genuine cosmopolitan stance has been earned and not easily achieved. One Koestler speaks more for human unity, despite his rationalist assault on the cult of Zen and the pretensions of Ghandi, than a dozen committees of UNESCO. He deeply appreciates national culture differences, but attaches little value to them and adopts each in turn with a kind of ironic affection.

Ultimately, he should be pleased with himself as the super-reporter. What he has now given us is, in fact, in its temporal order and with its headnotes, a remarkably full and clear picture of the public activities of his life. The rest is silence.

To end, most tentatively, on a mischievous or an affectionate thought? His last novel was a rather lightweight, merry satire called *The Call Girls*: those great men, mainly, who wait for the letter or the phone to summon them to Alpbach, Pugwash, Villa Serbelloni (the Rockefeller Foundation's earthy paradise), or wherever, the eternal conference round of internationally famous intellectuals. It was a very knowing satire. How often had he played that game himself, as perhaps a widely translated professional writer must. He may have grown weary of it, found it no longer so useful to him, or even risen above it; but in the end I suspect that the old journalist simply had to report on the institution: to send it up simply by describing it. It was like that. He was a great descriptive writer. But what they were probably all talking about were themes as vast, but as times possible as vapid, as some of his 'fate of the species' books.

Surely it will be, rightly or wrongly, his earlier political books for which he will be best and longest remembered. He told the tale so compellingly of how a man came to look for utopias, but finally grew sceptical of political activity, except for small clear things; like abolition of capital punishment. It might fairly be objected that between utopianism and scepticism lies the whole range of practical politics, from the conservative to the democratic socialist. Orwell thought that Koestler should have explored the nature of a non-utopian political theory. But Koestler was not a political thinker. And no man, not even Koestler, can do everything. Koestler had a tendency to dramatise things to extremes, the Yogi or the commissar, and to exclude mundane middles. He was a reporter of great themes, however. If there were no immediate utopias to observe in the 1950s from that Graf Zeppelin still hovering over polar extremes, he would have to report on the evolution of the species itself. I cannot evaluate his success or not in this matter, only share a common scepticism, but with a shameful sense of not being brave or rash enough to try myself. But it does not diminish or change his earlier work, and one has to hope that he himself takes this view, either at peace with himself in his old age or properly proud of all the bricks he made so skilfully and in such difficulties as a great and dedicated professional writer and superjournalist.

Five

_____

Hannah Arendt: Hedgehog or Fox?

*A broadcast review of Elisabeth Young-Bruehl, *Hannah Arendt: For Love of the World* (Yale, 1982), printed in *The Listener*, 27 May 1982.

We learn that it was not without reason that Elfriede Heidegger, the philosopher's wife, distrusted his relationships with infatuated female students, particularly with the brilliant Jewess Hannah Arendt. She, perhaps his most precocious student, sat at his feet in the mornings, but he lay her in her attic full many an afternoon, all that long time ago in Marburg around 1925. Elfriede Heidegger was not always so perceptive. Once, after a merry housewarming party, singing and drinking around a Teutonic bonfire, she asked a handsome lad, who later became Arendt's first husband, whether he wouldn't like to join the local Nazi youth group. She was put out when he told her that he was Jewish.

Arendt kept this little secret for exactly fifty years, until after her sudden death in 1975 when letters and poems, clung to through flight, imprisonment and exile, revealed the student idyll. Fortunately, she did not follow her disorderly friend W.H. Auden's example and order the destruction of her letters (Auden who, after Arendt's second husband died, had suggested—to her embarrassment and horror—that they should have a companionate marriage); rather, she left her papers in the competent hands of Mary McCarthy, who sensibly commissioned a full-scale scholarly biography.

I must not give any false impression that Elisabeth Young-Bruehl's life of Hannah Arendt is a particularly lively book full of sexual exposé—though it is somehow good to discover that an existentialist preacher of humanity could be herself *menschlich, allzu menschlich*. Here is a philosophical biography of great weight and integrity that concentrates on the life of the mind—which was also, indeed, the title of Arendt's unfinished and posthumously published last work, a work of pure philosophy, returning to her youth as the student of the unhappy Heidegger and then of the noble Jaspers. Young-Bruehl is a former American student of Arendt's. She writes as a philosopher. The personal life is

72

incidental. But there is enough of the background to make a sad and interesting tale in its own right—a tale of three cultures: the old German universities, Paris and New York.

Oddly, I find that Elisabeth Young-Bruehl is more successful in bringing to life the unfamiliar ambience of German universities in the 1920s, and of the Paris of the exiles in the 1930s, than she is of her own New York intellectual scene of the 1950s and 1960s. Perhaps familiarity creates flatness, and unfamiliarity is a challenge. Only the very skilled writer can make the familiar appear as extraordinary as it usually is. Yet, despite being a student and admirer of Arendt's, her biographer keeps a cool and proper critical distance: a considerable achievement in describing someone who has been so over-maligned, and occasionally over-praised—or, rather, praised in everything. Young-Bruehl's method inspires confidence. She reflects in her Preface on the reliability on memory:

> Stories about her adulthood are plentiful, and often exist—memories being what they are—in as many versions as there are tellers. From versions of a story not significantly different, I have woven a single story for this book and cut loose threads away. In these cases, the criteria familiar to historians—and detectives—have been employed in the weaving: inner consistency and plausibility; conformity with written sources, other stories, and documents; reliability of the storyteller in terms of vantage-point and knowledge. In those few instances where irreconcilable versions of stories exist, I have noted all the versions . . .

Good. If biography is to tell the truth, we amateur biographers—or, rather, scholars doing a one-off job—often produce something more reliable, if more dull, than the professional biographer primarily concerned to tell a tale in a lively way. And this life of Arendt does throw light on the nature of her work.

Her life has a parabolic pattern: in the Twenties, she is philosophical; in the Thirties and Forties practical activities dominate; in the 1950s comes the flood of sociological or quasi-empirical writings; and through the 1960s, into her seventieth year, she returns again to philosophy.

What is surprising is how much practical activity there was. After fleeing from Germany in 1933, resolute and lucky to be released after withstanding interrogation by the Gestapo, she had to keep herself by odd jobs in Paris. Helped by Jewish organisations, she became director of the Paris branch of Youth Aliyah, training orphan children for a new life in Palestine. Her second husband, Heinrich Blucher, was an ex-Communist and self-taught intel-

lectual, not a university man. Even while in Germany, anti-
semitism had turned her mind towards politics. Her Heidelberg
doctoral thesis, on St Augustine's concept of love, was not quite
what it seemed: there was love as *appetitus*, or desire, there was love
of God, and there was neighbourly love—and it was neighbourly
love, she argued, love of one's fellows, which unites and transcends
both carnal and divine love.

And while still in Germany she began her life of Rahel
Varnhagen, the 18th-century Jewish intellectual who remarked on
her deathbed: 'The thing which all my life seemed to me the
greatest shame, which was the misery and misfortune of my life–
having been born a Jewess—this I should on no account now wish
to have missed.' Arendt, like Varnhagen, was not opposed to
assimilation as such, but came to learn from bitter experience—
strengthened by the years in France—that while the Jew was
welcome, indeed, to assimilate, she or he also assimilated to
gentile anti-semitism.

Yet Arendt's Jewishness was humanistic: she could not react to
anti-Semitism either by espousing the anti-Arab fervour of
Zionism or by accepting myths that the stateless, unpolitical
people had resisted like citizens in the grim days to come when the
passive round-up before the unknown slaughter had begun.

She herself was rounded up by the French in May 1940 and put
in a camp for German, mainly Jewish, women. In the confusion
before the handover to the Germans she had the sense and
courage to walk out, whereas most remained, fearful that their
relatives would not otherwise find them, accepting that they would
suffer but not fearing worse than indignity. And by 1941 she and
her husband—even her mother, luckily—had reached America.
Then there was another language to learn and more odd jobs to do,
with Jewish agencies and publishers, simply to stay alive. But
somehow she began work on a huge book on anti-semitism and
imperialism that grew into the famous *Origins of Totalitarianism* of
1951.

We learn a lot about that book. It was originally planned as a
study of the nature of anti-semitism, imperialism and racism, and
to be called *The Three Pillars of Hell*. The famous last section on
totalitarian society was a formidable afterthought. And the
misleading title *The Origins of Totalitarianism* was thrust upon her,
though she afterwards protested that she was not writing history,
as many critics had assumed she was. The aim of the book, she told
the publisher, was 'to find out the main elements of Nazism . . .
and to discover the underlying real political problems . . . not to
give answers but, rather, to prepare the ground'. The pity is that she

didn't say this to her readers; rather, she plunged in with a messy splash and created a wake that could last for ever. She was trying to characterise the basic nature of the totalitarian impulse and show *how* it became plausible, not to explain fully *why* or comprehensively *what*.

Most British scholars pedantically rejected the unhistorical nature of *Origins*, and, unlike their American counterparts, few British literary intellectuals were prepared to wrestle with such an odd mixture of politics, sociology and philosophy. A.A. Alvarcz was a notable exception but Isaiah Berlin denounced her works as 'metaphysical free-association', and herself as 'most over-rated.' She was hard to accommodate to our neat and somewhat parochial philosophical categories. Personally, I think that had our literary critics read Arendt's *Origins* they would not have given such a warm reception to Anthony Burgess's *Earthy Powers* or even, though a far better novel, to D.M. Thomas's *The White Hotel,* both of which seemed to me to exploit the Holocaust for literary effect rather than to find appropriate forms in which to reflect imaginatively on how, man being man, it was even possible.

Some of us have argued that *The Origins of Totalitarianism* is not merely Arendt's most famous book but also her main concern and lasting achievement: it can be shown that all her subsequent major works, *The Human Condition, Eichmann in Jerusalem, On Revolution, On Violence* and the unfinished trilogy *The Life of the Mind,* take up unresolved or problematic issues from the *Origins.* This makes her fundamentally a political theorist who saw totalitarianism as both the fundamental flaw in, and the greatest challenge to, our whole Western civilisation, a civilisation which can only remain civilised while it continues and extends the Graeco-Romano idea of free citizenship. Politics and culture can never be separated.

And, like a good New York intellectual, Arendt plunged into many current political controversies—living up to her own preaching of the virtue of political activity as well as the life of the mind. Not all these forays or escapades were equally wise. To alienate most of the American black community one year and the Jewish community the next was no mean feat of negative politics. She didn't always approach audiences in the best way to get a hearing.

Some admirers of Arendt, however, see her political writings as a kind of massive contingent diversion from her real preoccupation, the so-called 'passionate thinking' of Heidegger, though far more Kantian than he, more affected by his teacher Husserl and his critic Jaspers, but pure philosophy none the less. Then her first work on Augustine, and her last on mind—or, rather, on thinking itself—became the key both to her life and her achievement.

Certainly the biography makes me think twice about the argument I made in Melvyn Hill's symposium, *Hannah Arendt: The Recovery of the Public World,* for the centrality of *The Origins of Totalitarianism.* And while is makes me admire Bhikhu Parekh even more for his recent *Hannah Arendt and the Search for a Political Philosophy*, yet now I share more of his doubts as to whether she really brought it off. Is she a hedgehog who found a system, or a fox who illuminated a thousand truths vainly searching for a wholeness? Elisabeth Young Bruehl certainly shows the continuity of her thinking. Some of us have rashly dismissed both *St Augustine* and the worldly *Rahel Varnhagen*. The early books are now shown as crucial. But they also emerge as more politically motivated than one had suspected: love, as neighbourliness and fraternity, emerges from *Augustine*; and if her fellow Jews had read her life of Rahel Varnhagen, they would have been more prepared and reflective and less wildly angry over *Eichmann in Jerusalem*.

Yet the politics in these two early books is a relatively traditional deduction from moral philosophy, whereas in *The Human Condition* and in *Eichmann* political activity, as the free actions of free men, is held to be autonomous and worth doing in its own right, closer to Kant's aesthetics than to his critique of practical reason: we *should* act politically, irrespective both of hopes of good consequences or clear philosophical grounds for action, which are rarely to be found.

Perhaps, then, it is a false argument between the predominance of the political and the philosophical in Arendt's thought: they were both there from so early on and so dependent on each other. Crudely but simply put, no utilitarian consideration should override the life of the mind—or what the older J.S. Mill in a different discourse called 'the free spirit'; but philosophers and free spirits do not survive at all in the long run, or without dishonour in the short run (like Martin Heidegger), if the polity is not free—and free actions cannot be left entirely to somebody else, not merely for prudential reasons, but because, Arendt simply holds, we are not existing as full human beings if we are not doing things publicly in concert with others.

From this abstract perspective Elisabeth Young-Bruehl is able to solve the apparent paradox of Arendt's conservatism and her radicalism. Her radicalism lay in her roots and in her husband's socialism, and she did wish for a more communitarian and participatory society; indeed, she attached exaggerated importance to the Workers' Councils in Hungary in 1956 and even invented a few that didn't exist in America in 1776. She opposed the Vietnam War, of course, and welcomed the student unrest of the 1960s. But this participation was for the sake of the human spirit, not for material advantage: she accused both liberals and Marxists of making a god of 'labour'—what must be done to stay alive, the realm of natural necessity—and of neglecting 'work'—what is worth doing for its own sake, the realm of human freedom.

A last thought. The biographer says quite casually that the big books don't always hang together well, for Arendt conceived them as essays. After reading this fine biography, I think I would advise our native sceptics to try reading Arendt again, but through her essays, 'Men in Dark Times' and 'Between Past and Future' especially. I'm still not sure of she is most usefully labelled 'philosopher' or 'political theorist', or as fox or hedgehog. But I'm more sure than ever after reading this book that she is, for all her faults, contradictions and occasional arrogancies (as in her quite dreadful and wilful misreadings of Brecht), a very great thinker and a most exemplary, as you wish, woman or man.

Six

Beatrice Webb as English Diarist

A review in *The Political Quarterly,* April-June 1986, of *The Diary of Beatrice Webb,* Edited by Norman & Jeanne Mackenzie Volume One 1873-1892 *Glitter Around and Darkness Within (Virago.* 386pp £20.) Volume Two 1892-1905 *All the Good Thins of Life (Virago.* 376 pp. £20.) Volume Three 1905-1924 *The Power to Alter Things (Virago.* 460pp. £20.) Volume Four *The Wheel of Life (Virago.* 519pp. £22.)

Now that all four volumes of Beatrice Webb's diaries are out and can be read through at leisure and continually dipped into for pleasure, there can be no doubt that they are not merely a major source for modern British social and intellectual history but also show that Beatrice Webb must be numbered, however unexpectedly to some, among the great English diarists.

Sidney Webb, the socialist, dined here to meet the Booths. A remarkable little man with a huge head on a very tiny body, a breadth of forehead quite sufficient to account for the encyclopaedic character of his knowledge, a Jewish nose, prominent eyes and mouth, black hair, somewhat unkempt, spectacles and a most bourgeois black coat shiny with wear; regarded as a whole, somewhat between a London card and a German professor. To keep to essentials: his pronunciation is cockney, his H's are shaky, his attitudes by no means eloquent, with his thumbs fixed pugnaciously in a far from immaculate waistcoat, with his bulky head thrown back and his little body forward his struts even when he stands, delivering himself with extraordinary rapidity of thought and utterance and with and expression of inexhaustible self-complacency. But I like the man. There is a directness of speech, an open-mindedness, an imaginative warm-heartedness which should carry him far ... (14 Feb 1890)
They cover an amazing time-scale of seventy years and she herself constantly reflects on time: her hopes for the future, memories of the past, wry and candid admissions that not all social change pleases her, and her fears that increasing bodily debility could spread to the mind; but the very last entry is a rational account of the ending of personal time. There are a few mundane passages, certainly, and the Mackenzies have sensibly printed little from their foreign travel world tours—out of her British environment she could be banal; but generally her profundity of observation,

both of events and of people, and the mixture of light malice towards others and honest, even torturing self-criticism, makes this both an authentic and a great diary.

It is an authentic diary. Beatrice supervised the typing of most of her diaries late in her life, but the editors have checked them against the originals, and there is no rewriting for the sake of hindsight. Only some spellings and punctuation are altered. The editing is truly exemplary. Some diaries are almost certainly touched up in an author's life-time, with perfect hindsight, to reflect the interests and tastes of present readers and thus make them more publishable. The diaries of her nephew, Malcolm Muggeridge, for instance, have not been reviewed critically and authenticated, to my knowledge, by historians or biographers professionally suspicious of the 'provenance' and dating of records. To my sad eye they carry many signs either of careful hindsight or of supernatural precognition. Literary reviewers generally take diaries at their face value. But some, even if not revamped, are begun with future profit and publication in mind: the suspicion that attaches to so many of even the youthful intimate diarties as well as private letters of the Bloomsbury group. Beatrice's diaries genuinely seem to have written from the first not for publication and posterity but to help her memory in later years, and to offer a running account, like many a Puritan, with a dead or dying censorious God. Certainly in middle life she was aware that she might write autobiography, first *My Apprenticeship* (that made people realise, with surprise, that she was a considerable writer) and then the unfinished *Our Partnership*; but this did not change the essential private informality of the diaries: they were to be a source for published autobiography, not a substitute.

It is a great diary because of its mixture of objectivity and subjectivity, the public world and the worried heart, the mixture of record and reflection, and the tension between writing to keep herself up to scratch, to craft an ideal self-image, and the self-doubting, at times almost destructive, reproofs at her own pride, even arrogance, sometimes snobbery and always an exaggerated public certainty. Nothing that could be said against the Webbs as people cannot be found as harshly in Beatrice against herself. Looking back, she wrote of 'disabling gaps' in their knowledge of Victorian England:

> . . . of sport, games and racing . . . foreign affairs, generally speaking were a closed book to us . . . owing to our concentration in research, municipal administration and Fabian propaganda, we had neither the time nor the energy, nor yet the means, to listen to music and the drama, to brood

over classical literature, ancient and modern, to visit picture
galleries, or to view with an informed intelligence the
wonders of architecture. Such dim inklings as we had of
these ... reached us second-hand through our friendship
with Bernard Shaw.

In fact, she did herself, even Sidney, less than justice—as the editors
properly comment. The diaries themselves show this: they were
not even averagely philistine, they were only averagely cultured.
She judged themselves by Shaw's extraordinary standards and
versatility or by analogy with her own work. Some reviewers have
taken her at her face value and have been unable, or politically
unwilling (like Shirley Letwin in *The Listener*), to break from the
caricature stereotype of unfeeling Webbs, and have used her own
accusations against herself literally, rather missing the significance
of the fact that they use her own words which are often
contradicted by her own behaviour. Perhaps some reviewers
simply struck back at her repeated explicit scorn for those who are
so cultivated and sensitive but have no effective human sympathies
for poverty or deprivation. And Enoch Powell in *The Spectator*
found 'an obsession' in the first volume with 'unrealised woman-
hood' and 'fear of spinsterhood' which 'sometimes verged on
nymphomania', a view that may tell one more about his lack of
experience than of hers.

   A celebrated cartoon of Max Beerbohm's once showed 'Mr
Sidney Webb on his birthday', playing toy soldiers with real
people. Such stereotypes of the Webbs are, indeed, hard to avoid,
indeed a wider stereotype: that all political activists (and some
would generously add all social scientists) are philistines. The
culture of so many English literary intellectuals, who make such
assumptions, is itself notoriously narrow. To them all politics is
activism, occasionally to be condoned for its sincerity ('dear
Stephen in the Thirties'), but part of a world of indiscriminate
telegrams and anger. Freedom is choosing and defending friends
not working the Republic. Politics is a world that one may visit for
a moment of crisis (or for a lark, or for experiences from which to
write a book), but not one of permanence, hence not of 'culture' in
either sense of the term, certainly not a world (as in the Aristotelean
tradition of politics) of speculation and reflection. In other words,
most English, unlike most American, French, German, Italian,
Czech, and even Irish, Scottish and Welsh literary intellectuals,
are politically ignorant and insensitive, say 'philistine'.

   Beatrice Webb certainly believed that an intellectual elite must
lead social change. 'Democracy', she once remarked, 'is not the
multiplication of ignorant opinions.' And they both took a long

time to be convinced that socialism was best promoted by commitment to a single mass party. As late as 1925 she thought that Sidney 'in his heart of hearts ... still believes in Fabian permeation of other parties as a more rapid way than the advert of a distinctly socialist government.' But that permeating elite were to be people of, as it were, 'two cultures' not one. 'One wonders when a generation of leaders of the people will arise who will have learnt that love and pity for the downtrodden cannot achieve its end', she wrote in 1920, 'unless the emotion is accompanied with honesty of reasoning, careful and accurate statements of facts. Religious ends and scientific methods are indivisible if mankind is to rise above the brute's battle for life.'

Her observations can be acid but culturally acute. '[John Morley] and Sidney anxious to be pleasant to each other. A charming person for a talk on literature but a most depressing spectacle as a Liberal leader ... a pitiable person as a politician— all the more so because he is conscientious and upright. It makes one groan to think of that moral force absolutely useless.' And in July that same 1897 she heard H.W. Massingham call Chamberlain 'no more than a great political artist'.

> 'Surely', I rejoined, 'we shall look back on the last fifty years ... as the peculiar period of political artists: we have no statesmen—all our successful politicians, the men who lead the parties are artists and nothing else: Gladstone, Disraeli, Randolph Churchill, Chamberlain, and the unsuccessful Rosebery, all these men have the characteristics of actors— personal charm, extraordinary pliability and quick-witted-ness.'

Her view of the world was far from mechanistic. She did not argue against 'artists' in politics, only against 'mere artists'. Her exasperation with Shaw's recurrent frivolity and his 'outrageous behaviour' towards women (outrageous not because he was a seducer, like Wells, but because he was more often a pretend passionate flirt) arose because, when at his best (or her idea of his best), she saw in him a unique combination of the artist and the social engineer. The friendship of Shaw for the Webbs was also no accident.

Beatrice ceased to be a Christian when a young woman but a sense of religious awe and duty never left her. She could work with religious organisations, appreciating their dedication and useful-ness, if they were equally tolerant. She resigned in 1897 from the National Union of Women Workers because 'the bishops wives' defeated her resolution that meetings should not begin with prayers. But she noted:

Louise Creighton has distinctly a statesmanlike mind, and
the group of women who now control the policy are a good
sort—large minded and pleasant-mannered. The 'screaming
sisterhood' are trying to invade them but Louise's battalions
of hardworking, religious and somewhat stupid women will,
I think, resist the attack.

She described the Derbyshire miners as 'A stupid, stolid lot of men
characterised by their fair mindedness and kindness.' Some things
never change and are never to be said, except in diaries. That is
why authentic diaries can be so entertaining.

Heroes of the early Labour movement get short shrift. 'Keir
Hardie, who impressed me very unfavourably, choose this policy
as the only one he can boss. His only chance of leadership lies in
the creation of an organisation "agin the government"; he knows
little and cares less for any constructive thought and action.' But
with Tom Mann, she noted, it was different: 'He is possessed with
the idea of a "church",—of a body of men all professing exactly the
same creed and working in exact uniformity to exactly the same
end. No idea which is not "absolute", which admits of any
compromise or qualification, no adhesion which is tempered with
doubt, has the slightest attraction to him.' And for fair measure she
adds Shaw's opinion that 'stumping the country, taking abstractions and raving emotions, is not good for a man's judgement, and
the perpetual excitement leads, among other things, to too much
whisky' (23 Jan. 1895). 'What (Josiah) Wedgewood demands is
fervent partisanship. Unless you are a partisan you must be a
scoundrel' (28 Nov. 1929). Against such views she put forward not
just Sidney's 'the inevitability of gradualism' (if coaxed, poked and
pushed continually) but her own 'policy of inoculation, of giving
to each class, to each person, that came under our influence the
exact dose of collectivism that they were prepared to assimilate.'
'There is some truth', she admitted, 'in Keir Hardie's remarks that
we are the worst enemies of the social revolution. No great
transformation is possible in a free democratic state like England
unless you alter the opinions of all classes of the community.' (23
Jan. 1895).(?)

Some of her portraits are, indeed, etched in acid but remarkably
timeless. She describes Susan Lawrence, MP for East Ham North,
in the general Strike:

> . . . the amazing change in [her] mentality–from a hard-
> sensed lawyer-like mind and the conventional manner of the
> moderate member of the London School Board, whose
> acquaintance I had made five-and-twenty years ago, to the
> somewhat wild woman of demagogic speech addressing her

constitutents as 'comrades' and abasing herself and her class before the real wealth producers. Today Susan is a victim to spasms of emotional excitement which drive her from one weird suggestion to another. She lives in an unreal world. In order to keep in touch with what she imagines to be the proletarian mind she has lost touch with facts as they are. And yet she is a real good soul, devoted and public-spirited. It is a bad case of the occupational disease so common among high-strung men and women who come out of a conservative environment into proleterian politics. (14 May 1926).

Ten years later, with the publication of *Soviet Communism: A New Civilisation?* (from which the question mark vanished in the Left Book Club edition of the following year), this might seem a case of pot calling kettle black, apart from the calmer tone of the 'work of supererogation' by the 'two aged mortals, both nearing their ninth decade', as they said in the Preface. A more flagrant case was her comment on Beveridge and his report: 'He agrees that there must be a revolution in the economic structure of society; but it must be guided by persons with training and knowledge—i.e. by himself and those he chooses as his colleagues.' By then they obviously did not think that Beveridge was the right person, even morally, to have been at the helm of 'their' good ship LSE. (Yes, it all comes out, in Beatrice's entries and the Mackenzie's ever accurate but unobstrusive commentary, what Sir Sidney Caine so carefully avoided discussing in his history of the LSE).

I remember Beveridge delivering the Webb Memorial lecture at LSE in 1959 and, being senile, unhappily devoting nearly all of it to praise of 'my Jane' without whose good management of the house and the servants, he told us, he would have never had the time to write the great works that had so changed the course of our national history. Of course, as I remember telling puzzled students afterwards, both he and Beatrice Webb were 'Whigs' and not self-made radicals: their incredible industry depended, albeit fairly modestly by the standards of their friends, on having domestic servants. Foundations can give one a research assistant, whom one spends half one's time training, but never a house-keeper.

Beatrice's handling of the characters of both the great and the not so great are equally entertaining—the mark of a true diarist. She comments that 'Malcolm is rabidly abusive of the USSR . . . he has discarded the *Manchester Guardian* and taken on the *Daily Telegraph*. Apparently his revulsion against Communism began on the boat out, as he "watched the expression on the faces of the crew".' She suggests that 'if you see so much of the devil and the idiot in human society, you have better believe in a god to set it right. And confession and absolution would suit poor Malcolm's complexes; he needs spiritual discipline, and would find peace in religious rites. "Malcolm would do well to join the Roman Catholic Church", I suggested' (21 Oct. 1933). Forty years later he took the advice. He caricatured the Webbs, incidentally, as Mr and Mrs Daniel Bret in a novel, *In the Valley of the Restless Mind.* Beatrice commented that 'these pages are one amusing and quite harmless episode', although 'What distresses me about this strange autobiographical work is the horrid mixture of religious strivings and continuous amatory adventure'—but then, she is said to be no judge of literature.

Larger prophecies did not come to pass. They both died in the belief that 'collectivism' had become the common propoerty of all the main British political parties. 'Collectivism' to them certainly meant centralism. Despite their forays into the field, theirs was always a London-centred view of England; and it was always 'England', never United Kingdom. It meant bureaucracy, but a civilised as well as a trained bureaucracy. It first meant municipal and then came more and more to mean state ownership, where rationally applicable; but until their Soviet delusion, influence and control over industry would ordinarily be enought. But it was, for England if not for Russia, always a democratic and parliamentary collectivism. Fortunately the Webbs brilliantly exemplified the accuracy of David Caute's definition of 'fellow travellers'— those who believed in socialism in somebody else's country. And mostly 'collectivism' meant to them no more nor less than common responsibility for common interests, less clearly attached to any single method than defined by its contradicting the vision of a wholly individualistic society leaving all major decisions of policy and welfare to natural selection and market mechanisms. This theory and sentiment they believed had lost its plausibility for ever, perhaps with the death of that tetchy old family friend Herbert Spencer. There are no references to Hayek in the book and only glancing references to Lionel Robbins: but the enemy was already in the gate of their beloved only-begotten child, LSE.

Seven

Words

These were originally three-minute broadcast talks (very concentrating to the mind) from a series of the same title, reprinted in *Words: Reflections In The Use of Language* (British Broadcasting Corporation, 1975).

Against Promiscuity

'Words, words, words', answered the Lord Hamlet. 'The ball seemed in the net, Montgomery[1] lifted himself off the ground, somehow he got his fingers to it, a miracle, deflected it off the cross-bar; he was there by some supernatural instinct. Words fail me to describe the scene...!!' No they blooming well didn't, or if so, then only for the briefest moment. He was just getting his breath back. Then out flowed the words again. Never at a loss for words, but sometimes perhaps *homo sapiens, ludens,* the Fallen Angel or the Naked Ape is at a loss for the right words.

So I am not so sanguine (which is a lovely word to look up in the full *Oxford English Dictionary*) as Marghanita Laski said she was about the coinage of new words. Yes, indeed, it is one of the glories of our double-rooted English language that with it we can so readily make new words and extend the meanings of others. But they had better be good ones. Since we haven't got a French or a Hebrew Academy trying to steer the language, rather as governments try to steer the economy, and since even Sir Ernest Gowers in his great book, *Plain Words,* was just a little bit up-tight, then it is up to all of us who love the language to be a little sceptical, conservative or preservationist about the coiners and developers. I am wide open to be convinced, but I hate promiscuity with words.

Take just two innocent sounding extensions like 'extremist' and 'dialogue'.

How often is the concept 'religious extremist' used when what is really meant is 'fanatic' or 'zealot', both good old words, someone extreme in his claims or action, but not necessarily the extreme point of a common tendency of the religious. He may be a logical *reducio ad absurdsam* of orthodoxy or he may be plain idiosyncratic. But with the common phrase 'student extremist' the tar-brush of extended meaning is often deliberate. In any precise sense 'student

85

extremist' usually refers to either Revolutionary Socialists or to anarchists: but the phrase carries the naughty implication that the extremist exemplifies what is latent in all students—I mean that they are an extrapolation from a rising curve of homogenous student response. If the others were not a right lazy set of bastards, or slackers in a Dr Arnold or Mr Gladstone sense, they would be out there with the 'student extremists' on the streets fighting for liberation against repression, or with them in the teach-ins reifying or deifying the Young Marx (who never grows old). But students are in fact a pretty mixed bunch—I mean are functionally differentiable into a plurality of sub-cultures. If the slackers did pull their socks up, some of them would be out there on the streets, some would be boozing and brawling with the rugby club; some would be swotting and cramming even harder; some of them would be having religious revivals; others would be even nicer than they are now, and some still wouldn't have a clue what they are doing. The so-called extremist is, in fact, more likely to be way-out, isolated and—however righteous—on his own, not the tip of a tendency as the loosely used word implies.

'Dialogue' is a more beautiful but an arrogant word. Can't we just meet and talk together anymore without the salad-dressing pretence that there will be a dramatised and personified absolute reason confronting, with platonic clarity, such another? 'O Kosygin, consider that we Americans believe that all men are born free.' 'O Nixon, consider that we Russians believe that all men are born equal.' The dialogue between East and West, presumably. But it even creeps into my telephone. 'Bernie, I think you and I must have a dialogue at some approximate date about our emerging points of substantive difference.' Or 'Crick, could you come round to talk to me soon. A quiet word together might be useful at this stage.' Somewhere between overstatement and understatement there must be ways of saying more clearly what the character of a meeting is to be. 'Dialogue' is such a pretentious, trendy, mid-Atlantic *Encounter*-magazine sort of word, either the obvious on well-gilded stilts or else delusive fairy gold.

And when I hear that a 'meaningful dialogue' is promised, then I weep for all the others. I would that I could render dialogue 'inoperative'.

(ii) Proper authority

It is said that the Mandarin officials of ancient China believed that the business of good government demanded an official 'rectification of terms': that if every word by imperial edict were returned to its original, precise and distinct meaning, justice and tranquillity would be assured. Such a programme would, indeed, be authoritarian. But I do want, none the less, some proper authority. Simply because there is neither any single original meaning of a word, say like 'authority' itself, not any single demonstrably correct usage, it is all the more important, not less, that those who are commonly admitted to use words well, and hence are given some slight authority about the usage of words, should not accept that anything goes. Power is useless if it cannot influence people. The Mandarins had the power to order the freezing or reform of language, but it would have had no effect unless people accepted their authority. And it is unlikely that they would have done. Their authority was accepted, presumably, for the business of government, not for the rectification of language. 'Authoritarian' is the abuse of authority. All authority is not authoritarian. Proper authority is exercised by people who are recognised to be skilful in fulfilling a function that is accepted as needed. I have authority, while I am skilful and knowledgeable, as a teacher of my subject; and usually have no difficulty in exercising my authority in relevant ways. But if I use my narrow authority as a teacher of a subject to lay down the law to my students about their morals or about the benificence or inquity of the Government of the day, then I am abusing that authority and I would expect them to interrupt, switch off or drift away. It is foolish to be against authority as such: but we should always be against the extension of one type of authority, however relevant and good, into other and irrelevant fields. In the same way we should be against the arbitrary extension of the meaning of words which already have burden enough to carry.

So let us not be authoritarian about the defence of our language, particularly since it is now—*pardonnez-moi, messieurs*—the new *lingua franca* and used by so many other peoples; but let us not be frightened to use any brief authority we still happen to be dressed in, or else the result may be a cumulative vagueness of meaning, a gradual debasement of language. That is why I, unlike Marghanita Laski, admit to a prejudice against new words. Not intolerance mind, simply initial prejudice. I want to put them through some pretty stiff hoops before accepting them fully. Do they add to clarity, or subtract from it? Do they have a greater resonance, or simply a sloppy vagueness?

If I had authority, if I were King of Words for a day, a word I would specially like to persecute and crack down on is 'escalation'. I knock it out of *Political Quarterly* articles and student essays every time I can catch it. As when people talk about 'the escalation of violence', seeming to mean that a single or a few observed instances of something they don't like is the beginning of an inevitable process of cumulatively horrendous events. Built into 'escalation' is a concept of inevitability and also of things getting out of control, but getting out of control—paradoxically—in a predictable sort of way. Not the 'explosion' of violence, for that is too unique and unpredictable an event, nor a fashionable 'implosion' of violence either, but a full-scale lumbering 'escalation': a getting worse step by predictable and irresistible step.

Of course, people who use the word are just trying to frighten us, or themselves: they never in fact believe that the processes are (as they seem to say) irreversible or irresistible. They are usually meaning to say that if you don't accept quickly my well-meant but arbitrary wonder-cure, so far untested, things will get so out of hand as to remove all possibilities of choice. Well, as a student of society I'm not taking that unless the evidence is put on the table, or unless it is at least admitted that there is time to stand on the same step together and to ask precisely and for what reasons one is thought to be part of this spiral escalator. And doesn't, by the way, an escalator turn round and come down again? The middle-class 'backlash' will then set in just as rigidly as our tired old Marxist friend, 'inevitable reaction'. I wonder if the dialectic can escalate?

Pornography, pollution, drug addiction and violence are nasty and wrong things, but they are not simply 'escalating', as that other old traditionalist in *The Times* keeps on saying who would do better to defend the tradition of the language itself than to use such words. No, I am not facetiously complacent. Things may get worse if such and such conditions continue, arise and coincide. But to combat them, we must specify them. And to be specific is to see that there are choices of action. 'Escalate' has become as shoddy a blanket concept among the political right as was ever 'inevitable tendencies' among the left. Some degree of graduated deescalation is overdue.

(iii) Only disconnect

It occurred to me once that social science jargon has a kind of latent poetry in it:

> Come correlate hypotheses
> And if thou thinkst as I
> We'll soon conceptualize a hunch
> In one subjective sigh.
> Let interdisciplinary zeal
> Now count the feedbacks down
> And spark the old bi-polar urge
> Neath thy conceptual gown.

There are in fact three literary quotations and only three which turn up regularly in the textbooks of social scientists. The first is Yeats's 'Things fall apart, the centre cannot hold'—which can be applied to anything; the second is W.H. Auden's 'Hunger is something which hurts the citizen and the police. We must love one another or die'—which he got so fed up with, presumably because of its glib falsity, that he removed it from later editions of his *Collected Poems*; and, thirdly, of course, E.M. Forster's 'only connect'.

Someone wrote a textbook on British politics with that legend, no names no pack drill, a rose by any other name etc. And the trouble was that he did connect everything. He had a theory about what the essential functions of government are, full of words like in-put and out-put, affect and effect, upon which facts were strung like coloured bulbs on the arms of a plastic Christmas tree. Everything was connected, simply because he assumed that there was a SYSTEM. Now whether everything in British politics and society is related systematically is, you might innocently think, a matter of fact, an empirical matter. But no, it turned out to be a theoretical assumption: it was assumed that there was a system. Indeed the word 'model' was used; but the model didn't really claim to be a replica of an actual social system, but rather something like an old-fashioned clothes horse, on which any old country can hang its wet clothes in some kind of order.

Thus 'system' and 'model' can, in the social sciences, either claim that an intllectual framework must be imposed on an otherwise random world of events, or that the world of events consists in fact of mutually consistent regularities. The one sense of system is a tautology, whatever one sets up then is true by definition, but the other is true presumably only if it can be empirically verified. But, in fact, it never is. All we get is words, words, words. How do we form our basic conceptions about politics? By processes of socialisation. Why should we obey the state? To meet the functional prerequisites of mechanisms of legitimation. Do we want different things out of politics? Yes, we are cross-pressured by differential role perceptions. There is better to be found, of course, but there is too much of this kind of thing: purely verbal answers: opium puts one to sleep because it has a soporific quality. As I sit editing an article which may actually have something to say, beneath the ingrained verbiage, and as I try to put nouns back into verbs, passives into actives, and to remove 'isms' and 'isations' from nearly everything, I shudder to think at the amount of congested and unclear writing that the social sciences tolerate, and at their enshrinement of banalities. To write plainly is to be suspect of being merely literary.

Consider the great Yale scholar Harold Lasswell ruminating about content analysis of the word 'democracy;'

'Our problem may therefore be posed as follows: Under what conditions do words affect power responses? If we let the "power responses" in which we are interested be referred to be the letter R, the problem is to find what words in the environment of the responders will affect R in one way rather than another, given certain predispositions on the part of the audience (other environmental factors being held "constant").' Tristram Shandy long ago analysed these things more exactly: 'Now there are such an infinitude of notes, tunes, cants, chants, airs, looks, and accents with which the word fiddlestick may be pronounced in all such cases as this, everyone of 'em impressing a sense and meaning as different from the other as dirt from cleanliness—that causists (for it is an affair of conscience upon that score) reckon up no less than fourteen thousand in which you may do either right or wrong. Mrs Wadman hit upon the *fiddlestick which summoned up all my Uncle Toby's modest blood into his cheeks*'.

(iv) Plain propaganda

How well I remember my acure embarrassment on first reading George Orwell's great essay 'Politics and the English Language' when, after nodding at every line of the first page with vigorous and amazed delight, I ran into his very first example of combined ugliness of style, tiredness of imagery and imprecision of meaning—coming from the pen as if from the very lips of my late teacher:

> I am not, indeed, sure whether it is not true to say that the Milton who once seemed not unlike a seventeenth century Shelley had not become, out of an experience ever more bitter in each year, more alien to the founder of that Jesuit sect which nothing could induce him to tolerate.

Harold Laski, of course, alas—my teacher. And five negatives in fifty-three words, rubs in Orwell. Orwell's essay was, of course, concerned with obscurity of utterance both through incompetence and for deliberate political effect. Now one can defend language against abuse and argue for a plain, direct and lively style in the name of meaning and comprehension or in the name of taste and aesthtics. 'Kind hearts count more than coronets, and Saxon roots than Latin synthesis'. But Orwell was eager to show the precise political advantage of a clear and simple language.

This precise advantage was made more clear in an earlier essay, 'Propaganda and Demotic Speech'. There he wishes, simply or perhaps grandly, 'to bridge the intellectual gulf', he says, 'between rulers and ruled ... the same gulf which lies always between the intelligentsia and the common man'. His theory of style was indeed part of his doctrine of politics. 'The whole idea of trying to find out what the average man thinks,' he says, 'instead of assuming that he thinks what he ought to think, is novel and wholesome ... What is wanted is some way of getting ordinary, slipshod, colloquial English on paper'.

But why, one may ask, is this wanted at all? His answer is plain and political: to demonstrate that there is nothing important politically which cannot be explained to ordinary people in ordinary words. But even if 'slipshod'? Here he surely goes too far, and shows that his own socialist arguments have a special kind of rhetoric about them too, not a technical or pseudo-scientific one, such as he mocks so well, but a colloquial rhetoric. Does one by using a colloquial style necessarily understand better the common man? This suggestion can be as dangerous as the rhetoric of pseudo-science. There are dangers in a populist theory of style. Some thoughts of philosophy, religion and social theory are very difficult and are more likely to be misunderstood if put in too homely and conversational a style. To be precise and to be colloquial is not always easy.

Once more he came down like a ton of bricks on the unfortunate Laski who had rashly criticised T.S. Eliot for 'writing only for the few'. What rubbish, says Orwell, to say this 'of one of the few writers of our times who have seriously tried to write English as it is spoken, like (he quotes):

And nobody came, and nobody went,
But he took in the milk and he paid the rent
although I think Orwell might have conceded that there are lines somewhat less clear in some of Eliot's other poems. 'On the other hand (continues Orwell), here is an entirely typical sentence from Laski's own writing':

As a whole, our system was a compromise between democracy in the political realm—itself a very recent development in our history—and an economic power oligarchically organised which was in its turn related to a certain aristocratic vestigia still able to influence profoundly the habits of our society.

And as the offending sentence came from a printed lecture, asks Orwell, did he actually stand up and spout it forth, parenthesis and all? And the odd thing is that he did. I heard him many many times. And it was very effective. Laski was often above the heads of his audience, but they respected the visible sincerity of this professorial gentleman in trying so hard to explain difficult things to them. Orwell, on the contrary, was a poor platform speaker and indeed an indifferent broadcaster. Perhaps he was too honest to perform those funny tricks one has to do in order to appear even half-way natural. Now I'm not defending Laski's over-rhetorical and over-congested style. But it is easier to be colloquial when attacking the abuse of power, as did Swift, Hazlitt, Cobbett and Orwell himself, than in trying to set out new and positive doctrines and theories. So many of us are deeply affected both by Orwell's style and his politics. But I sometimes wonder if his theory of language didn't doom him to being far more appreciated as a critic than as a positive moralist—as he also wished to be.

NOTES
1.   The year Newcastle won the F.A. Cup.

Eight

My LSE

From the anthology, *My LSE*, ed. Joan Abse (Robson Books, 1977).

My LSE was a year or more as an inter-collegiate undergraduate student, then two years as a post-graduate student (1950-2), and then from January 1957 to June 1965 as a member of the staff. But I am only going to write about what I can *now* remember about what it *seemed* to me to be like then as a student.

So this has no pretensions to be either history or premature autobiography. True, I've dipped into some old files labelled 'Student Junk' to get some colour, but they are almost as incomplete and as idiosyncratic as memory; and from my work on Orwell's biography I've discovered that human memory even over twenty years is unreliable, patchy, rationalizing and imaginative unless checked point by point with the written record.

The great tradition of LSE as the Sacred College of Social Democracy, the advance guard—if not the whole army—of the social sciences in Great Britain, and of 'the empire on which the concrete never set' (whose joke was that really?), all that I saw later but not then. How accidental it is that any individual goes to any particular place and, I scorn teleology, to feel part of an academic tradition is always hindsight. True, I was never more pleased than when *The Guardian* made me part of that tradition. The back cover of the Pelican edition of my *In Defence of Politics* has their reviewer saying:

> One of the most thoughtful products of the political dialogues of the London School of Economics since the great days of Tawney, Dalton, Wallas and Hobhouse.

Youthful ambition fulfilled? No, in fact, socialist though I was as a sixth former, I neither knew of LSE in these terms nor wished 'above all else to go there'. It was accident. I was simply a late developer, nothing but a formidable rugby player, until I prematurely ceased to grown and did unexpectedly well at the old Matric in the Fifth Form and even better in Higher Schools, except that I stubbornly refused to pass Latin even at the lower level.

What, at such a school at Whitgift, could be done with me? A socialist sixth-form master spotted that the Economics Faculty at London required no Latin. So he coached me for the now long-abandoned London General Entrance Examination. Almost all of what he taught me, somehow I unloaded on to the paper.

My first contact was, however, a false dawn. I was interviewed by both LSE and by University College for scholarships. My memory of the LSE interview is cloudy, except that there were too many people there, at least six. They took scholarships seriously then, so outnumbered, outgunned and overawed, my stammer kept locking me up as they bombarded me with difficult and even trick questions (of a kind that they had probably had in Army Officer Selection Tests), showing off to each other furiously. No, I do remember one question and I still blush. 'Why do you want to study Economics particularly?' I should have said: 'Because I have no Latin and didn't realize until now that there are other options in the B.Sc. (Econ).' But I had already rationalized my history, so I said: 'Because the post-war world in many vital respects needs changing, particularly as regards the sharing of incomes more equally.' I still remember the savage, almost tipsy, academic laughter of those brutes. The interview at UC was much more calm and gentle: an immediate offer of a place to do History, as long as I caught up my Latin by the end of the first year. But the Latin frightened me off and the unknown God of Economics called me on. A formal offer, despite the interview, came from LSE first. But I hung on a few days in hope and fear, and an offer came from UC to enter their small but excellent Economics Department.

Within two years I had so rationalized my decision that when fellow activists in the young NALSO would ask why I had gone to UC for Economics rather than LSE, I'd reply (with an ignorant knowingness): 'It's a smaller department; you see more of the staff; LSE is too impersonal; the staff are all wrapped up in research or public service or making money in the city.' But the real truth slipped out years later when Sir Alexander Carr-Saunders conducted his last appointment's committee for an unexpectedly vacant post in the Government Department. The only candidate put forward was me. It should have been a very relaxed occasion. But not for Carr-Saunders. He cross-examined me like a QC trying to discredit a hostile witness in a murder trial. Suddenly he said: 'I see from your file that we offered you a Leverhulme scholarship ten years ago and you turned us down in favour of UC. Why?' Isn't it said that in interrogation sometimes the sudden, disconnected, unexpected question based on a small, intimate truth will break down even an experienced double-agent? 'I didn't know the least thing about it at the time,' I blurted out. 'This place looked to me just like my father's insurance office. The portico at UC looked what I expected a university to look like.' To everyone's surprise Carr-Saunders thumped the table and said to the others: 'He's quite right. Just what I'm always telling you all this place is like and that's what we're up against.'

The point I'm trying to make is that part of the excellence of LSE is that it is part of London University and that inter-collegiate arrangements can work. It is at its worst when it forgets that. This is not hindsight. I have felt this as man and as boy and was persistently irritating in saying so while on the staff at LSE.

In fact, although I enjoyed UC greatly for the variety of students there, I was at odds with my subject. My tutor, Alfred Stonier, a brilliant man, in the first week of the first term of my third year, gave me back a vacation essay on 'Value Theory' marked Alpha Plus, but said: 'Get out. I advise you to get out. You plainly don't believe in the subject. You will be a brilliant critic of it if you go on. But you don't believe that economic theory is anything else but an analytical card-castle. If you go on, you'll end up by hating your subject, hating yourself, and feeling you've wasted your life.' Both our pipes went out and I gaped at him. The vehemence of the advice and, in every sense, its personal nature, was obvious. I rallied and relit with a kind of sarcastic meekness: 'I see what you mean, but I am taking finals this summer. A bit late to switch?' 'Nonsense, not if you really want to get out of Economics. You're going along to LSE for Laski's lectures for subsidiary. Government's easy, just reading books. Switch to that till you're clear what to do.' I said: 'Will you give me till tomorrow morning to make up my mind?' 'Of course. Come back tomorrow. I'll make time for you.' I only consulted with my girl-friend in the Philosophy Department. She had already reached the same conclusion about me; and Freddie Ayer and his circle had already reached the same conclusion about Economics—that it just didn't live up to the verification principle.

So I heard Laski's lectures for two years. I got to know him a little, since I was welcomed as a kind of sinner who had repented when I told the tale of my 'conversion'. Doing Government at LSE then was to sit at the feet of Laski. His lectures had a Gibbonean rhetoric about them and he sounded like a Churchill of the Left. No wonder, when chairman of the Labour Party in 1945, he had tried to take on the great man himself; and that the great man had condescended to notice him, trading blows and insults. He was in the Pantheon, of course, of Sagittarius, whose satiric verses we read weekly in the *New Statesman*. Vicky drew him in cartoons as we saw him when he lectured: all head, only a frail and irrelevant body, and standing absolutely still. He poured out his alternately majestic and sarcastic periods without notes to crowded and often excited audiences, seemingly as if it was General Will himself (who had been to Oxford and Harvard) speaking to us directly. By 1949-50, however, he looked tired and ill. The jokes and quips were always the same. In lecturing on the political thought of the French Wars of Religion one waited, not in vain, for the famous quip to follow the famous quotation: 'the wars lasted until Henri of Navarre decided that "Paris was worth a Mass"—which indeed, I can personally assure you, it is'. But that year I heard him give the same lecture twice. We did not interrupt him. The mood was anxiety and sympathy. His tiredness was obvious. A few nights later he spoke at the Conway Hall in support of Santo Jeger (Lena's husband) in the General Election Campaign. His name filled and flooded the hall. I was organizing the over-flow meeting in Red Lion Square outside, having knocked off from preparing for Finals to be Assistant Agent for Holborn and St Pancras for a month. Laski was very late. I remember the anxious expression on the face of Norman MacKenzie, who seemed to be in charge of getting him from one meeting to another. A job to get him through the crowd; but to give a rather tired replay of old passages, good for the students, perhaps, but what would the constituency make of: 'It can be said of the leaders of the Tory party, as Bagehot said of the House of Lords, "the cure for admiring them was to go and see them" '? Who was Bagehot? And were they that repulsive to look upon and where could one see them?

Yet he moved one deeply. He was concerned with the matter of Britain, the future of the world, and was both an egalitarian and a libertarian. It was not a matter of philosophy or logic that the academic subject should be relevant to political practice, it was a matter of basic belief; and that I've never wanted to shake off—though the relationships of theory to practice are more varied than Laski would ever admit. He mocked Hobhouse's version of the 'General Will'—'one is unlikely to meet it walking down Houghton Street'—but he invoked, promiscuously and imprecisely, something called 'the felt needs of our time'. He was a great influence on many who went to LSE and others far beyond. His greatness was as a teacher and preacher, not as a political philosopher. Herbert Dean of Columbia University wrote a solemn book about the political thought of Harold Laski which simply applied the dreadful Oxford textual critique, the witch-hunt for contradictions and inconsistencies with which Laski's writings were riddled. He missed the point. The same thing had been done to Rousseau, but

the man remains. Laski was wise on Rousseau: 'Do not falter at the
formal contradictions of his arguments, which are legion, but
endeavour to discover what is the animating inwardness of the
man.' Kingsley Martin's biographical memoir of Laski should
have caught his inwardness, but it was a hasty and (some say) a
largely ghost-written book (and the poor ghost might have done
better on his own). We thought at the time that Ralph Miliband
was the truest and strongest of the disciples. Perhaps he will write
about Laski one day. Or perhaps Ralph, from his very different
Marxist perspective, felt, as I did, a certain intellectual embarrassment at reading the books again, some of them anyway, shortly
after Laski's death, after the voice that carried conviction was
silent. All but the early ones are so repetitive and rhetorical.

Another great teacher dominated my undergraduate LSE,
Lionel Robbins. What a contrast! No rhetoric, but well-ordered
notes and a slow, logically constructed and ponderously delivered
argument. He took his time. For although his introductory
Economics course began in October, he would not, so thoroughly
was each basic assumption of classical economics argued, even
allow Man Friday to join Robinson Crusoe on that hypothetical
island for an exchange economy to begin until nearly Christmas.
Some were bored and appalled. But most did see what the game was
about. He realized that it was absolutely necessary to convince
people that Economics is about price, not about the creation of
wealth. The Marxists, even then, called this ideological. But I
accepted it as part of the human condition and still do. Everything
purchased, everything gained, is at the cost of something else.
Demand will always exceed supply, particularly in relatively free
societies. I would, of course, moralize and politicize all this. The
price for political progress may be worth paying, but we had best
not deny that it is paid, especially if paid by others. Then, as now, I
saw these basic propositions as being equally applicable to
socialist and capitalist economies. Also Robbin's basic method
made a great impression. Did he say in so many words—he
certainly implied it—that the great mistakes and choices are made
at the very beginning of thinking about basic concepts in the social
sciences, not on the postgraduate or high scholarly levels of
elaborating and quantifying theories? Any educated fool can
elaborate but it takes a very special kind of wise simplicity to
establish the elements of a subject.

That there was a coolness between Laski and Robbins somehow
percolated downstairs, even in those remote days of discretion. It
was thought to be personal and political, but at the time I saw it as
primary intellectual, seeing only what showed. And I see no need

to revise that judgement. Laski's crowd rarely went on, for instance, to Popper's seminars. But Robbins was plainly reading Popper closely (though the clash of personalities may have been just as great for all I knew), and something of this came over. Yet Laski and Robbins had in common two very important things for LSE. They each taught the basic first-year course in their subjects and they taught it at a time (five or six o'clock, I forget) when the evening students could attend as well. So we all heard the two great men and they saw the importance of impressing their views of the subject directly on the undergraduates. It gave an intellectual coherence to the whole school. My private theory of the peculiarly local conditions for the *troubles* at LSE of 1966 (and after) was the neglect of undergraduate teaching when Robbins gave up his lectures, sometime in the late 1950s, and went off to become Lord High Everythingelse. 'Neglect' is perhaps the wrong word, for when he gave up these lectures, whole committees gave thought to how best to develop them; and the best of the young economists went in as a team to introduce the new models and mathematical theorems of the discipline to the ranks, having been somewhat impatient of Robbin's literary and philosophical approach which left them 'the real work to do', they grumbled, in the second and third years. But they went right over the heads of most students and forgot to establish those basic propositions that can make the difference between Economics being a humane and politically relevant discipline or a technical tool for the biggest paymaster.

Postgraduate LSE was very different. After Laski's death, there was no centre to anything in the Government Department. My temporary supervisor, Kingsley Smellie, said: 'My lips are sealed, but someone very extraordinary is coming who will bring great changes!' Already there was a sense in the whole of LSE that the great political days were over. Indeed they were never as purely socialist as legend has it. In the outside world, the Labour Government had won the 1950 election but was plainly on its last legs. The talk was of 'consolidation', not of any extension of socialist achievements. We socialists summed it up fairly well by realizing that we had just seen five years of reform, irreversible reform, as I argued fiercely against the 'calamity men' who expected the Tories to put the clock back rather than to accept the new time, but, none the less, it was simply reform. Nothing would ever be as bad again as pre-war, but nothing as good as we had hoped. And the new generation of undergraduates had mostly done their two years' military service (I eventually dodged out by pretending to be barmy), were that much older, but had not been through the war like those who had come up in 1946 and 1947.

In my own case, LSE meant less to me than others and its student politics seemed to me less interesting than the UC Debating Society, of which I actually became President after leaving the College. At UC also I had been in on the founding of a Labour Club to rival, very successfully, the Socialist Society (affiliated to the Communist-dominated Student Labour Federation), and as chairman of the London Association of Labour Students, I was wise enough to see that the LSE Labour Club was a kingdom to itself. The London Association did waste one meeting on LSE (bringing coals to Newcastle) with Nye Bevan as speaker. Actually, he disappointed the huge audience. He tried to be academic for the occasion, repeating most of Laski's favourite quotes from the Putney Debates, 'The poorest he that is in England has a life to live as the greatest he', etc., which I later discovered mostly came from a little book by H.N. Brailsford. But afterwards at the urinals, he really did say to me—for he was a sensitive and empathetic man, and plainly I had had a regressive effect on him when I had introduced and thanked him: 'Lad, I con-g-g-g-g-g-ratulate you. You've g-g-g-reat c-c-c-courage. I had to c-c-cure myself of stammering when a young man by t-t-t-aking up p-p-public speaking.' I loved him from that day, never met him again, but went to his Memorial Meeting years afterwards on the tops above Dowlais and wept.

Perhaps also the University Scholarship of £275 a year, twenty-five more than the maximum Ministry undergraduate award, kept me out of LSE a good deal, being able to afford, with that extra ten bob a week and beer at about ninepence a pint, something of that life of 'sub-Bloomsbury', the pubs where there was always someone one half-knew, talking politics or literature, in Frith Street, Rathbone Place, Charlotte, Marchmont, Lambs Conduit or Great Russell Street. LSE types rarely got up into Bloomsbury or even the Museum area. They stuck close to home in the White Horse, the George IV, and their very own good Union bar, The Three Tuns, which used to be on the corner of Houghton Street and the alley way to the Law Courts, and was always well used by the more matey sort of staff.

And yet, if I had no sense of an intellectual centre to the School and if my interim supervisor, Kingsley Smellie, showed little interest in my thesis topic, 'The Method and Scope of Political Science: the problem of the integration of empirical social research into the study of politics', yet, on reflection, I did nevertheless sample a lot of other things. I went to Popper's seminar. I had been to his brilliant undergraduate lectures on Method, but only the inner circle were allowed to speak in the

seminar, except for a specially invited 'victim of the week'. His
function was to explicate in a long paper, of which he could get out
but a few paragraphs before the dogs attacked him, some fallacy
like Psychologism, Historicism, Holism, Determinism, Marxism,
or Essentialism, which the truly great man had already refuted. No
wonder they called him 'the totalitarian liberal'. The way he
conducted a seminar was intolerable. One felt a mixture of shame
and sorrow for his acolytes; but many of us learned more from his
lectures and his writings than from anyone. His influence has
been incalculable.

In my trade I am one of those who has always tried to carry
institutions and ideas forward together. But recollecting for this
essay, why did I, already plainly philosopher and theorist, go
voluntarily or just for fun to William Robson's seminar on Public
Administration, however great his reputation in that field? The
dualism must have been there already. Robson's seminars were
important, dry and terrifying occasions: he was learned Fabianism
personified. We were expected to deliver Webb-like judgements
based on Webb-like readings on the whole of post-war planning.
Passengers were not spared. William (as I may now call almost my
oldest friend) had everything categorized. When I came back from
North America without a job, it was Robson who, without power
or patronage in that then strangely autocratic department, went
through the dutiful gestures of asking me to tea a couple of times,
to his house once, even though the power of the keys lay with
Oakeshott who in June 1956 had given me my Ph.D., and 'Oh you
probably want a job, but there isn't any money in the kitty' all in
one breath, then total silence (not a cup of tea, a sherry or a lunch)
until November, when miraculously 'It seems probable that we
shall now be allowed to appoint a new assistant ... It is a quite
unforeseen opportunity, and I shall be most disappointed if you
are not available.' Basically I preferred Oakeshott's bohemian
informality and terse epistolary practicality, but I came to share
Robson's sense of duty and learned much from him as a colleague
and, finally, as joint editor of his *Political Quarterly*.

To listen to H.L. Beales was my other great optional extra as a
postgraduate at LSE. He wandered, like Dr Who, over all time and
space. But his lectures were of the very stuff of Social History—
whether or not they were called 'Economic History'. Largely
unprepared, immensely erudite and suggestive, bristling with
political implications, many would rank them in memory alongside
Laski, Robins and Tawney—although for the published record one
has to look not to his own hand but to over a hundred and twenty
(O.M. MacGregor has counted) dedications or major thanks to

him as the prime mover which have appeared in books or Ph.D. theses by his students. The chair became vacant one year before his retirement. To LSE's shame, they held his lack of publications against him. After the Robbins' Report went off, chairs were filled left, right and centre on publication lists far less important than his. The very concentration of talent in one place with very few alternatives, could create much bitterness in LSE—too many people whose eggs were all in one basket, too many people who had lived together for far too long. But he continued to teach from home and some of us still drop in, twenty years later, to cadge a good idea and a good drink.

As for fellow students, I viewed them rather ironically as a pretty serious lot. No rags or raids for mascots as at UC. They stood by while a raiding party from King's removed the Beaver himself, disdaining to indulge in infantile rowdyism. But you could sit down at any table in the cafeteria and join in a serious political discussion or a wrangle about Laski's, Robbin's or Beales's latest pontification. Undergraduate facetiousness there was, but it seemed deliberate and pointed to the annual satirical reviews and special occasions, none of the odd, spontaneous happenings that would break out in the other colleges—rags, raids and mock candidates at the Union elections. But at that time I didn't go to those famous cabarets. So I didn't meet Ron Moody and can only hazily remember Bernard Levin, though when pressed by contemporaries over cans of brown memory juice I begin to recall that I was at the famous review when Bernard Levin not merely imitated Laski, but wrote a sketch in which several rival Laski imitators did the great man debating with himself, exposing his own 'stages' or contradictions. Perhaps I was really there but have forgotten. Or perhaps it is all myth. Bernard could phone unto Bernard and ask, but I can't explain all this through his secretary. Anyway, I'm recalling the past, not history.

Yet I have an extract from the Students' Union Publication for 1950 which shows Levin as secretary of the Chess Club, John Stonehouse as chairman and a very rum character called Ken Watkins as treasurer. I can never understand how Stonehouse ever got so far. His nickname at the time was 'Lord John' and his conversation was openly and restlessly about how best to get a parliamentary seat. He seemed to assume that that was the main motive for anyone being active in student Labour politics. We teased him with fantastic schemes, most of which he gravely rejected as impractical or 'unrealistic'! He wooed not merely the Cooperative Party, but their Women's Guilds specifically. In the old Coop movement the hand that held the teapot rocked the throne. One afternoon he asked me at short notice to fill in for him at Kentish Town, perhaps trusting the semi-outsider either not to not to notice or not, until now, to blow the gaff. I began on international affairs and in those days I was a Pacifist, and they were with me to a woman. Elated by this Left-wing surge of motherly approval, I moved on to attack Mr Attlee's inadequacy and Mr Herbert Morrison's reactionary policies. They radiated dislike. Over violently strong cups of tea, they indicated that 'dear Mr Stonehouse' or 'our dear John' would have spoken very differently. He had, indeed, rumbled that the Woman's Cooperative Guild was the one group in the country at that time that was Left-wing in foreign policy (i.e. anti-war: 'we don't want the boys going again') and yet Right-wing loyalists on nearly every domestic issue ('dear Mr Attlee' and 'dear Mr Morrison, not having people getting at them after all they've done for us'). Were they split-minded or were we stereotyped? But, anyway, John Stonehouse rode those two horses together and rode them well. He got his job in the circus.

This essay has become all persons. But that is how LSE seemed to me, not a concept, idea or principle. I only began to think of it in those terms when I was myself a lecturer there (and became disaffected with the reality as a result). So two more people must figure. Before Oakeshott, there was Kingsley Smellie. He tutored me for the year before Oakeshott came in 1951, but I didn't get on at all well with him then, only appreciating his provocative qualities (how well his needling began to move me from positivism) when a colleague. He was a brave man who had gone up to Cambridge on two wooden legs after the First World War. He played table tennis; he kept his socks up with drawing pins; he turned taking the chair at meetings and public lectures from a boring duty into a scene-stealing art form ('It could be said that Isaiah Berlin here, Sir Isaiah, Professor Sir Isaiah, is too well known to need any introduction; but if I said that, you might think it was bluff on both sides, so here goes . . .'); and he learnt to drive at about the age of 60.

> *My name it is Smellie I say*
> *I drive to the School every day*
> *Like a tiger on wheels*
> *I delight in the squeals*
> *Of colleagues who get in the way.*

As a colleague I found him brilliant at putting down (or answering truthfully) those direct questions of visiting American Professors which appeared to break the code. 'What do you do, Professor Smellie?' 'Well, in the morning I listen to a few students read essays to me and then give them a "B+?−", which is a very safe mark to give; in the afternoon I go to the cinema, there's always something new in London; and in the evening I must wend home to Stephanie and Wimbledon.' He gave a famous briefing to new examiners: 'It's a Fail and it must be a Fail if there's *nothing* on the paper or utter gibberish; if there's something on the paper paraphrasing and embroidering the words of the question, that's a clear Pass; if they try to unpack the question to see what it's after, that's a Lower Second; if they make a shot at answering it with a lot in it you can understand, that's an Upper Second; and if they make a shot at answering it at considerable length with a lot in it you can't understand, that's almost certainly a First.' I've found it in practice almost as good as any other set of Performance Criteria.

When Smellie learned that I was going on to Harvard to finish my Ph.D., he urged me to read Matthew Arnold's *Discourses in America* of 1885, George Santayana's *Philosophical Opinion in America* of 1917, and a funny book by Douglas Woodruff called, if I remembered, *Socrates in America.* Oakeshott nodded gravely when I took this remarkable news to him and suggested, in addition, William Faulkner's novel, *Light in August.*

In 1951 I was one of Oakeshott's first students when he came to LSE. Initially, he made little impact upon me. At first he seemed shy and reserved, but then one saw that, unlike Laski, he didn't enjoy argument for its own sake, and didn't care to extend himself towards people who didn't already understand his position or quickly take the trouble to do so. And his position was, after all, a method of understanding, deliberately removed from practice, far more intellectual and academic than Laski's doctrines which could be asserted, simplified and learnt. Unlike most of my contemporaries, I had no sense of shock at his inaugural lecture, only bewilderment. A pity, but why shouldn't there be a conservative political philosopher (I've always read Burke deeply and admired him much) to follow a socialist? I didn't like their 'but it's not LSE' attitude. I liked Oakeshott's phrase that an academic should not be 'a hedge-priest for some doubtful orthodoxy'. I still thought of LSE as a college of the university that happened to specialize in all these things, not as having a sacred and peculiar mission; and, anyway, I knew that the economists had some right to complain that the public image of LSE ('I'm sure you're not all Communists there, are you, Dr Crick?' an old army man said to me) was somewhat exaggerated. But I misread Oakeshott's inaugural on 'Political Education' as being more party political than it was. I didn't at that time understand his philosophical position, so totally different was it from 'mainstream' logical positivist or linguistic schools, yet also sceptical, plainly not 'ethical' (a sceptical Hegelian, was it possible?). Few people understood it. The story Morris Ginsberg's colleagues put around was that they asked him what he thought of the lecture. 'I thought it obscurantist,' he said. But added that he wasn't sure that 'obscurantist' commonly meant exactly what he meant to mean by it, so 'I went to the Oxford Dictionary to check, and it did.' The external examiner in Political Thought told me that in Laski's day it was all simple parrot Laski, but two years later it was incomprehensible and uncomprehending parrot Oakeshott. 'Which would I prefer?' I only began to understand Oakeshott's philosophical position when I read his *Experience and Its Modes* while at Harvard, fortunately having already been introduced to Collingwood's *Idea of History* by Kingsley Smellie. And when I returned, over four years later, I found a polarized department into which I fitted firmly but uncomfortably.

So 'my LSE' was the undergraduate and postgraduate creative confusion. When appointed to the staff, I was disappointed. The Common Room was too large and impersonal. Beales and Tawney had gone, though I was able to meet them both outside the school. But most departments kept themselves to themselves and generally shop, particularly interdisciplinary shop, seemed (unlike at Harvard and Berkeley) taboo. The librarian did not lack for companions in talking mainly about roses—useful to me at the time. The Government Department had already grown too large, so we were always treading on each other's toes, however many small sections the syllabus was chopped up into and however many options were introduced; and it had partly the air of a court (Oakeshott's new appointments), and partly the heaviness of a good many people who had lost all sense of direction (mainly Laski's old appointees).

Truth to tell, I found LSE a narrow place compared to University College and to Harvard, where the company of colleagues and students in Arts and Sciences relieved the ingrown imperial claustrophobia of so many social scientists locked up together. Certainly I earned no love by almost alone, except for Donald Watt, Ernest Gellner, and, I think, John Griffith, opposing the general desire in the School to do our bit and more for expansion when the Robbins Report finally went off and the whole line lurched forward mindlessly. *Beaver* interviewed me, so this is not hindsight:

> We are becoming an ant heap so large that we are losing common themes of conversation . . . LSE ceased to be a

scholarly community when the Common Room grew so
large that members of the staff did not even know the names
of all their colleagues ... What London needs is not a larger
LSE, but a new college of social sciences. I agree with the
economists for once: LSE would benefit from a stiff dose of
competition ... [And] we should never allow ourselves to
become more than half a graduate school; for divorce of
research from teaching is as bad as the divorce of teaching
from research. It is the first year's lectures that matters–to the
scholar as much as the student ... The School is now
increasingly dominated by peripheral activities of research
and vocational pursuits and the hard academic centre seems
to be declining.

I would not now argue for another college of the social sciences,
like the Yugoslav joke, 'Who wants a two party system? One is bad
enough.' I would simply argue that historically the existence and
expansion of LSE has held back the development of the full range
of the social sciences in the other large colleges in London where
they would have influenced and been influenced by other
disciplines. We (for once an LSE man, even of my difficult sort
always an LSE man) once needed protection in the social sciences,
but we came to need free trade and both local and national
competition.

I still interpret the student troubles of 1966 and after largely in
terms of the size of LSE, the relative neglect of the undergraduates
and *les folie des grandeurs* that result from such a concentration of
so many research-minded social scientists all together. And like
our poor old country itself, the memory of unique power outlives
the reality. Everywhere in Great Britain universities suffer from
immobility. But the consequences are worse where subjects are so
concentrated. I told a student cabaret, with more public spirit than
complete personal honesty, that I was leaving *'pour encourager les
autres'*. Yet it was a very tolerant and amusing place to have been
in, both as man and boy, and had the overwhelming advantage of
being in London, the cultural and political capital, even if its great
days both of scholarship and influence were plainly in the past. It
is simply that, like the ocean liners, the cinema organs, the cavalry
and the Kibbutzim, it has had its finest days. It should not rage against
old age but live modestly and remember with pleasure the virile
days of its youth beyond recall. My essay has been a middle-aged
reflection on what was already, in my youth, a middle-aged
institution. *'Odi et amo ...'*, as Catallus remarked.

Nine

Reading *The Observer* as a complex text

From *The Political Quarterly,* April 1985. The editors rejected my original title 'Deconstructing *The Observer*' and substituted sadly *'The Observer'.* Some of the features have changed considerably since I wrote, especially the Review Section; but overall *la plus change le meme chose.*

'I have spent a most dismal day, first in going to church, then in reading the *Sunday Times* which grows duller and duller . . . then in reading through the rough draft of my novel which depresses me horribly. I really don't know which is the more stinking, the *Sunday Times* or the *Observer.* I go from one to the other like an invalid turing from side to side in bed and getting no comfort whichever way he turns.

(From a letter of Eric Blair written on a Sunday in 1932)

In the October 1984 issue of this journal, Hugo Young began this occasional series on newspapers with a most interesting inside account of the internal politics of the *Sunday Times,* the struggle for control between owner and editor and its changing policies. All this could be done for the *Observer,* indeed. But I want to essay something simple but rare and difficult, to read the newspaper as a product, to read it closely and externally as an entire and self-contained text. The proof of the pudding is in the eating—as our mothers taught us before the colour supplements' cookery inserts: just for once to look at the thing in itself and not *how* it came to be, or what it *should* be doing. And to look at it in its entirety. Hugo Young created the impression that the *Sunday Times* is composed of political matter! Did he ever read the whole astonishing artefact?

My quotation from Orwell is a little self-indulgent and external to the text, but it does serve to bring out two basic structural factors. The first is that for most educated, thoughtful, lively and well-informed people, there is only the choice of the one Sunday or the other—or both.[1] No wonder that, hunting for the same market, the two rivals look so like each other, embodying the same kind of 'improving consensus' as the two main political parties used to do in pre-Thatcher days—and for much the same reason. 'Like Tweedledum and Tweedledee', it was often said, which still looks

106

largely true, by content, make-up and values, apart from the *Sunday Times'* lurch to the Thatcher camp in its few political pages. The second structural factor shown by Orwell's sardonic agony is that Sunday newspapers are designed to be read on *Sundays*, originally to fill the yawning gaps of the Protestant sabbath and now, more and more, to assist people in planning a day of leisure– either in fantasy or reality: what to do, what's on, DIY, vicarious pleasures, fashionable loves and hates, or a score or more of varieties of medical scares and hopes, and a certain amount of catching up with the week, including but by no means pre- dominantly politics. Both papers contain a few controversies of a kind suitable for discussion at a family dinner table, or for couples who have breakfast in bed, often swapping from one 'stinking' paper to the other. For solitaries and lonelies, the Sunday papers are, of course, like Radio 4: a whole culture and surrogate society.

My procedure was this. I took the first issue of each month in 1984, if that was not available substituted by another. Then I read them closely and in their entirety, except for the small ads, but including the larger advertisements which form part of a newspaper's meaning, inescapably. Now, in fact I read the *Observer* every week except when I am abroad, but I 'read' it in a very different way: selecting things that interest me, very much guided by headlines and sub-heads. I often ignore some sections entirely: skip and dip.[2] Perhaps I have done something now that nobody does, not even the editor, in reading the whole thing.

The issue of July 1, 1984, had about 99,600 words in it. That excludes advertisements, headlines, capitons and the colour supplement. To talk only about what I normally read, or what I speculate about other people's choice from the 'magazine' would beg the question. All newspapers nowadays are, in fact, magazines containing varying proportions of news or reports of recent events. It could well emerge from this series that the very term 'newspaper' needs redefining, both as to the main content of the dailies and the probable motives of their readers. On those rare occasions when news is both important and pressing, urgent and changing rapidly, most of us turn to radio or television, don't we?

Overall Structure and Up-Front

The make-up of a paper is revealing. With occasional variations as for a Travel section in February, the paper has settled down into the front section, Review, Business and Weekend sections and the colour supplement. The proportions are interesting. In my sample, the front section varied between fourteen and twenty pages–four issues were fourteen and three sixteen pages. Review is always eight pages, Weekend always four pages, and Business varied between fourteen and twenty in almost exactly the same way as the front section (Business includes the four Sports pages). The colour supplement varied between forty and a hundred and twenty-eight pages, according to the seasonal supply of advertising.

The front section could be loosely called the political section. Most people who write regularly for it talk about this section as the policy end. They play an old-fashioned role which stoically ignores what is happening in the rest of the paper: whether the overall content could also, in any possibe sense, be a political factor, contradicting or affirming their own proferred values. The front section carries domestic news, foreign news (relatively well covered), editorials, usually two feature articles on the leader page, and a single, long article on the right-hand inside page; also a 'personality column' immediately before the leader page (during the year it was Conor Cruise O'Brien, replaced by Katherine Whitehorn, who joined the paper in 1963 as Fashion Editor); a 'Political Diary' by Alan Watkins (more and more a personality column), and a more traditional column headed 'Politics' by the political correspondent, Adam Raphael, commenting on the most important events of the week. What I mean by 'personality column', by the way, and all papers have carried them since the 1930s, is writing that the editors believe the readers like for characterfulness, forcefuless, quirkiness, unpredictability, rather than for regular and responsible coverage of a subject: the campaigning essayist as it were. The Levins, the Watkinses, and the O'Briens are usually better writers than their American counterparts, but they do not appear to have research assistants: they write from the top of their heads, a quirky or forceful view on the same stock of news. The *Observer* has never been much taken with 'the investigative columnist' or 'the Whitehall correspondent', let alone an 'Insight team' given time to dig, as the *Sunday Times* attempted before the money ran out and the iron heel came down.

The leader pages are obviously written with seriousness, perhaps a mite too solemn, for unlike the political columns there is every sign that too many cooks dilute the broth. They obviously favour the Alliance, not so much as a policy decision but as temperamental believers in what Arthur Schlesinger once called (without intending the least self-parody) 'the vital centre'. But they are careful not to break with Labour entirely. It probably doesn't matter very much. I suspect that the underlying belief of their leader writers, now that Alliance-boosting has abated, is that the real difference in British politics lie within the two main parties rather than between them. The editorials are all very sensible and decent, but somehow 'wet', in the sense of dealing in generalities, never thought through into consistent and practical policies. This middle of the road, considered, over-compromised framework somehow infects as well as selects the signed feature articles on the leader page: not having a decisive the of policies, just decent and predictable values. The *Observer* could open up its leader page to the full range and strength of political and social viewpoints argued outside in our society—as *The Times* imagines it is doing. But, with a few exceptions, the diminishing number of outside contributors all sound as if they have been exposed to the remorseless drip, drip of friendly *Observer* consensual pressure, so that the forceful ideas of a Tuesday become presentable to the majority of readers by the Sunday (who, to judge by the rest of the paper, are little interested in politics anyway).

A fifteen-hundred word 'Profile' each week maintains a very high standard of, so to speak, living obituaries of the famous. It is a speciality of the house, as is the Pendennis column which forms the back page of the front section, less room for advertisements which take up half. It deals largely in the personalities of public life. What becomes clear on reading closely the whole front section is that there is a house style, and its basic philosophy is still profoundly liberal in the way they look at the world and the presuppositions they accept—and never bother, of course, to argue. And liberalism in its broadest sense: that events (both historical and contemporary) are to be explained basically by the initiative, enterprise, talent and originality of individuals. The front section is linked to the other sections by the belief that events, whether in politics, art or sport, are to be explained primarily in terms of individual performance and motivation. All issues have to be personalised, which does not mean the writers are writing down to the readers; it is obvious that they themselves believe this. Not for them 'long-term factors', social and economic trends, 'impersonal forces', 'the structuration of society', etc. (Or perhaps for no one of a Sunday.) But this obsession with personal achievement does make their perennial concern for the decline of the British economy and the breakdown of consensus politics (which I have read every Sunday of my adult life) perpetually impotent, trivial and short-sighted. But they are liberal, indeed, so they do not adopt a conservative epistemology either, as *The Times* does so naturally, and as the proprietors are trying to impose on a naturally *Observer*-like *Sunday Times* staff: by conservative I mean experience, tradition, hierarchy, the skill of a traditional elite (plus socialising the best of the creeps, climbers, thrusters and gallopers). The *Observer* is cheerfully radical about mocking 'the Establishment', despite the pleasant voyeurism of the colour supplement's glimpses of Show Biz people and other personalities. But, of course, it is also a very conscious provider of the information that people think they need to rise in the world, for the upwardly mobile (just as the *Sun* is certainly the paper for those who think they have got stuck down unjustly or unluckily).

If the back page of the front section has to be half advertisement, editorial belief in the primacy of the political (even though their practice denies it) comes across strongly on the front page: only sixteen inches of advertising matter is allowed out of a hundred and eighteen column inches. The front page has a good, clean, fresh design, and tries hard to find and feature some exclusive and important-sounding political story not already run in the weekly Press. Dubious spy stories may now replace the old 'Impending Cabinet Reshuffle?' as the perennial first reserve for this eye-catching position. 'MI5 Double Agent Defects to *The Observer*' was a good one. Medical scares are another standby: 'Secret Deal Over Britain's First Test-Tube Quads.'

The front page carries a selective index to the four mainly political/serious special features, yet much more prominence is given to a two-inch strip across the top of the front page under the title. This picks out with illustrations special features obviously highlighted to reassure the reader at once, despite the traditional political front page, that the *Observer* caters brightly for 'the whole of life', as it sees life. I pick out three issues at random just to remind you of what kind of things are thus featured. March 11, 1984: A major new magazine partwork, British cookery; Katharine Whitehorn on alternative living; Germain Greer, Eunuch into Mother; The Other War, Gulf (on the oil industry) and Little White Hope (on Zola Budd). August 5: Yoko Ono, life without Lennon; Clive James and the Big Guns (reporting the *Observer's* own celebrity shooting contest); Seaside Britain, the Kent Coast; Chariots of Gold, Hugh McIlvanney at the Olympics; and Living the Life (on conspicuopus consumption). November 4: Paul McCartney talks about the new film; America's Other Election (beauty queens); Castle Battlements, Roy Jenkins on Barbara Castle's diaries; and Heroine of the Wightman Flop (tennis).

The 'Review' Section

'The Review' used to be thought of as 'the literary pages', but that was never really true. Reviews of books take up two pages out of eight. The issue of September 2, for instance, had about 165

column inches of book reviews, 16 inches of book advertisements
and 108 inches of Holiday and Travel ads on these two pages. Not
much is published in July and August. But on November 4 there
were 176 inches of book reviews and 154 inches of book ads. April
15 saw 44 inches of book ads, but then 'What's On' ads moved to
take up two-fifths of the left-hand book page. Long gone are the
days when Gollancz used to advertise his books on the editorial
page of the front section. Publishers' ads are highly seasonal
anyway and these figures suggest some doubt in their minds about
whether readers of the newspaper buy books for themselves and
not just for Christmas presents. And the books advertised show
little congruence with the books reviewed. The selection of books
for review seems a curious running compromise between a good
old-fashioned view of Literature with a capital 'L', a frame of
reference that only intellectuals will share, and a belief that
readers of this part of the section are interested in almost any
biography, whether of a literary figure, a general or a royal
princess. It is good on modern English and French novels, poor on
literary criticism and academic Eng. Lit. and surprisingly good (if,
of course, terribly selective) in doing one general or academic
history book a week. It tries hard to keep its literary readers abreast
of modern poetry. But either because the literary editor, Terence
Kilmartin, who has done the job for thirty-two years, has no
personal interest in pure philosophy, moral or political philosophy,
even the best of books in what is after all quite a strong national
hand, rarely get reviewed.

And again, with rare exceptions it is as though the social
sciences did not exist. But for some book ads, readers would not
know that important works get published that need popularising.
And the feature writers or serious columnists up-front don't seem
to have time to read even the best of social science, though *New
Society* does all the gutting for them. Space, of course, as every
literary editor knows, is terribly tight; but some are less defensively
purely literary than others. The *Guardian*, with less space, throws
its net wider.

A few people do nearly all the reviewing. Any editor must rely on
trusties. But the number in the *Observer* is so few that the close
reader suspects that the ideology of personality is at work again. A
commissioning editor believes that readers read for the personality
rather than the subject matter. 'What's old A.J.P. on about this
week?' Or what mixture of great sense and perverse provocation
will flow from Anthony Burgess's pen? 'What a pity they never
really found a substitute for Philip Toynbee (or was it Cyril
Connolly?) whom I used to enjoy every Sunday.' Specialists are a

nuisance and cannot write English. Also one suspects that once in the family, the reviewers to a large extent pick their own books—which makes for lively writing, but also eccentric coverage and occasional blatant nepotism.'

A few political books get reviewed by staff writers from the front section—either a sign of economy or an editorial concern with trying to make precise the necessarily nebulous or consensual '*Observer* editorial line'. Statesmen's memoirs tend to get reviewed by other statesmen, so are rarely given a serious criticial appraisal.

The tension between politics and literature (and a very narrow view of each emerges) is made plain on the front page of the Review section. This page carries a single article which normally carries over. It is the big read of the week. My sample was divided between broadly political topics and broadly literary, even if 'literary' usually means the 'private life' of some leading personality. Typical was the headline. 'Get on that stage you little bitch', and the box, 'Garry O'Connor ends his study of the tragic, doomed marriage of Laurence Olivier and Vivien Leigh'; or 'Blind Boy on a Bicycle. Ved Mehta . . . tells how he struggled for the right to a normal childhood.' And I now know a lot more than I want to about the sex life of H.G. Wells, Rebecca West and the psychology of Anthony West by-lined as 'their illegitimate son'; but it won't stop me reading them. And Eliot's private life ran a strong second to Lawrence's this section. The 'political' features tend to be dominated excruciatingly intricate and boring spy stories, wives of great men, and Second World War battles (the last of which I oddly enjoy. *De gustibus.* They do have to spread it wide).

Film, theatre and music reviews strike me, overall, as extremely good: they contain some of the best writing in the paper, giving a mixture of reportage and critique—but usually fairly clear which is which. Many of us rely on their excellent 'Briefings' as well as the advertisements for news of cultural events. For dance and art reviews I cannot judge: blind spots. But it obvious that in all these performing arts the reviewers or columnists are allowed to assume a degree of prior knowledge and cultural reference in the readership which would neither be assumed nor tolerated in the political pages.

And that is unfortunately another way of saying that the level of political writing in the front section is lower than that in the Review section. One can see how this occurs. The good liberal conscience says that the paper's political writings must be accessible to everyone, but that the rest of the pages cater to special interests, often demanding a degree of specialised knowledge in the reader. That political knowledge can be made public and that the public should be involved in politics is a great liberal cultural ideal. But to reflect thoughtfully on that process is not the same thing as involvement in that process: political discussion on a level which matches the best on art and sport need not be exclusive. Shakespeare, after all, solved the problem, of talking to different levels at once, often with less space. Good teachers do it. Good doctors move easily from one patient's level of understanding to another's.

'Business' and 'Weekend' Sections

The length of the Business Section tells a tale. The amount of reportage of company news, developments and new issues is about equal to political news reportage. There is a similar love of personalising issues and also some really dramatic writing about boardroom purges and take-over bids (it was a treat to see how well they described the bitter struggle for the control of Harrods between their proprietor and that professor),[4] yet the issues never vanish into middle-of-the-road generalities. Their readers, like punters, want precise suggestions and good judgment. If their front section columnists are sometimes diffuse, the named writers in the Business section are admirably urgent and concise, and so write good English into the bargain, nearly as good as in the *Economist* or the *Financial Times*. They run a lot on computer developments: section editors talk to each other apparently, for the colour supplement also ran a good series during the year on the uses of computers.

Most of the Business section is taken up with advertising, but its quality (or to be less sweeping, its cost) shows that insurance companies, investment trusts, mortgage companies and airlines have a greater faith that they influence people with money to spend than publishers show in the book section. Travel and holiday advertising appear in the back of this section, for obvious reasons, even if that may be the only thing that brings some people into it at all. People like myself who, previously, never read the main Business section, are missing, I have discovered, a good deal of much more specialised material on the state of the economy, economic policy and industrial relations than one can find among the more generalised, general-reader politics of the front.[5]

Rather incongruously, perhaps because they both have to be printed late, the Sports section is tacked on to Business. Here, too, is some of the best writing and photography in the paper. The level of knowledge assumed is higher than in the more popular Sundays which give proportionally more space to sport. A technical phrase like 'primary election' or 'single transferable vote' up-front has to be explained (or fudged in a general haze about 'PR'); but 'off-side trap' or 'double fault' get by every time. An historical allusion in a political column to, say, 'Mr Thatcher playing the Opposition so differently to Baldwin' would need explaining and therefore (counting words) be dropped; but 'like Arsenal played the wings in the 1930s' is rightly assumed to be part of the knowledge of anyone who cares for the sport at all. An interesting sign of social change is that football reportage clearly exceeds rugby reportage, both in column inches and in quality.

As the *Observer* is so reader-conscious, it is surprising that 'the whole of human life' as a sport gets such relatively short shrift in pages. Not merely sport in general, but so many sports. Yet 'market conscious' may be the more fruitful concept. There is little big advertising directly related to sport, so often the sporting section has three clean pages.

'Weekend' evolved out of the Women's pages. And though Katherine Whitehorn moved up front during the year to take O'Brien's column, 'Weekend' is still very much her kind of thing: 'intelligent woman' giving personal opinions on everything from fashion to tokenism to PTAs and what to do about dog droppings. Indeed, like the colour supplement, this section tries to be ahead of fashion whether in cars, clothes or cookery: to play the game of 'spot or start the trend'—literally trendy, but slightly ironically, as if one knows all along that it is a joke and that one day one will be serious again, and not wish for electric can-openers or 1930s French knickers until every child is fed in a world beyond the notional 'NW1' in which the section is set.

'Weekend' always begins with a feature of some seriousness, but again heavily personalised: 'Family Writer: Ann Chisholm talks to Hilary Spurling about her biography of Ivy Compton-Burnett and how she combines having children with her career.' (This may also be a case of building up a relative newcomer to the *Observer* family in order to offer another 'personality' to its readers.) Or ' "To Prove a Villain" . . . Antony Sher who plays Richard in the current RSC production, puts Shakespeare's character into historical perspective.' He is a fine actor, but one might just as well have Olivier on the history of Cyprus, or the decline of the music hall. This section ends with a half-page 'Notebook' essay by Michael David—thoughtful, varied and sociological and not needing the hype of personality to keep my interest.

The Colour Supplement Ends It

What really struck me about the *Observer Magazine* is the

photography. No wonder so much of it ends up as collage on bathroom or bedroom wall, let alone on Anthony Powell's famous ceiling—itself once featured. The contents are remarkably like an illustrated 'Weekend'. There doesn't seem to be much more to say, only that the cookery is now in colour. And a famous politician, artist, performer or writer shows 'A Room of My Own', something for us to criticise, emulate, or envy. There is the odd serious piece embedded in all the good living and how the other half copulate or contracept sort of stuff. One of the best tabular presentations of regional unemployment statistics appeared between lingerie and car ads on October 7. I hope schoolteachers found it. Roy Hattersley's '100 Years of the Fabians' did get a caption on the cover alongside 'Putting the Skates under Starlight Express', 'Heyday of the Horror Comix' and 'British Cookery—East Anglia'. If one is very clever or pedantic, one can find on pages 5 or 7 a Table of Contents to the magazine. But from the catch-penny cover right through to 'Peanuts', the design of it is as a lucky dip, difficult to extract what one wants and get out quick: one has to turn all those pages of colour ads wondering if there might be something interesting; there sometimes is. It has to be done, one might be at a loss for the sub-text on a Sunday night in some unexpectedly specific conversion. Talking points. Here one sees the graphic breakdown of any attempt, which both the political and the literary pages still try to make, at rational discrimination: a kaleidoscope of consumer delights and instant issues are put before us. Or is that what we demand? 'Who the rider, who the horse?' as Yeats remarked.

☆   ☆   ☆

What emerges is a clear picture of what is best and what is worst in the culture of modernity. 'Have we come all this way for this?' What is best is the sheer lively range of choice, open to those in employment. What is worst is the cynicism or self-deception needed to put all this together week by week to please everybody and offend no one; and for the reader to take it seriously. There is a kind of modern eunuch who is brilliantly expert in mentioning issues as if by so doing they are resolved. Just as most of us now are political voyeurs more than actors, and are grateful for the weekly magic theatre.

The *Observer's* writers have a clear, common epistemology: that there is true knowledge, but that it is always and only about people's motives. Psychology is king. In the world of competing individualism even 'character' is now replaced by 'personality'. The paper also has an ontology: that the world consists of nothing but momentary pleasures and stimuli—ethically Hobbesian sensationalism. Said the master, 'Felicity is a continual progress of desire, from one object to another ... I put for a general inclination of all mankind, a perpetual and restless desire of Power after Power, that ceaseth only in Death.'

So at the end of the day, reading the whole of the actual text, the difference between the *Observer* and its rival and other down-market Sunday papers becomes one of degree, not kind. John Stuart Mill attempted to escape from Hobbes, Bentham and his father by distinguishing (or asserting that there was a distinction) between higher and lower felicities: yet even his argument suffers the fatal flaw and anti-humanistic horror of any utilitarian culture, that 'the greatest happiness of the greatest number' whether high or low can indeed be achieved, economically, culturally and politically, while leaving the lesser number outside— even if they number millions—if they are an electoral minority or cannot influence the market. And these millions have no other values than these put before them, useless though they are. The highest aspiration becomes individual escape if *you* are worthy enough, or in truth luckily enough, to rise into the wonderful narcissistic solipsist, hedonistic world of the 'Weekend' section and the colour supplement (not to mention its own new monthly pull-out section called 'Living Extra'). If one could not laugh, as if in a theatre, one would howl as if with Lear on the Heath.

NOTES
1.   Certainly just as some people vote Conservative in order to appear to be middle class, so some may read the *Sunday Observer/Times* in order to appear educated, thoughtful, lively, concerned, well-informed, and attractive.
2.   In fact I read the headlines on p. 1 quickly, then more slowly the Football League Division One results to see how badly Arsenal and QPR are doing, and then the evening television recommendations in order if necessary to make a pre-emptory joint policy statement over breakfast. Then I start skimming any section anyone else hasn't grabbed. Does anyone read a newspaper sequentially like most books?
3.   Just by reading the whole text it is clear how much they puff each other; not out of vanity, I'm sure, but from a professional belief that readers are more interested in personalities than in ideas. I will stray outside the text to recall the colour supplement of May 8, 1983, which celebrated their 10,000 issue. The main feature was 'The Paper's People' a definitive list of the personable among the inner family.
4.   Though the stories never reminded readers of who he was. But I know a lot of ordinary readers who don't know a Rowlands from a Murdoch: that is specialised knowledge.
5.   Perhaps there could be a box on the leader page signalling advanced political readers to items in 'Business'. Some good may come of this article.

Ten

On the Difficulties of Writing Biography in General and of Orwell's in particular

A lecture delivered at the Biographical Research Centre, University of Hawaii and published in *Biography*, Vol. 10 No. 4, Fall 1987, which was a revision of the Orwell Memorial Lecture for 1985 of which a shortened version appeared in the *London Review of Books*.

The word 'biography' can create as many different expectations as the word 'Orwell'. There is 'Orwell' as Orwellian—the gloomy prophet-pessimist of *Nineteen Eighty-Four,* so it is said, though I see the book as Swiftian satire if only marginally more cheerful for that; and there is Orwell as 'Orwell-like', the essayist, the humourist, the humanist, the lover of nature and of all small, curious things. The word 'biography' can mean a memorial or a panegyric; it can mean a hatchet job, or it can simply mean a good read. Now, of course, the hatchet job, whether literary journalism (stemming from Lytton Strachey) or of political journalism (stemming from W.T. Stead) was itself simply a reaction both to the Moneypenny and Buckle-like monumental 'good' lives, in which as among Lutheran pietists all mundane facts are held to be equal and to be equally sacred and all lively facts are suppressed; and also a reaction to the mercifully shorter celebratory lives, exemplary lives, Robert Southey on Nelson or Samuel Smiles on the great explorers and inventors, often published in series well-called 'Popular Lives'. This tradition has not died out, nor should it. 'Let us now praise famous men' and women indeed: 'There is a time and place for all things'. I notice that Michael Foot now calls his *Life of Aneurin Bevan* in its paperback edition, 'a polemical biography'. Perhaps he is reacting to some criticism by pedantic historians that his book was a trifle partial. And so splendidly it was. There is a place in our culture for holding up certain lives as noble examples, whether of Nye Bevan, the Queen Mother or Ms. Onassis, according to the reader's values. I do not wish to say that these are not biography, any more than to deny that their mirror-image hatchet jobs are. They are precisely what many people still mean by biography. Names are not sacred; only actions are good or bad.

Others, I've said, simply see a biography as 'a good read' about an actual person, whether praising, knocking or tolerably fair.

117

Wyndham Lewis once said that good biographies are like novels. Certainly the common reader seldom looks for or follows up footnotes; rather he welcomes a coherent, evenly flowing story and a clear portrait of a character. And this kind of biography can exist for different levels of readership, just like novels. Publishers seem to know three broad levels; popular—mostly lives of sportsmen and 'show-biz' celebrities; 'middle-brow'—mostly of heads of state, royal families, generals and famous criminals; and 'intellectual'—mostly famous statesmen, writers or thinkers.

The next move in the argument is obvious, but I want to put my case minimally and negatively: so long as the difference can be perceived between those aforementioned types of biography and scholarly, academic or definitive—call them what you will—biographies, I don't need to call my sort legitimate biography and the rest bastards; I would only need, if time allowed, to point to some of the crucial differences between them. Biographies whose primary intent is not to tell the truth, the whole truth and nothing but the truth, often fulfill some useful, cultural role. But just let us not confuse the categories. I found some sophisticated reviewers who obviously expected that I should either 'put the case for Orwell' or 'cut him down to size at last,' and were not merely disappointed when I didn't, but then accused me of doing the other. Some friends of Orwell said I was attacking him and most of his enemies said I was finding excuses for him, though they all conceded that I provided a vast amount of factual information that might one day be useful to someone else, to save someone of more delicate sensibilities from having to sweat.

At times while taking all criticism seriously, I did feel a bit like the BBC reporting the Northern Ireland and Falklands crises. Being hit by both sides at once, I felt that theoretically discredited attempts to be balanced and objective might occasionally more or less have worked. Epistemologically I know that the position is absurd, but practically one cannot help feeling a little bit smug, nailed up there on one's cross when the blood flows down from both cheeks at once.

Yet scholarly biographies have peculiar difficulties. I referred to some of them in my Introduction, so I won't labour the obvious. The novelist has a reasonable control over his or her characters, the plot, the length of chapters and the balance of one part of the narrative against another. But the scholarly biographer in limiting himself to what can be said truthfully is limited by the availability of the evidence and the reliability of witnesses. And evidence comes in all shapes and sizes and with all kinds of gaps: skill, patience and energy are necessary, but they are useless without luck, and they cannot recreate lost or destroyed papers. The final evidence can look very like that celebrated Irish description of a fishing net, a series of holes surrounded by string.

Sometimes one has more documentation than is needed or is easy to handle. Sometimes one has, as for the Burma period in Orwell's life, very little direct evidence. Nothing is rational, everything is accident. Orwell's letters to his agent, over almost thirty years, survive; but not his agent's letters to him. Two letters of George's to Sonia, his second wife, survive, and none from her to him. Quite simply in writing a scholarly biography there is no way, without excessive speculation and padding, to ensure any proportionality between the length of chapters and the probable importance of various episodes of someone's life. I was not being foolishly modest or nervously defensive when I said in the Introduction that I could have produced a better book. I am not being modest at all. I am aware that I can write as well as most academic biographers and better than nearly all other social scientists. But lumpiness and unevenness are necessarily there, if one's primary commitment is to truth based on evidence rather than to telling a good story based on intuition. Literary facility can prove deadly if it tempts a biographer into lack of respect for the limitations of the evidence available.

Now of course I admit that this is not an all or nothing proposition. I am no advocate of that school of historical biography who dish up documents raw and even uninterpreted on a scale only limited by the resources of university presses and Foundation subsidies, or as Leon Edel said in his 'A Manifesto' in the first issue of *Biography*, 'Like crushed cars in a car cemetery'. Who are such historians writing for—themselves? Or there is the extreme contrary response as when the writer A.J.A. Symons chose to write the life of a notorious if talented liar, Frederick Rolfe, who moved among men to whom secrecy and duplicity were second nature and where documentation was destroyed, forged or scarce, and all living memory suspect for self-interest: therefore he wrote his *Quest for Corvo* as an account of his quest and of his relationship with the witnesses, as if a novel. Decency, let alone the laws of libel, closed that door to me.

A biographer who presumes a serious readership, however, must present the evidence, must not merely have footnotes (which literary publishers and typographers hate) but must bind himself or herself to saying nothing of importance that cannot be footnoted. But perhaps if the footnotes are detailed and sometimes long, as when one needs to discuss the reliability of evidence, and if they are tucked away at the back of the book, then the text can be kept reasonably clean and flowing. I certainly tried to keep both scholars in mind and those general readers—if they thought it worth the effort—who wanted the story of George Orwell. So the final result was, of course, as are most thing in life, a compromise.

I think that the writer and painter Wyndham Lewis was perverse to suggest that the good biography is like a novel. Some biographies and autobiographies are, but then, while enjoyable, they do have to be taken with as much salt as they have pepper. May I give a rather extreme, absurd but endearingly honest example from an English literary lady's biography?

> I owe an apology to those who expect, and are entitled to expect, accuracy, coherence, chronological order. This is not so much narrative as an anthology: selected moments, hand picked. Why burden the book with 'the long littleness of life' which the reader would only skip, and which I have skipped, for him? On other hand, may I remind him that *toute verite n'est pas bonne a dire*. I have not lied, I have merely by-passed the truth, whenever unpalatable.

Violet Trefusis does mention Vita Sackville West quite often in her book, but not that they were lovers and eloped together.

I am not saying that popular biography cannot be truthful. Most readers are prepared to believe that dear Mr So and So, who wouldn't know a footnote if he saw one, is telling the truth about the Duke of Edinburgh or about Mrs Onassis; or certainly believe that *they* would get *him* in the Courts if his make-believe was too lurid. But unless the biographer does the hard graft, even *he* is not to know if he is telling the truth or not; and hard graft means a lot more than relying on the memory of people who met one's subject and on the gossip of third parties. Strictly speaking, a truthful popular biography could only be a popular version of an existing scholarly biography, just as all school histories are taken from academic histories. For instance, Mr Peter Lewis's recent popular short life of Orwell is, despite some questionable political judgements (what Orwell should have believed had he not been a socialist), a very reliable and useful brief distillation of the evidence—only I'm bound to say that I found the remark in his Preface hard to accept that his own work was finished before mine appeared, unless being finished it then started up again. I make no complaint, it is the fate and function of scholarly works to raise the standards of popular journalism.

More seriously, what is biography really about? I deliberately called my work a 'Life' of Orwell because, as I argued in the Introduction, 'biography' has, since the time of Dr Johnson, come

to imply the portrait of a character. The main business of a
biographer has often been thought to be that of 'getting inside' his
subject, 'grasping the inwardness', 'knowing another person', or
'revealing the true personality'—in a word, empathy. And this is
why, presumably, Wyndham Lewis would prefer the novelist to the
historians as biographer. Now I set out with this common view in
mind, which I now hold to be romantic. I'm not wholly sure how I
came to change my mind, only that I did as I became impressed
with the ambiguity of much evidence and even, in order to make
good some well-established readings of Orwell's character, with
the need to suppress contrary evidence (i.e., if we cut out Act I,
Scene 1, then the ghost can be purely in Hamlet's schizoid mind).
Critics are entitled to believe that in justifying an external, almost
alienated approach, I was rationalising a defeat. Several leading
reviews, not merely by old friends of Orwell's, paid great tribute to
my energy, industry, sense of period, grasp of history, etcetera,
before saying either that I failed to paint a credible character, or
that it was not as they remembered. But I'm unrepentant and
though sentimentally I would love to have met him—he feels like a
lost lover whom I never knew; yet for the stern purposes of
biography I see advantages in having no personal memories. For I
must say publicly that, while each of those reviewers was able to
paint, in a few paragraphs, a more coherent picture of Orwell's
character than I was able to do in a quarter of a million words, yet
these miniatures were, while all life-like and beautiful, each quite
different from the other and each fused with autobiography. I
made the same point in the book about the obituaries of George
Orwell: fine and noble writing but showing considerable diversity
in characterisation.

The point is an epistemological one: in the nature of knowing
and being, can we really know *the* character even of people we are
very close to, lovers, friends and family, in such a way that we can
surmise accurately (as adolescents torture each other) 'what are
you *really* thinking'? Can we use such 'knowledge' of character,
such as it is, to entail facts: actually to fill gaps in the record of what
she was doing in the many years before she remade our life, still
less to be sure what her former motivations were? Yet English
biographers, famous for their good judgement of people (which in
itself may be a national stereotype, vice or collective delusion)
commonly do just that. They follow the great Dr Johnson in his
Lives of the English Poets—'I knew that poor wretch, Savage':
probably he and Savage drank together on two or three occasions.
Then they infer a life from a character. If we live with people or
meet them often, we can build up a fair knowledge—and abilities

differ in this respect—of their likes and dislikes, even of their probable behaviour in response to past and future events. We can become fair judges of each other's probable behaviour, allowing for a good many surprises and misunderstandings. Don't misunderstand me. I am not a behaviourist. These things cannot be measured. Amid necessity there is human freedom. I'm not a behaviourist; but I suspect that most of the people who talk so confidently about the character of George Orwell or anyone else, don't really want to commit themselves to *radical intuitionism*. A radical intuitionist is someone who thinks that you can have direct knowledge of somebody else's motives.

There are many wise and helpful things in Professor Leon Edel's book *Literary Biography* directly based on his experience of writing his truly great and monumental biography of Henry James. Yet in my terms he *almost* professes to be a radical intuitionist:

> The biographer is called upon to take the base metals that are his disparate facts and turn them into the gold of human personality, and no chemical process has yet been discovered by which this change can be accomplished. It is a kind of alchemy of the spirit; to succeed the biographer must perform the anusual—and the well-nigh impossible—act of incorporating himself into the experience of another person, even while remaining himself.

I'm glad that in fact he kept his distance. A biographer of Henry James written by a Jamesean simulacrum would be almost as weird and over-complex as an Orwellian biography of Orwell would be falsely simple.

No names, no pack drill, but if I heard once on my trail, I heard a dozen times something like this: 'I really didn't know Orwell awfully well; to tell the truth, Professor, we only met over lunch or drinks three or four times by way of business; but somehow, I really cannot explain, very different people you know, but somehow we clicked at once . . .'

When, occasionally, this kind of understanding could be put into words, specific enough to say something, all I could do was to put it alongside several other different revelations and puzzle: usually I couldn't count them as evidence at all or only by default if they related to some specific and problematic event in Orwell's life for which documentation was lacking—why did he go to Burma? Why did he go to Spain? Why did he go to Jura? Why did he want a second marriage so much? Only then did I think it right to trouble the reader, and then only with this frankly quasi-evidence of different opinions. As with Brecht and the art of acting: if people must demand what *the* true interpretation of Hamlet is, I'd rather they, or rather each one of the audience, made up their own mind differently rather than the actor and the producer should try to solve the enigma definitively and smooth it all out for them.

I think it is possible to give, as far as surviving evidence allows, a reasonable objective and reliable account of how someone led their life. Even then, the evidence may overwhelm one, so of course one makes judgements as to what was important. In Orwell's case I chose (or rather I came to find myself choosing), not very surprisingly, to concentrate on his attempts to write and publish his book—as Marxists and structuralists would say, on his 'literary production'; a useful enough phrase, on its own. But I note that if Malcolm Muggeridge had carried out his original commission to write a biography of Orwell, it would have been an account of the struggles of a Christian without God to find a cause, just as gentle and well-meaning Sir Richard Rees, who had known Orwell very well, did write a book about Orwell as 'almost a saint'.

If one must say that biographies are about character rather than about the lives that people led, then at least it is prudent to adopt, as philosophers would say, a soft rather than hard usage of the concept. Consider this dialogue in *Middlemarch* about Lydgate, suspected of crime:

'. . . there is no proof in favour of the man outside his own consciousness and assertion.'

'Oh how cruel!' said Dorothea, clasping her hands. 'And would you not like to be the one person who believed in that man's innocence, if the rest of the world belied him? Besides, there is a man's character beforehand to speak for him.'

'But, my dear Mrs Casaubon, said Mr Farebrother, smiling gently at her ardour, 'character is not cut in marble—it is not something solid and unalterable. It is something living and changing . . .'

If I concede that there is 'character' in Farebrother's sense, then at least I must remind, in very friendly spirit, four good old friends of Orwell's, who have all said kind things about my work except that I miss his character, that they only knew his 'living and changing character' relatively late in his life. And that what he told each of them about his earlier life and states of mind is not conclusive evidence: our own interpretations of the past live and change, one reveals different things about oneself to different people, and if one never lies, as a lady once said to me, one seldom tells the whole truth. And their own readings of his character, not surprisingly, thinking of their own diverse backgrounds, viewpoints and talents, differ. Friends see friends as part of their own lives. Part of how we now see him is through the very diversity of the testimony of all who knew him well, quite as much as in the common ground. I presumed a reader who might actually for once like being left alone with divergent testimony to make up his or her own mind, not offered a solution by some superintelligent and superempathetic biographer. The externalising, the distancing, the alienation-effect, if you like, became deliberate; indeed I now think it the only proper stance for a biographer to take if telling a true tale about a life is the aim, not the presumption of final godlike judgement on character or achievement. Too much English biography is an extended version of the Headmaster's report.

Preconceptions about character, even by those who knew the subject well, can actually end up in contradiction to the actual course of the life. Sonia Orwell was genuinely convinced that it was not in his real character to be so political, and that in turning to her he was showing the dominance of his literary over his political self. Leaving aside whether this 'politics' versus 'literature' is not a false disjunction—he said that above all else he wanted to make 'political writing into an art'—and leaving aside any speculations that there might have been other good reasons why a man would turn to Sonia, her view involves what I have called 'speculative teleology': what he should have done had he lived differently or longer, the logic of the 'real character,' not the grossly empirical course of the actual life. Sonia wrote in her Introduction to the Collected Essays:

> If political events had made less impact on him, he would have lived in the country, written a book—preferably a novel—once a year, pursued his interest in the essay form and, when money was badly lacking, done straightforward book reviews which, he said, he enjoyed writing ... War made him a political activist.

But if she meant the Second World War, he was by them already a political activist; and if she meant the Spanish War, that was a war that he chose to fight in, went out of his way actually to fight in, not simply to visit Spain for conferences like Connolly, Auden and Spender. I'm not quoting this passage simply to show that Sonia was wrong in her judgement of his 'character', making it indeed an article of faith among her own friends that she would have saved him for 'literature' from 'politics'; rather I quote it to show the danger of all such judgements based on the concept of 'character.' Since she was so clear what his real character was, several important or revealing political essays were discarded from the *Collected Essays, Journalism and Letters*, as being inferior, not typical or repetitive.

A 'character study' is simply not the same as a 'life'. Arthur Koestler regretted that I failed in those laborious 473 pages to grasp Orwell's character as well as the aforementioned Mr Peter Lewis in his sprightly picture book (which, incidentally, largely reflected Sonia's view of the true George, though no reviewers noticed this). Perhaps so. I'm only irritated that Koestler failed to notice why I was so explicitly sceptical of the concept of character.

Let me try once more. I had talked to Koestler once at length and twice briefly and read most of his English works: from this I could have written a decent character sketch, certainly good enough for a *Times* obituary or an *Observer* profile; but this would be as far from a Life or a biography as Hyperion to a Satyr. A life must be a true account of what somebody actually did. Mr Iain Hamilton wrote a biography of Koestler in his lifetime in which he did not bother to look for any primary sources whatever for the first thirty-five years of Koestler's life, on the odd grounds that Koestler has himself written autobiographies covering that period. But surely a prime duty of any biographer of a writer is to examine critically the relationship between the writer's own autobiographical writings and what actually happened. The distance between there two things may not discredit the man so much as enhance the writer, and show, incidentally, some of his critics and commentators to be singularly naive in accepting the professional writer's use of the first person as always an attestation of public truth. With Koestler, as with Orwell, scepticism and research are crucial.

Sonia Orwell, as is well known, was very upset both by some of my judgements and by my 'putting Orwell in the box,' she said, as if it was wrong to doubt the literal truth of anything he wrote in the first person. Such scepticism seemed to me the elementary duty of any scholarly biographer. One of the practical difficulties of modern biography in general is with owners of the copyright in words, especially widows and sisters—women live longer: Nietzsche, Wagner, Kipling, Eliot, Keynes, Orwell, etcetera. To be fair to Sonia Orwell, when she asked me to do the biography, quite out of the blue, not knowing me nor I knowing her, she agreed to my firm condition that as well as complete access to the papers, I should have an absolute and prior waiver of copyright so that I could quote what I like and write what I liked. These were hard terms, even if the only terms on which, I think, a scholar should and can take on a contemporary biography. It was courageous of her to meet them. That she signed such a contract should be a noble example to what she would often racily call 'the widows' union'.

There are, of course, specific difficulties of contemporary biography. The advantage of having living witnesses is partially balanced by the personal involvement of some of them, particularly if writers themselves, in the reputation of the subject. And also publication itself stimulates both new witnesses and unexpected reactions from old witnesses to the actual text. For instance George Mikes and Andre Deutch, no less, had been sitting on yet another authentic rejection of *Animal Farm* by a leading publisher. I had thought that Reg Groves was long dead, who worked in the bookshop immediately before Orwell and was one of the original 'Balham secession', the founding of British Trotskyism. His testimony strengthens the view that Orwell's conversion to socialism was far less suden than he himself implied. The British anarchists kindly sent me a collective review that added considerably to knowledge of his ambivalence and contacts with them in the *Animal Farm* period. I knew that Orwell's consultant physician at University College Hospital was long dead and all medical records destroyed, so had given up that trail; but I very foolishly forgot that the young houseman does the day to day work, and he wrote to me with important new evidence. Apparently Orwell didn't stand a chance; but they did not tell him nor did they tell Sonia, nor did she ask.

Things in Orwell's own writings and life raise three particular difficulties for a biographer. Firstly, he was unusually secretive or perhaps simply private, liking to keep different groups of friends apart, for instance, and yet he let his pen name develop in the *Tribune* days into a public character—'good old George' or 'that damned Orwell stirring it again.' Secondly, his fame came late, but then came fast—therefore many writers, who only knew him well after the publication of *Animal Farm* (so if well, also relatively briefly), committed themselves to critical judgements in print about him long before it was possible to read his books and essays as a whole; and they also committed themselves to broad statements about his development in the 1920s and 1930s that were not based on first-hand observation. Thirdly, the nature of some of his best writings raise difficult problems of *genre*, are they fact or are they fiction? If one shows fictional elements in 'Such, Such Were the Joys', or in 'Down and Out in Paris and London,' is one to be accused of doubting the word of 'the crystal spirit' and destroying his reputation for integrity and honesty, or is one paying tribute to a craftsman less naive than some of his Chelsea and Bloomsbury literary friends of the days of his fame seemed, enthusiastically but patronisingly, to assume? A word on each of these problems.

Orwell valued his privacy greatly and was not given to self-revealing monologues, even to girl friends. Now personally I do not find anything psychologically abnormal about this. I suspect that more people are of that kind than those who must always be telling all to everyone; and certainly when we meet, whether as friends, teachers or as involuntary travelling companions, extreme cases of such talkative people, we commonly suspect that not everything they say is true. Courts often are rightly sceptical about convicting on the basis of unchecked confessions. Orwell was simply not that type, and he had no thought, until very close to the end, that he would be a household name throughout the world. To say that he was careless about keeping 'his papers' is pure hindsight, for why should he have had any care? He was not born to the literary purple and while he wanted to live by his novels, he showed no signs of thinking himself a great man or a great writer. Some of the Bloomsbury group, for instance, seem to have secreted papers and exlcuded letters even before their first works were published in the calm expectation that one day they would be useful to their family biographer. Not so old George. If he became famous with *Animal Farm*, consider that even though he had worked for the BBC and did scripts for them even after *Animal Farm*, including a bad adaptation of *Animal Farm*, yet nobody thought to record his voice. Old BBC hands told me that it would have seemed a comic disproportion then, 'old George' was simply one of the boys who had a very lucky break with one book. Disc recordings for the archive were only set up for the very great, like Wells and Shaw, or for people absolutely assured of a permanent place in the history of English letters, like Sir Max Beerbohm and J.B. Priestley.

Orwell's privacy was not pathological, it was perfectly normal: however, it makes difficulties for a biographer. But he was not seeking to help a biographer, nor expecting one until the last year of his life when the reception of *Nineteen Eighty-Four* both impressed and worried him. Frankly I do not think that the 'Eric Blair/George Orwell' disjunction need trouble one greatly. Even Stansky and Abrahams had dropped it by their second volume: I think the idea of a character change when he adopted the pseudonym was always more a formal excuse that they were not writing about 'George Orwell' rather than a genuine and sustained (albeit dubious) psychological hypothesis. Certainly in the *Tribune* columns he produced a kind of ideal image of himself: the plain, blunt, free-speaking man of common sense and common decency, something that I call 'Orwell-like' in contrast to what 'Orwellian' meant after *Nineteen Eight-Four*. But this image was an extension of part of himself, not a mask. If he was role-playing a bit, it was with different proportions of genuine aspects of himself. I think of the late Richard Hofstadter's classic essay on Abraham Lincoln: how, while an honest and straightforward man, he quite consciously exploited 'Honest Abe' for political effect. Similarly Eric Blair was always George Orwell for literary effect. Julian Symons has put this better than I can: there was no war of two selves, only a continual growth in his powers and range as a writer, and 'Orwell' was the writer's name. So compelling did the name become, almost an English institution, that Sonia Brownell, Mrs. Eric Blair, late—for a while—Ms. Pitt-Rivers, perhaps had very little choice but to appear as Mrs. George Orwell in the phone book.

The second problem peculiar to Orwell biography is that since his fame came late, many of those who wrote about him on the basis of personal acquaintance have been less than cautious at times in recalling precisely when it was they first got to know him. Perhaps because the man was so unusually private when writers are necessarily involved in self-publicity, and so irritatingly unwilling to talk about personal things, yet so interesting and provocative, that there was an unusual amount of rather dubious biographical interpretation of him, rather than of literary criticism, right from the first writings. And writers on Orwell have been apt to place great weight on their own diverse memories of him and, even more difficult for a biographer, on their memories of what he said to them about his memories of earlier periods of his life. Much of this evidence was difficult to use. Some people are surprised that I did not repeat in my book important anecdotes they told to me of what he said to them or did. But like a detective, the biographer must always seek corroboration and can never rest a case on hearsay evidence. Rarely do people seek to deceive, even themselves. But is it to some a quite unholy thought that Orwell could have occasionally teased people who either pressed him too hard or ignored him completely by giving them deliberate pieces of misinformation? This biographer must sadly report that he learned to be scpetical of memory unchecked by document or independent witness. I'm sure I've suppressed some revealing incidents that did take place. But, alas, I also discovered that several anecdotes to which people genuinely claim to have been eye-witnesses are in fact found in Orwell's own writing. It is not merely that memory over thirty or forty years commonly matures and grows and occasionally even decays, but that memories of a famous man in his days of obscurity can become badly confused by reading and recalling subsequent writing on him. The past is remembered not just directly, but also filtered through what one subsequently learns.

Memories are valuable evidence. But they are not history in themselves. I'm all for aural history so long as people don't think that its authenticity makes it true, that it is history: it is only part of the evidence.

Not merely Cherokee chiefs read books on anthropology before being interviewed by anthropologists, distinguished men of letters can re-read their early essays on Orwell shortly before being interviewed and the recount them with commendable accuracy and beguiling freshness. It is simply very difficult to get through to genuine remembrances or re-remembrances: people defend what they wrote long ago, however, incomplete or inaccurate. Imagine trying to ask Proust on the one hand, or Nixon, on the other, 'what *really* happened?' Their memories would be self-induced rationalizations. Fred Warburg did not commission Orwell to go to Spain and write *Homage to Catalonia*, though he remembered it vividly in his memoirs, even supplying a dialogue. But then publishers' memories are in a class of their own.

The interviewer can only approach contradictions in the evidence, between what people once wrote and what is now known, with great delicacy. People don't like being contradicted in their own homes. And, by the way, thinking of some manuals that are from time to time written for research students, there is no such thing as a 'structured interview', or if you impose it, you get very little beyond 'yes' or 'no'. When interviewed most people enjoy talking at large, a discursive conversation takes place. Then one is in the world of an English novel, not in the interrogation cells of Koestler's *Darkness at Noon* or Le Carre's *Tinker, Tailor, Soldier, Spy*. One or two things that are not already clear from the written record have to wait their turn in a long and patient process of mutual exploration. Just like in bed, those manuals are useless.

People who knew him well and had neither written about him nor been interviewed by the BBC were more rare and in some ways more precious to me, so then it was sometimes worth taking down every word (although normally I found that a verbatim record was not worth the risk of people being resistant to recording). But when every word was taken down, sometimes I discovered afterwards that precisely because Orwell had become such a *popular* writer, that they too, even the non-writers, had memories of Orwell or views about him that could only have been formed by a subsequent reading his works or works about him. His sister, Avril, plainly only glanced at most of his works in his lifetime and did not like them. When I met her twenty years later, she had accepted that her brother's fame was justified, so famous were his friends, had forgiven him, as she saw it, for letting the family down (his resignation from the Imperial Service, his tramping, his socialism, his poverty) and she had become a cultivated and sensitive reader of his works, really worth talking to on many points of literary criticism; it was as if she had given herself an adult education from her brother's books and the commentaries about them. But this searching also contaminated her memories of the past. Fortunately she was interviewed at length by the BBC not long after her brother's death and those transcripts, while far less perceptive about the writer, contain the more authentic memories of the man.

Again I must point out that it was simply not possible for even critics and scholars to make a proper assessment of Orwell until the so-called *Collected Essays, Journalism and Letters* of 1968 appeared; and by then most people had committed themselves and continued to defend entrenched positions. A new edition is now unfolding which should contain interesting and important matter not included in the original four volumes. This will be the chance for fresh critical assessments. The third and last peculiarity of Orwell's biography is the *genre* problem of some of his major works. Crudely, are they fact or fiction? I realised right from the beginning how complex was the relationship between his writings and his life. While the closeness of the relationship was generally appreciated, its complexity was less recognised, despite some clear warnings he himself made. In *The Road to Wigan Pier,* he said of *Down and Out in Paris and London* that 'Nearly all the incidents described there actually happened, but they have been rearranged'. That is why I have to say again that I cannot agree with Sonia when she said in her introduction to *The Collected Essays* that all his novels except *Animal Farm* and *Nineteen Eight-Four* 'contain straight descriptions of himself' or that 'a whole chapter of *The Road to Wigan Pier* suddenly turns into straight autobiography'. The man was straightforward, but the writer was not naive. Each of his autobiographical passages serves some different literary and political purpose. Some of his friends of the brief days of his fame seem to have typecast him as the Douanier Rousseau of English letters, forgetting that he had gone to Eton just as some art critics were to forget that the 'primitive, visionary' painter, Stanley Spencer, had been to the Slade School of Art.

So it is not easy to distinguish between the autobiographical 'I' and the storyteller's 'I'. When Penguin books reprinted *Down and Out in Paris and London* during the war, the first printing was in the old orange fiction covers. It was then reprinted in the famous non-fiction blue. Records have vanished. But I have some sympathy with what may have been simply a mistake at a low administrative level. Did all those people who told the author such lurid tales in *Down and Out* really exist? There's no documentary evidence, but in a literary judgement of the text I would have bound the Penguin reissue in a candy stripe of orange and blue. For *The Road to Wigan Pier* there is more evidence, which simply suggests that he did not invent, but that he did rearrange the order of events, touch up, and heighten skilfully and make the timescales involved appear longer than they were (as George Painter said of Proust, 'though he invented nothing, he altered everything')—so a blue cover with an orange surround. For *Homage to Catalonia* there is quite as much evidence as for Wigan and all of it supports the most literal veracity of what he described: true-blue all through. I suppose that since he was writing the book as a polemic against false pictures of the war, he knew he must give his opponents no possible opening to fault him on points of fact.

The sheer difficulty of how to use 'Such, Such Were the Joys' as biographical evidence is still painful to me. The need to explore carefully its truth, since so much bad speculation about the genesis of *Nineteen Eight-Four* has been built on it, held up the telling of a story and made the opening both hard to digest and made it contentious. Perhaps I should have simply ignored all those silly and arbitrary, at least infinitely reversible, pseudo-Freudian short cuts, or simply referred them to Richard Ellmann's marvellously sensible chapter on the subject 'Literary Biography' in his essays, *Golden Codgers*. Nonetheless, I'm unrepentant about the truth of the matter: if 'Such, Such Were the Joys' had ever been printed by Penguin separately, there could well be much blue on the cover, so long as there was a large and dramatic blob of cautionary orange as well. I see it as a polemic against private schooling based on his own experiences, but with fictional supports to widen the attack. Yet somehow the literal truth of it became an article of faith to some. My troubles with Mrs Orwell began on this score as well as with the usual American publisher to the Orwell estate.

Certainly I and my helpers wasted a lot of time trying to find from the *Rangoon Times* and the *Mandalay Gazette* whether an elephant was shot, and I certainly established from Burma Police manuals that someone in Blair's job would have had no business whatsoever at a hanging. But this kind of boring research is purely for the narrow purpose of recounting his life. It cannot affect our appreciation of his art. May I quote from David Lodge's essay 'A Hanging' in his *The Modes of Modern Writing*:

> When I first read 'A Hanging' I certainly assumed it was a true story. The more I studied it, the more I suspected that Orwell has added or altered some details for literary effect,

but I did not doubt that the piece was essentially factual and historical. I think this is probably the response of most readers . . .

But he then goes on to relate that Stansky and Abrams in their biography found a lady whom Orwell had told that he never saw a hanging, despite subsequently claiming to have done so twice more in print; and I found (unknown to Mr. Lodge) another such lady.

So there is at least an element of doubt about the eye-witness authenticity of 'A Hanging', a possibility that it is a fiction . . .

It is very unlikely, at this date, that we shall ever be able to establish definitely whether Orwell attended a hanging or not, and more or less impossible that we should ever be able to check the particular circumstances of 'A Hanging' against historical fact. It may be completely factual, it may be partly based on experience, or partly on the reported experience of others, or partly fictional, or wholly fictional—though the last possibility seems to me the least likely. The point I wish to make is that it doesn't really matter. As a text, 'A Hanging' is self-sufficient, self-authenticating.

Indeed, 'it doesn't really matter' from the point of view of his art. It does matter from the point of view of his biography, but even in using a sledgehammer to crack a nut, quite unsuccessfully int his case, the biographer cannot reduce the work of art to some other dimension.

How strange that some have honestly thought that one was diminishing Orwell if one pointed out that some of his essays in the first person are more like short stories than true confessions. His reputation must finally rest on being a writer, not simply as an exceptionally honest and decent human being. And despite his reputation as a writer, in the simple sense that ever so many people read him, some of his old friends, even Sonia Brownell, Cyril Connolly and Richard Rees, still felt so uneasy at the content of what he wrote and so dissatisfied with his formal qualities as a novelist that they made too much of the personal virtues rather than the literary craft of the man. Part of his literary craft was his use of his own virtues and, of course, his own experiences, which makes it very difficult to tell fact from fiction—certainly I could not always succeed. But an artist deals in speculative truths whereas a biographer must—as Leon Edel has remarked, citing Desmond MacCarthy—put himself or herself under oath, however much at times that limits a good story.

Eleven

Reading Nineteen Eighty-Four As Satire

From Robert Mulvihill, ed. *Reflections on America, 1984: an Orwell Symposium* (University of Georgia Press, London: 1986).

Nineteen Eighty-Four has been read with amazingly diverse interpretations. Serious people have seen it as a deterministic prophecy, as a conditional projection, as a humanistic satire of events, as nihilistic misanthrophy, as a libertian socialist satire of power in general, as predominantly an attack on the Soviet Union. At times the reader needs to be reminded that it is a novel and not a monograph or tract. Anthony Burgess has seen it as a comic novel. For a man who cultivated the skills and reputation of plain living, plain thinking and plain writing, this diversity of reception, this propensity to be body-snatched by nearly everyone (except the Communists), is at least curious.

Partly Orwell brought the trouble on himself. The book is indeed a novel, but specifically a satirical novel and it is also the most complex and ambitious work he ever undertook, probably too complex for its own good, both aesthetically considered (compared to *Animal Farm*, for instance) and in the crowded jostle of its substantive ideas. Orwell appeared to use *satire and parody* synonymously. In the now well-known press release he issued after reading the first reviews of *Nineteen Eighty-Four*, he denied that he was saying that 'something like this will happen,' but that 'Allowing for the book being after all a parody, something like *Nineteen Eight-Four* could happen.'[1] And in his letter to an official of the United Automobile Workers, also worried at some of the American reviews, he says: 'I do not believe that the kind of society I describe necessarily will arrive, but I believe (allowing of course for the fact that the book is a satire) that something resembling it could arrive.'[2] In the same letter he called it a 'show-up' of the 'perversions to which a centralised economy is liable and which have already been partly realised in Communism and Fascism.' And in the letter to his publishers about the 'blurb,' he had said that he was 'parodying ... the intellectual implications of totalitarianism,' which he then links, as in the press release, to the division of the world by the Great Powers;[3] but in the press release he had added the specific dangers to freedom in having to rearm with the new atomic weapons. Strictly speaking, parody mocks a style or the external characteristics of a person, whereas satire mocks ideas, institutions, or behaviour purporting to be good. In the vernacular, *take-off* and *show up* express the difference. But the line is fine in some writing. *Nineteen Eighty-Four* as a whole is clearly satire, although with some elements of parody to be found in the Goldstein section and in the appendix.

The targets of the satire in the actual text are more than Orwell's two statements might imply. In my reading of the internal symbolic structure, seven main satiric themes emerge: the division of the world by the superstates; the mass media as an agent of prolerisation; power hunger in general and totalitarianism in particular; the untrustworthiness of the intellectuals; the abuse and degradation of language; the control of history for political purposes; and the theses of James Burnham.

However, all that is interpretation. And what an author intends a book to be or says that it was is not always what we find in the text. So I simply want to demonstrate by a slow reading of the text following the actual plot or story line that the book is a satire of continuing events, not a prophecy of the future. This is tedious (or scholarly) but it is seldom done; commentators tend to seize on one element or other in the book and then preach a sermon upon it.

First, there is the title. A title or a name creates preconceptions. Orwell first intended it to be called, as he had headed his outline of 1943, 'The Last Man in Europe.'[4] As late as October 1948, when he was beginning to revise and retype the final version of the manuscript (an effort that brought on his final collapse), he told his publisher, 'I haven't definitely fixed on the title but I am hesitating between NINETEEN EIGHTY-FOUR and THE LAST MAN IN EUROPE.'[5] Perhaps the publisher felt strongly that *'The Last Man in Europe'* would give too much of the game away, was too leading and gloomily didactic. *'Nineteen Eighty-Four'* would invoke more of a surprise, arousing expectations of some new *Brave New World* or Utopia. The dashing of those expectations would then add to the satiric effect.

Consider the title as if we are reading the book in 1949. If thirty-five or under, the reader will think to himself that he will probably be alive to see if it is so. He may quickly realise that any precise date is a joke, but he will relish the joke that though it sounds like a utopian, anti-utopian or possibly science-fiction novel, the date is well adjusted to be within the lifetime of some of us and in their childrens' lifetime for others, sounding both closer and more precise than Huxley's year 2000. It is overwhelmingly probable that the date is simply 1948, when Orwell finished the book, turned inside out; the date had been used before by other writers, but it is most unlikely that they could have influenced Orwell's choice.

In other words, the novel inhabits what Julian Symons well calls 'a near future': 'In one of its aspects *Nineteen Eighty-Four* was about a world familiar to anybody who lived in Britain during the war that began in 1939. The reductions in rations, the odious food, the sometimes unobtainable and always dubiously authentic drink, these were with us still when the book appeared.' And he concluded a perceptive 'Appreciation' of Orwell: '*Nineteen Eighty-Four* is about a possible future, but through the fantasy we see always the outline of our own real world'[6]—the same point but with a different emphasis. Surely it looks both at his present and, allowing for fantasy, at a near future. Anthony Burgess's *A Clockwork Orange* and Doris Lessing's *The Memoirs of a Survivor* are other examples of 'near futures'; and they can worry us more than dystopias because they are less easy to distance. Nonetheless, commentators try to distance *Nineteen Eighty-Four* by putting it in the tradition of Wells, Zamyatin, and Huxley, rather than seeing it as a mutant of social novel and satiric polemic. This is made easier if the title is misrendered (as is the usual American custom) as a date, *1984*, rather than spelled out. A date suggests a prophecy, whereas a spelling suggests a fictive name.

The opening pages are full of recognisable images of immediate postwar London, albeit with sardonic exaggeration. The experience described in the very first paragraph of not being able to close the door quickly 'to prevent a swirl of gritty dust from entering along with him' was a familiar experience: the dust from the bombsites and from the rarely cleaned streets. 'Victory Mansions' was familiar, and what a victory it seemed: food shortages and rationing had actually increased after the end of the war with the end of Lend-Lease and a world shipping shortage. 'The clocks were striking thirteen': the armed forces, civil defence, and railways had gone over to the 'Continental' twenty-four hour system during the war, but the man in the street still dragged his unprogressive feet, and still does. And the next two paragraphs have the smell of 'boiled cabbage' (something never in short supply), propaganda posters, elevators that don't work, the electric current cut off for certain hours as part of the economy drive (indeed the winter of 1947 saw widespread power failures; in London one was forever getting stuck in lifts); also Winston's tiredness, his blue overalls, coarse soap, and blunt razor blades.

All these things were very familiar to the British reader in 1949. Winston drags himself up 'seven flights' of stairs: few apartment buildings in London were then of that height, but Orwell was the kind of gloomy person who feared that in the future they all would be so, and the elevators still no better. Some of the posters are torn and flapping and 'little eddies of wind were swirling dust and torn paper into spirals'—most familiar. How bold and bright the design of wartime exhortatory posters and of political campaigns; how dirty and torn they quickly became.

The only new inventions we meet immediately are the telescreen and the helicopter, and these only new in their adaptation for surveillance. All this is consistent with a 'near future,' quite unlike science fiction or fantasies. The BBC had begun television broadcasting just before the war and had recently resumed, so all Orwell did was to imagine its extension, as now used for security in banks and supermarkets. Helicopters had been used by the American army during the invasion of Europe for artillery observation and guidance, so the fantasy of police using them for general surveillance was not a very great one and soon came true. And when in the fourth paragraph the telescreen is 'still babbling away about pig-iron and the over-fulfillment of the Ninth Three-Year Plan,' while the last phase would take the politically literate reader's mind to the USSR, the general gabbling of triumphant and possibly imaginary production statistics was not unfamiliar to wartime listeners to the BBC. And while the BBC's morning exercises were not compulsory (as in Oceania), they were there and made absurd claims that millions of patriotic people did them to keep fit for the war effort.

As we read on into the first section, the inventions continue to be familiar, recognisable caricatures that look a little way ahead and a little way back, quite unlike the biological fantasies of Aldous Huxley or the engineering fantasies of Zamyatin. 'Ink-pens' were simply the new and still-expensive Biros; 'Speakwrites' were simply dictaphones that typed, though we can't quite yet dispense with human secretaries; and the 'pneumatic tubes' that transmitted Winston's work in the ministry had linked, since the 1920s, the sales staff to the cashiers in big department stores. The great ministries are named Minitrue, Minipax, Miniluv, and Mini-plenty. Abbreviated names and acronyms became a fashion in the 1930s—it seemed very modern and futuristic to be CP, Nazi, FBI, or Coop, for example—and during the war the fashion became a contagion and spread rapidly.

'The Ministry of Truth ... was startingly different from any other object in sight. It was an enormous pyramidal structure of glittering

white concrete, soaring up, terrace after terrace, three hundred
metres into the air.' Now the Senate House Tower of the University
of London is a mere 64.5 metres high, but it was the tallest building
in London in 1930s and 1940s and, more to the point, housed the
wartime Ministry of Information, which everybody knew to be
Newspeak for Ministry of Propaganda. Admittedly, working
conditions within Minitrue closely resemble those of the wartime
BBC, with which Orwell was very familar, but the terraced
structure and the location of the Ministry of Information make
Senate House the primary, primary of Orwell's detestation. And
the first of the three great Party slogans on the wall of the tower,
'War Is Peace', is pleasantly reminiscent of the 'Fight for Peace'
beloved of Communist Front organisations in the Popular Front
days and revived after the war to oppose British and American
intervention in the Greek civil war, and anything else that ran
counter to Russian interests.

The more we see through Winston Smith's eyes of the townscape
of London as the provincial capital of Airstrip One (the genial
anti-Americanism of the name escapes most commentators, even
though the United States Air Force bases of 1942 have since
reopened, and some never closed), the more we are aware of a
desolate and colourless world. ('Colourless' is used in the descriptions almost as often as 'dust'.) A bleak contrast is painted between
the glittering machines in the modern-style ministries and the
drab grime and dirt of the streets and the crumbling homes of both
the Outer Party and the proles. This awful gulf between theory and
practice, the idea and the actual, the best and the ordinary, is
literally Swiftian: despite all the marvellous schemes of the
projecteers of Balnibari, 'the whole country lies miserably waste.'
Dust means a dead world—not literally dead, but with all the
liveliness and humanity gone out of it.

One of the later passages on this theme, however, while it brings
totalitarian projects and pretensions down to London earth, is yet
of such power that a prophetic note is undeniable.

> Life, if you looked about you, bore no resemblance not only
> to the lies that poured out of the telescreens, but even to the
> ideals that the Party was trying to achieve. Great areas of it,
> even for a Party members, were neutral and non-political, a
> matter of slogging through dreary jobs, fighting for a place
> on the Tube, darning a worn-out sock, cadging a saccharine
> tablet, saving a cigarette end. The ideal set up by the Party
> was something huge, terrible, and glittering—a world of steel
> and concrete, of monstrous machines and terrible weapons—
> a nation of warriors and fanatics, marching forward in

perfect unity, all thinking the same thoughts and shouting
the same slogans, perpetually working, fighting, triumphing,
persecuting—three hundred million people all with the same
face. The reality was decaying, dingy cities where underfed
people shuffled to and fro in leaky shoes, in patched up
nineteenth century houses that smelt always of cabbage and
bad lavatories. He seemed to see a vision of London, vast and
ruinous, city of a million dustbins.

This vision must go far beyond (though it still includes) the
actuality of London in 1948. Different readers will read very
different things into it: the essence of our own time, the decaying
'inner city,' or various precise locations ranging from Eastern
Europe to China through sundry pretentious, cruel, but inefficient
military dictatorships.

Winston begins his diary. The keeping of the diary is the major
theme of the plot until two minor themes, his interest in Julia and
then O'Brien, introduced quietly and casually early in Part One,
suddenly and dramatically become dominant in Part Two, but
not until Part Two. The diary thus carries the story through the first
third of the book, serving both to tell us a lot about Winston and to
broach the two-edged theme of memory: private memory as
essential to humanity, but also its terrible uncertainty. The diary
itself 'was a peculiarly beautiful book. Its smooth creamy paper, a
little yellowed by age, was of a kind that had not been
manufactured for at least forty years past.' So it was manufactured
about the time he was born, 'since he was fairly sure that his age
was thirty-nine, and he believed that he had been born in 1944 or
1945; but it was never possible nowadays to pin down any date
within a year or two.' His probable year of birth accounts for his
first name, of course, but the important point is that the diary exists
in itself physically, even before it becomes a diary by his writing in
it, before his memory. The author writes in an empiricist tradition:
he shows no doubt that there is an external world independent of
the consciousness of the observer. And though finally Winston
Smith is attacked and destroyed by O'Brien in this very point, the
author does give us, very early on, this simple, external point of
reference. We are never meant to doubt that two plus two equals
four.

The first thing Winston sets down is a tense account of a night at
'the flicks,' a sadistic newsreel of the war during which the prole
woman starts shouting 'they didn't oughter of showed it not in
front of the kids.' And Winston 'did not know what had made him
pour out the stream of rubbish.' 'Pour out' suggests an instinctive
attempt at cleansing himself, trying to use the diary as therapy;

indeed the sadism of the scene he describes, the audience applauding the killing of the child, makes him think of the hateful-looking young woman from the novel-writing machines, who wore the 'narrow scarlet sash, emblem of the Junior Anti-Sex League.' Orwell thus deliberately links the sadistic with the erotic; the regime turns sexual frustration into violent hatred—the famous orgiastic Two Minutes Hate is a daily event, and it even affects Winston's perceptions. When later Winston recounts to his diary his visit to the horrible prostitute, the naturalistic vividness of the description suggests not just another embellishment of the consequences of an imaginary regime, but a fairly conventional progressive view that modern society creates sexual frustration of the kind of Winston's marriage.

Yet the same film also makes him think of a member of the Inner Party whom he had seen from time to time but never talked to, but to whom 'he felt deeply drawn.' As the relationship develops, even into the final torture chambers of Miniluv, he thinks he finds a father figure, almost a god; but in fact O'Brien becomes antifather, almost anti-Christ.

The next thing he writes in the diary is 'Down With Big Brother,' repeatedly, although the trust he is to give to O'Brien shows that he wants a real big brother, father, family even. For as we read on, more and more of Winston's diary entries, to which are soon added his dreams, are concerned with memories of his mother, his childhood, and not just his vanished wife's sexual coldness and Party warmth but the specific fact that he and his wife failed, however many times they went at 'making a baby' or 'our duty to the Party,' to produce a child. Immediately after the first diary-writing scene, Orwell takes Winston in next door to help Mrs. Parsons clear a blocked pipe. I don't think that small piece of symbolism is very important; he had used it before and far more effectively in *The Road to Wigan Pier*, when he himself watches remotely from a train the helplessness of a young working-class woman trying to clear a blocked external drainpipe. The image is Sisyphean, of squalor and oppression, not sexual. But what is important is to meet the truly horrible children so early: ' "You'r a traitor!" yelled the boy. "You're a thought-criminal! You're a Eurasian spy! I'll shoot you, I'll vaporise you, I'll send you to the salt mines!" "Want to see the hanging! Want to see the hanging!" chanted the little girl, still capering round.' How ghastly that a regime can render the time of innocence so sadistic—and that these young members of 'the Spies' do finally betray their proud father, the zealous Parsons. All this makes us think of both the Soviet Young Pioneers and the Nazi Youth groups (and I suspect that

Orwell had dark suspicions that the Boys Brigade and the Boy Scouts were potential paramilitaries). But there is something about these neighbours, not shared by Winston, that is so obvious that we might miss it: they are a family, a satiric family, a black joke on the real thing, but a family nonetheless.

Winston tells his diary that he had bullied his mother and stolen his frail sister's chocolate ration just before they both disappeared. His memories of his family life were bad, but nonetheless he want a child. So there is a strong suggestion in the text that the family should be the primary school of that 'mutual trust' which is the precondition of a wider fraternity and general decency towards others. Some moralists, like Plato, or social philosophers, like Marx, have seen the family, or rather family ties and affections, as inherently a vested, selfish interest, corrupting to justice. The socialist Orwell did not like family privilege, still less rule or influence by privileged families; but he did quite sensibly suggest that any regime that destroys the primary institution in which we first learn mutual aid and how to behave toward others, destroys any possibility that morality rather than force will govern general social relations. Despite his strong belief in the influence and injustice of the class system, he had called England 'a family with the wrong members in control'—a metaphor that still embarrasses some socialists.

The diary quickly returns to the theme of mutuality when Winston addresses the future—an important passage because it is his first clear statement of what he believes in, this last man in Europe:

> To the future or the past, a time when thought is free, when men are different from one another and do not live alone—to a time when truth exists and what is done cannot be undone: From the age of uniformity, from the age of solitude, from the age of Big Brother, from the age of doublethink—greetings!

Freedom and *truth* are great and obvious affirmations. Not merely their defence but examples of their use run through all Orwell's writings and the way he led his life, and at the very least *Nineteen Eighty-Four* is a satire of all attempts to justify the unfree and the untrue. Only in this passage are they explicit; elsewhere and throughout they are found in the negation of their negation (the technique of satire). The importance of freedom and truth both in the text and to the author is common ground among critics, but not so the theme of mutuality, mutual trust, sociability, even fraternity. Some critics see Orwell as always an individualist, in a strict liberal or neo-conservative sense, or as returning right at the end, in crisis and under stress, to the individualism that had preceded his socialist writings.[7] But notice that in this passage, far from defending individualism as privacy and autonomy, he looks to a time 'when men are different' but also one in which 'they do not live alone,' and he makes, paradoxically to some, 'the age of uniformity' also 'the age of solitude.' Orwell's individualism was not of a liberal kind but either of a republican (sometimes called 'civic humanism') or of a modern socialist kind: a person cannot be truly human except in relationship with others. My uniqueness consists not on my 'personality' but in the 'identity' by which others recognise my actions: it is a mutual, social process, not solitude.[8] Privacy is important to Orwell, but it depends on political action to preserve it: the whole man must move backwards and forward, constantly and easily, between public and private: man must be both citizen and individual. Orwell is closer to Rousseau than to Adam Smith or John Stuart Mill.

The ideals are clear, far clearer than the hope of ever regaining what we could lose. Winston has a panic sense of doom, in which Julia shares, when they embark on their illicit affair, 'free love' indeed. He had begun actually writing the illegal diary 'in sheer panic, only imperfectly aware of what he was setting down'; just before he was interrupted while writing his first entry, he had been 'seized by a kind of hysteria' and scribbled: 'theyll shoot me i dont care theyll shoot me in the back of the neck i dont care down with big brother.' Even when he writes more calmly, 'to the future or to the past,' he has no confidence that anyone in the future will read his diary or know freedom, truth, and sociability ever again; and he enters the foreboding words: '*Thoughtcrime does not entail death: thoughtcrime* IS *death.*' Orwell is clearly saying that once one gets into a totalitarian regime there is no way out, no hope through conspiracy or rebellion. This view is far from irrationally pessimistic: the Nazis were only defeated externally by war, and it is unlikely that Orwell would have believed that the death of Stalin meant the end of totalitarianism. 'The moral to be drawn from this dangerous nightmare situation,' he said in the post-publication press release, 'is a simple one: *Don't let it happen. It depends on you.*' Our resistance to totalitarian tendencies will be greater if we fight without illusions, above all with no false belief in the inevitability of progress. The worst could happen. And here Orwell drops prudential calculation, as in effect did Winston Smith. Implicitly he is saying that a man, to remain human, *must* exercise his freedom; he must rebel, however hopelessly: '*theyll shoot me i dont care.*' Winston, often dismissed, or labeled as an anti-hero, is actually a very brave man: he holds out for truth under torture astonishingly long, though it can do him no good at all—'pointless,' says O'Brien.

This part of the satire is specifically anti-totalitarian. The autocracies of the past had only demanded passive obedience; ceremonies of occasional conformity were all that was needed for law and order. But Orwell implies that totalitarianism demands *complete* loyalty, no reservations being allowed, and continuous enthusiasm, not just occasional conformity.[9] Hence even to think a heterodox thought is a crime, and life without the Party is impossible: *'Thoughtcrime IS death.'* But precisely because this is *not* typical of autocracies in general, some of the satire, aimed at the power-hungry in general or the Party seen as a savage caricature of all bureaucracies, appears both implausible and diffuse. *Totalitarianism* is both too big and too precise to appear relevant to every jack-in.office. Most bureaucrats 'let sleeping dogs lie' rather that prosecute vigorously for 'Thoughtcrime.' Neither bureaucratisation nor totalitarianism is to be commended; but they are different phenomena, and threaten each other. Orwell attacks both, but using the same imagery can be confusing. Two Birds are hard to kill with the same stone.

'Thoughtcrime' is not commonly found in autocracies, unless Orwell shifts and blurs the focus of the argument from totalitarian regimes to totalitarian *tendencies* (of which there may be some in quite unlikely places). Matthew 5:28–'Whosoever looketh on a woman to lust after her hath committed adultery with her already in his heart' expresses a kind of Thoughtcrime; and Boy Scouts in Orwell's day took a famous and much-mocked oath to be 'clean in *thought*, word and deed' (my italics).[10] This was precisely the aspect of Christian teaching that the humanist in Orwell detested. There is also a conscious parody of the Catholic church in the text, especially in the meeting and ceremony in O'Brien's apartment. We know that Orwell was anti-Catholic in the 1920s and 1930s, and attacked the anti-socialist influence of the church in postwar Europe. Yet this direct satire of the Catholic church in *Nineteen Eighty-Four* can blur the focus. The church may have some total—itarian tendencies, but Orwell is *not* saying that it *is* totalitarian: it is self-evidently a very traditional kind of autocracy, but also a very special kind. So the satire of total power moves ambivalently between totalitarianism proper and any autocracy, with the Catholic church singled out for special mention in the latter category. It is as if the configuration of powers in the novel form an isosceles triangle with a small, ill-defined, but tangible base of Catholicism between the two long, strong arms of totalitarianism and bureaucratic autocracy (or 'managerialism').

The treatment of the proles involves this ambivalence. The

Party is plainly a totalitarian party, but the proles are anomalous; they seem familiar and closer to home. They are not mobilised or put into uniform marching columns, and 'no attempt was made to indoctrinate them with the ideaology of the party'—precisely what Orwell had argued in essays and book reviews was the mark of totalitarianism. This can only be because their main function in the story is to serve as a satire of what the mass media, poor schools, and the selfishness of the intelligentsia are doing to the actual working class of Orwell's time. 'Heavy physical work, the care of home and children, petty quarrels with neighbours, films, football, beer and, above all, gambling, filled up the horizon of their minds.' All that was required of them was a 'primitive patriotism' so as 'to make them accept longer working hours or shorter rations,' and 'a vast amount of criminality,' including prostitution and drug peddling, was allowed among them. Also 'in all questions of morals they were allowed to follow their ancestral code. The sexual puritanism of the Party was not imposed upon them.' So the devices of political control most practised are not indoctrination and terror, as the Inner Party controls the Outer Party or as in Orwell's conception of real totalitarian regimes, but degradation and fragmentation: 'even when they became discontented, as they sometimes did, their discontent led nowhere, because being without general ideas, they could only focus it on petty specific grievances.' 'Without general ideas' implies that the intellectuals have deserted the working-class movement for the security of desk jobs (the Outer Party).

Yet there is something more to the proles than a Swiftian satire on confounded hopes for the socialist ideal of proletarian man and Orwell's version of the betrayal of the intellectuals. We are told that 'they were beneath suspicion' for, 'as the Party slogan put it: "Proles and animals are free." ' And 'the Party taught that the proles were natural inferiors who must be kept in subjection, like animals, by a few simple rules.' Sir Victor Pritchett once brilliantly described Orwell as 'a man who went native in his own country'; and Orwell himself stated in *The Road to Wigan Pier* that he had been led to live among tramps to see if we treated our own working class as he and his fellows had treated the native inhabitants of Burma. So in part at least the proles are 'white niggers,' a symbol of colonialism: a caricature of the British working class as if they were Burmans or Indians.

Yet despite their degradation, 'the proles had stayed human. They had not become hardened inside.' 'If there is hope,' Winston wrote, 'it lies in the proles,' and the thought is repeated three times. After all, they were '85 percent of the population of Oceania,' reasoned Winston (a figure that is repeated in Goldstein's testimony) and 'if only they could somehow become conscious of their own strength . . . They needed only to rise up and shake themselves like a horse shaking off flies.' 'And yet—!' he adds. For he remembered at once how he had heard a tremendous shouting in the street, had thought that the proles were 'breaking loose at last,' but it was only a fight in a crowd of women over scarce tin saucepans on a market stall. 'But if there was hope, it lay in the proles. You had to cling on to that. When you put it in words it sounded reasonable: it was when you looked at the human beings passing you on the street that it became an act of faith.' Of course Goldstein's testimony is absolutely confident that the proles will conquer in the end, and it provides the 'general ideas' that both Winston and the proles lack; but it was written by the Inner Party. 'Is it true, what it says?' asks Winston in the cells of Miniluv. 'As description, yes. The programme it sets forth is nonsense,' replies O'Brien. 'The proletarians will never revolt, not in a thousand years or a million.' Yet, as I will argue, we are not meant to believe all that O'Brien says either: he is mad, and I think we are meant to believe more of Goldstein than we at first believe (even if 'as in a glass darkly,' and through a subsidiary and rather confusing satire of Trotskyist rhetoric). So the text is perfectly unclear and deliberately ambiguous as to whether we are to believe in an inevitable victory of the common people. 'It must be so' wrestles with 'impossible if things go so far.' If one puts such historical questions to a fiction, the answer can only be, as Winston sees when he looks at the proles, 'an act of faith.' Commentators are being far too literal-minded, treating Oceania as Orwell's working model of the future, to argue whether rebellion is possible in such a regime and therefore whether Orwell (not Smith) had despaired. And some socialists are being very obtuse or humorless to say that Orwell had either broken with socialism or is unforgivably rude to the workers to liken them to animals; he had already said in *Burmese Days* that white administrators treated the natives like animals and had recounted in *The Road to Wigan Pier* that he had been brought up to believe that the working class smell (not that they do smell, as shocked left-wing activists angrily misread or wickedly distort him).

Leaving the empirical question aside, however, as being irresolvable in terms of the dramatic needs of a satirical story, there can be little doubt that the author intends us to take very seriously the noble passage, already quoted, 'the proles had stayed human.' And this is repeated in the nostalgic passage about the proles: 'They remembered a million useless things, a quarrel with a work-mate, a hunt for a lost bicycle pump, the expression on a long dead sister's face, the swirls of dust on a windy morning seventy years ago.' Irrespective of whether 'the last man in Europe' and humanity in general is destroyed or not, we are asked to honour the human spirit in its freedom and oddity: the proles have not been fully debased. Immediately after reading Goldstein's testimony and immediately before their arrest, Winston has a vision that the 'hard and red and coarse' prole women, singing while she hangs up her washing in the backyard, is 'beautiful.'

> The future belonged to the proles . . . at the least it would be a world of sanity. Where there is equality there can be sanity. Sooner or later it would happen, strength would change into consciousness. The proles were immortal, you could not doubt it when you looked at that valiant figure in the yard. . . . they would stay alive against all the odds, like birds, passing on from body to body the vitality which the Party did not share and could not kill.

Hope in the inevitability of rebellion is, of course, immediately dashed. The irony is dark and bitter indeed. But her 'vitality, which the Party did not share and yet could not kill,' remains. Orwell is not saying that the only things that are good are those that we believe are bound to succeed, a simple utilitarianism shared, in his opinion (and that of others) by both Marxists and market liberals. He is saying both that the spirit of the common people cannot be crushed and that even when individuals are crushed, memory of their spiritedness is good in itself.

Julia exhibits more of this prole vitality than Winston; or rather, in modern social terms, she seems as if she has risen from the people, whereas Winston has a middle-class intellectual's romantic attachment to the people. Julia is tough and resourceful, she seeks out Winston, trusts her own judgment about Winston's proneness to thoughtcrime, and organises the complicated separate itineraries to meet and make love in the countryside. She is harsh and unfeeling. She recounts how her first affair was at sixteen with a party member who later committed suicide to avoid arrest: 'And a good job too,' said Julia, 'otherwise they'd have had my name out of him.' She does not believe that the rumoured Brotherhood exists, and 'any kind of organised revolt against the Party, which was bound to be a failure, struck her as stupid. The clever thing was to break the rules and stay alive all the time.' She even falls asleep when Winston begins to read aloud to her *The Theory and Practice of Oligarchical Collectivism*, and she shows no interest in or comprehension of his tale of the photograph that gave objective proof that the *Times* was lying about Jones, Aaronson and

Rutherford, the dissident leaders. 'She was "not clever" but was fond of using her hands and felt at home with machinery.' 'She didn't care much for reading,' but she quite enjoyed her work 'servicing a powerful but tricky electric motor' on the novel-writing machines in 'Pornosec, the sub-section of the Fiction Department among the proles.' Yet we must admire her sheer vitality. She is not a very deep character, but she is far from two dimensional; and people like her in the real world make life very difficult for the puritanical boss who worries that he doesn't really known what is going on under his nose.

She is consciously nonpolitical, but in fact she challenges by her promiscuity the Party's assumption that 'there was a direct intimate connection between chastity and political orthodoxy.' And she hates the Party. She 'seemed unable to mention the Party, and especially the Inner Party, without using the kind of words that you saw chalked up in dripping alley-ways.' When they first try to make love, he fails, but she is splendidly practical: 'Never mind, dear. There's no hurry. We've got the whole afternoon.' But then what brings him on is not just the vision of 'the Golden Country' and the thrush singing its heart out—a very Orwell-like theme of nature undefiled, even if a stylistic lapse into an overwritten piece of purple prose—but also the dialogue of sexual contempt for the Party. ' "Have you done this before?" "Of course. Hundreds of times—well scores of times anyway" ' and 'always with party members.' Not with Inner Party members though, but she opines that 'those swine' would 'if they got half the chance. They're not so holy as they make out.' And Winston as he 'pulled her down' rather surprisingly announces: 'Listen. The more men you've had, the more I love you. Do you understand that? . . . I hate purity, I hate goodness! I don't want any virtue to exist anywhere. I want everyone to be corrupt to the bones.' Even though Winston plainly does *not* hate goodness and virtue, only the Ingsoc version of them, yet nothing has really prepared us for such a Julia-like cynicism on his part. And of course it ends famously (if a little ludicrously): 'Their embrace had been a battle, the climax a victory. It was a blow struck against the Party. It was a political act.' One could argue that this crudity is part of the satire, but it is not a well-written passage, though a crucial one.

It is crucial because it leads Julia to break her own rules. For even a short sexual affair in such a regime some mutual trust is needed. Her usual prudent rule is short and sweet or cut and run, but the affair develops into an obsessional entanglement, at the least, on Julia's part, and into love, or seeming love, on Winston's. He tells her early on that 'We are the dead,' and 'Folly, folly, his heart kept saying: conscious, gratuitous, suicidal folly.' But they persist with their damning infatuation. When they are tortured, Julia, according to O'Brien, betrayed Winston immediately: 'I have seldom seen anyone come over to us so promptly... everything has been burned out of her. It was a perfect conversion, a textbook case.' Plainly she has only vitality, love of freedom, and a hatred for the Party, whereas Winston, though physically more frail, can hold out longer because of his passion for truth: two plus two *do* equal four. A whole person is both heart and head, head and heart: for even when he accepts that two plus two can be five, he has the final reservation of loving Julia more than Big Brother, and only the ultimate fear can burn that out. And nothing can ever destroy the fact that they did trust each other.

They even trusted each other in the business of trusting Mr. Charrington and O'Brien, trust betrayed. Now most of us know the story too well. But would any normal first-time reader distrust Mr. Charrington—such a warm-sounding name and such a reassuring description? 'His spectacles, his gentle, fussy movements and the fact that he was wearing an aged jacket of black velvet, gave him a vague air of intellectuality, as though he had been some kind of literary man, or perhaps a musician. His voice was soft, as though faded, and his accent less debased than that of the majority of proles.' When the arrest comes, 'the cockney accent had disappeared.' This is a wry joke against Winston (and presumably against Orwell's old enemies, the condescending left-wing intellectuals): Winston finds hope in the proles and yet he trusts a man because his accent is better than the majority of proles. More sadly still, Smith trusts Charrington because he teaches him a nursery rhyme about the old church bells of London. This appeals to Winston's dreams of a better childhood. Perhaps the irony is too obvious when he tells Winston, 'How it goes on I don't remember, but I do know it ended up, "Here comes a candle to light you to bed, Here comes a chopper to chop off your head"' But the familiarity, almost the banality, of the rhyme to the English reader probably masks its meaning or softens the blow on first reading.

Before he rents the room he buys from Charrington the coral paperweight, just as on his first visit he had bought the diary. ' "It's a beautiful thing," said Winston. "It is a beautiful thing," said the other, appreciatively. "But there's not many that'd say so nowadays.' Winston even resolved to come back to 'buy further scraps of beautiful rubbish.' Of course everything becomes perverted from its natural state in Oceania. As soon as he walks out of the shop he sees that the unknown girl from the Fiction Department has been following him, obviously spying, and so he contemplates smashing in her skull with either a cobblestone or the coral paperweight. Nonethless, the object is 'beautiful rubbish.' And 'what appealed to him about it was not so much its beauty as the air it seemed to possess of belongings to an age quite different from the present one . . . The thing was doubly attractive because of its apparent uselessness.' He had noted that the proles 'remembered a million useless things.' So another positive value develops beneath the satiric form: there is liberty, equality (as the negation of hierarchy), truth, and sociability or mutual trust, but now to these must be added a wholly nonpolitical value, described as useless beauty: aesthetic judgment.

At this stage of the argument I am trying to stay within the text, but the weight that Orwell wants us to give to this symbolic piece of coral is suggested by that most famous passage in his essay of 1946, 'Why I Write':

> What I have most wanted to do throughout the past ten years is to make political writing into an art. My starting point is always a feeling of partisanship, a sense of injustice. . . . if it were not also an aesthetic experience. Anyone who cares to examine my work will find that even when it is downright propaganda it contains much that a full-time politician would consider irrelevant. I am not able, and I do not want, completely to abandon the world-view that I acquired in childhood. So long as I remain alive and well I shall continue to feel strongly about prose style, to love the surface of the earth, and to take pleasure in solid objects and scraps of useless information.[11]

He had once teased his fierce *Tribune* readership by devoting a precious wartime column to praise of 'sixpenny Woolworth's roses' (a scion is still alive); and on another occasion he told them that though 'the atom bombs are piling up in the factories, the police are prowling through the cities, the lies are streaming from the loudspeakers,' yet neither 'dictators nor bureaucrats, deeply as they disapprove of the process' are able to stop 'the earth going round the sun' nor such simple pleasures as 'watching the toads mating or a pair of hares having a boxing match in the new corn': 'Indeed it is remarkable how nature goes on existing unofficially, as it were, in the very heart of London. I have seen a kestrel flying over the Deptford gasworks, and I have heard a first-rate performance by a blackbird in the Euston Road.' His attitude to natural objects, both inanimate 'solid objects' and most animals, was almost mystical, pietistic. All this is evoked by the Golden Country episode and Winston's pleasure in possessing the 'almost useless' coral paperweight.

Yet, alas, there is nothing in nature that cannot be destroyed, perverted, or tainted by man. The coral is deliberatey smashed by the police in the arrest, and the irritation of Charrington of the Thought Police may only be because the smashing is done without his command. And even before this, the spare room is revealed as the trap it really is; its attractions are tarnished. Hardly have Julia and Winston entered when a rat appears. She reacts to 'the brutes' pragmatically, but he cries out melodramatically, 'Of all the horrors in the world—a rat!' and had 'the feeling of being back in a nightmare, a recurrent nightmare indeed.' Now, rats are generally admitted to be fairly unpleasant creatures, and rat phobia is common: they eat the dead, they spread disease, they multiply when public order and cities decline and they were once a favourite disguise for the Prince of Darkness. Even in *Animal Farm,* although the animals before the revolution voted 'that rats were comrades,' the Wild Comrades Re-Education Committee after the revolution completely failed with rats and rabbits. It failed with both, presumably, because Orwell holds that there will always be some evil and some silliness in men. Socialism, he said, could make people better, never perfect. And Orwell's pietism towards nature was mediated by his realism. To be conscious of being part of nature, he implies, is a necessary condition for man to be at his best, but not a sufficient condition: man needs reason, skills, and courage as well for civic action.

Even in his love for Julia, Winston's sense of the importance of a rational politics continues, especially of the question, Does the Brotherhood really exist? The sexual act may by itself be both freedom and rebellion for Julia, but it is not enough for Winston. This leads him to trust O'Brien when he approaches him with 'grave courtesy' to congratulate him on his facility with Newspeak and to offer him the loan of the latest edition of the *Newspeak Dictionary*, if he would care to call to pick it up. His readiness to trust is not just linked to the hope to find an active conspiracy, it is also linked to his failure to discover the truth on his own. It is not until Part Two, a third of the way through the book, that Winston gets to know Julia, and then O'Brien. The last section of Part One has dealt with the frustration of his hope to find the truth about the historical past by talking to proles, by evoking their memories. His dialogue with the old man is a marvellous comic invention. The old man is an unreconstructed traditionalist, all right: 'A 'alf litre ain't enough. I don't satisfy,' but the barman doesn't even know what a pint is—his ramblings are a chronologically jumbled parody of a misremembered and never fully understood *Daily Worker* or Communist Party prolefeed popular history. 'A sense of helplessness took hold of Winston. The old man's memory was nothing but a rubbish-heap of details.' (So much for oral history.) The significance of the incident is that it makes clear that however important is memory, it is useless without more formal knowledge—in this case documentary verification—and collaborators. The truth cannot be discovered on one's own. So quite apart from psychological need (though this is strongly hinted at too, in O'Brien as surrogate father), Winston needs to trust someone with access to the resources of the Inner Party and the Brotherhood.

Already, in the interview with O'Brien, the text contains forebodings that qualify Winston's moments of hope and should prevent the acute first-time readers hoping for that happy ending which the British version of the first film of the novel insisted upon. Even the first time Winston speaks to O'Brien, we are told that 'when the meanings of the words had sunk in, a chilly shuddering feeling had taken possession of his body. He had the sensation of stepping into the dampness of a grave, and it was not much better because he had always known that the grave was there and waiting for him.' 'Grave courtesy' indeed. Immediately before he and Julia visit O'Brien they discuss what will happen 'when once they get hold of us.' Winston stresses that they will be 'utterly alone,' and they both recognise that they will, everybody else does, confess under torture. He says that that doesn't matter: the only real betrayal would be if they could make him stop loving her.

> She thought it over. 'They can't do that,' she said firmly. 'It's the one thing they can't do. They can make you say anything—*anything*—but they can't make you believe it. They can't get inside you.'
>
> 'No,' he said a little more hopefully, 'no; that's quite true. They can't get inside you. If you can *feel* that staying human is worth while, even when it can't have any result whatever, you've beaten them.'

It is a humanist version of St. Paul's counsel not to fear those who hurt the body if they cannot hurt the soul. And it takes more courage (or folly) to mean this if one does not believe in life after death. But it shows that Orwell himself has moved beyond purely political, pragmatic, utilitarian, or hedonistic considerations, even if within the fiction 'they' do 'get inside' Winston and Julia.

The scene in O'Brien's apartment is tightly constructed and well crafted dramatically, compared to the florid scene in the Golden Country and elements of melodrama and didactic long-windedness in the torture scenes. Despite the very naturalistic setting, the text contains an unexpected symbolism. The door is opened by a little man 'in a white jacket.' O'Brien initiates them into wine (a privilege of the Inner Party, like being able to turn off the tele), catechizes them, and gives them both 'a flat white tablet' (to take away the smell of the wine) before they go. There is certainly more than a suggestion of a communion or even confirmation service, indeed of a black mass, considering the nature of the catechism. For they agree to a list of horrible actions if they would hurt the Party and help the Brotherhood, even 'to throw sulphuric acid in a child's face.' Only the last question throws them: 'You are prepared, the two of you, to separate and never see one another again?'

Julia immediately says 'No!' and Winston, only after a long pause and uncertainly, also says 'No,' (tellingly, there is no exclamation mark). The point is surely that their humanistic reservation is in vain, indeed mere selfishness after what they have agreed to do to a child. Now, of course, the scene has plenty of historic examples to draw on: as Orwell well knew, revolutionary brotherhoods of anarchists and nihilists in the nineteenth and early twentieth centuries had enjoyed such ceremonies and sworn such oaths. He also knew, incidentally, that both individual revolutionaries and police informers were prone to exaggerate the size of such bodies, occasionally inventing (for prestige or employment) huge, totally nonexistent ones.

It is difficult to be sure how consciously the author inserted this symbolism into the text, and if unconscious how important it was to him. No one writing in his tradition can avoid religious metaphor—militant atheistical socialists used to urge us 'forward to the New Jerusalem'—but one critic, at least, sees this scene as central to the book and to Orwell's concerns. The whole book is thus about the state replacing God, and Orwell's agonised despair at believing in neither. I find this argument far-fetched and missing the multiplicity of satiric targets in the book. It is true that the merging of church and state could be one of them, though it seems more likely that the satire is not on the great question of the impossibility of living without a belief in God (though Orwell saw difficulty, indeed, in the collapse of traditional morality), but more mundanely on the Catholic church as an organisation. He had disliked Catholicism as a young man, and he still feared its influence against socialism in Europe.[12] But while the text is charged, it is difficult to take a precise reading on this point. Yet whether or not the church in caricature is like the Party or whether or not it is impossible to oppose such parties without belief in God, Winston and Julia in their negative hatred for the Party have betrayed any possible morality, humanistic or Christian, that could universalise as a principle their experience of mutual trust.

In the cells of Miniluv, O'Brien plays back on a tape recorder Winston saying that he would throw acid into a child's face. Such a regime as is imagined would thus corrupt hopelessly even its bravest opponents, just as the concentration camps (as Orwell well knew) did succeed in dehumanising people before they were physically destroyed.

After meeting O'Brien, Winston is given 'the heavy black volume,' *The Theory and Practice of Oligarchical Collectivism* by Emmanuel Goldstein. Both mass movements and underground cells have their sacred books. 'Goldstein' recalls Bronstein, Trotsky's real name; and 'Emmanuel' is the Hebrew name for the Messiah or Saviour. Obviously Trotsky is parodied in the general style and the character of Goldstein's book, but the analysis of bureaucracy is the only intellectual point in common. 'Oligarchical collectivism' is not Trotsky's phrase. Orwell's Independent Labour Party company had fought in Spain as part of a brigade of the POUM who were Trotskyists so pure that their leader, Andres Nin, had broken with Trotsky (roughly speaking, for being too Stalinist, too dictatorial personally) although he had been Trotsky's confidential secretary in Russia. In 1941 H.G. Wells had called Orwell 'that Trotskyite with the big feet,' for between 1936 and 1942 Orwell was a bit hard to place politically, as a libertarian revolutionary socialist who hated the Communist Party and saw only milk and water in the veins of the Labour Party. However, there is no substance in Isaac Deutscher's claim that Goldstein's book is simply a 'paraphrase' of Trotsky's *Revolution Betrayed*,[13] any more than his dismissive claim that *Nineteen Eighty-Four* is simply a plagiarism of Zamyatin's *We*.[14] Even Jeffrey Meyers's assertion that 'Orwell's acute understanding of totalitarianism is most strongly influenced by Trotsky's *The Revolution Betrayed*' must be treated with caution: the book is only one source among many other obviously important. I share William Steinhoff's view that Goldstein's testament is much more closely linked to James Burnham's *The Managerial Revolution* and some later writings.[15] Burnham had once been a prominent follower of Trotsky, so there is a double edge to Orwell's parody.

Certainly there is a playful air to Orwell's use of the Trotsky persona and style to attack Burnham and to convey some truths and some dilemmas, though it can hardly be denied that the joke becomes laboured. There is an obvious structural clumsiness about the book-within-a-book that must make one examine with special interest why it is there at all and so important to the story. It holds up the action at a crucial point, though as Winston reads, Julia sleeps. Perhaps it is a needed intermezzo, a welcome lull before the storm of the arrest and the purposeful torturing. Or it could be argued that in this world of machines, memos and slogans, such substantial documentation, with a fair semblance of old-fashioned literacy, suits the atmosphere invoked in the descriptive passages of Part One. But the length is awkward. We quickly get the point and the joke of Newspeak as it is deftly worked into the general development of the story at several different points, so we can actually welcome the appendix on 'The Principles of Newspeak' as a useful consolidation or a supererogatory amusement. By contrast, Goldstein's book both is too long similarly to be threaded in and contains matter that we need to know before appreciating the final exchanges between Winston and O'Brien; yet its form if a heavy lump in the otherwise fast-flowing and clear structure of the book. I suspect that many ordinary readers skip it, and many profound psychological and philosophical interpreters of Orwell's 'message' make little reference to it (perhaps they skip it too): few people appeared eager to read it in any literal-minded spirit to see what Orwell really thought. This last would be a mistake, but not entirely—despite the double difficulty in the text of its being both O'Brien's invention (though he says that it is true as a description) and a parody of Burnham's thesis on the managerial elite written in a style that also parodies Trotsky's way of writing.

Winston begins reading chapter One, 'Ignorance Is Strength.' This title sounds more like a satire on Fascism than on Communism (until now the incidents or inventions of *Nineteen Eighty-Four* as a whole have been very balanced in this respect) but most of the rest of Goldstein's book draws more on Communist than on Fascist ideas and images. The chapter begins to tell us that from the beginning of time there have been 'three kinds of people in the world, the High, the Middle and the Low' and that 'the aims of these groups are entirely irreconcilable.' Mercifully, Winston skips on. We have heard all that before.

Chapter Three, 'War Is Peace,' is much more novel and intriguing. After relating that the world came to be divided into three great superstates around the middle of the twentieth century (as Burnham had prophesised and Orwell thought likely),[16] the book describes these three powers as having been 'permanently at war ... for the past twenty-five years.' War is not 'the desperate, annihilating struggle that it was in the early decades of the twentieth century. It is a warfare of limited aims between combatants who are unable to destroy one another, have no material cause for fighting and are not divided by any genuine ideological difference.' And 'it is impossible for it to be decisive.' We are told that 'atomic bombs first appeared as early as the nineteen-forties, and were first used on a large scale about ten years later.' After hundreds had been dropped on major industrial centres, the three ruling groups without any formal agreement, fearing for their own mutual destruction, ceased to use them; but they continued to manufacture and stockpile them.

> Meanwhile the art of war has remained almost stationary for thirty or forty years. Helicopters were more used than they were formerly, bombing planes have been largely superseded by self-propelled projectiles, and the fragile moveable battleship has given way to the almost unsinkable Floating Fortress; but otherwise there had been little development. The tank, the torpedo, the machine gun, even the rifle and the hand grenade are still in use.

Apart from the fact that mutual fear seems so far to have restrained the use of atom bombs even without that warfare of about 1955, and the minor matter of Floating Fortresses, the analysis is depressingly sensible and close to our own homes in the real world. And if not continuing warfare either, yet hardly peace, or what Thomas Hobbes would have counted as peace: 'The nature of War consisteth not in actual fighting but in a known disposition thereto, during all the time there is no assurance to the contrary.'[17]

But why, within the story, is such permanent though limited warfare (fought by small numbers of professionals over the former European colonial territories, not their own heartlands) continued at all? Up until now the account might suggest a parody of the Trotskyist, later to be the Maoist, doctrine of 'permanent revolution': that constant social upheaval and revolutionary renewal are needed to prevent bureaucratisation. But in the Oceanic world the violence is to ensure that the ruling elites are not challenged politically: to do so would risk giving an advantage to the enemy. The one thing the proles must and do believe in is the malevolence of the enemy. This theory of false or perpetual war could just be, is in part, a sophisticated version of the time-honoured tactic for maintaining domestic order that Shakespeare imputed to Henry IV and son. However, a new rationale emerges.

'The primary aim of modern warfare . . . is to use up the products of the machine without raising the general standard of living.' Winston reads. The Inner Party has realised that if the general rise in living standards of people typical of the 'end of the nineteenth and the beginning of the twentieth centuries' had continued, their own position would have been threatened.

For if leisure and security were enjoyed by all alike, the great

mass of human beings who are normally stupefied by
poverty would become literate and would learn to think for
themselves; and when once they had done this, they would
sooner or later realise that the privileged minority had no
function, and they would sweep it away. In the long run, a
hierarchical society was only possible on the basis of poverty
and ignorance.

So the problem become one of 'how to keep the wheels of industry
turning without increasing the real wealth of the world,' and the
answer is 'continuous warfare . . . Even when weapons of war are
not actually destroyed, their manufacture is still a convenient way
of expending labour power without producing anything that can
be consumed.' The object of war is not to conquer or defend
territoty 'but to keep the structure of society intact'—that is, a
hierarchical, anti-egalitarian structure.

All this is a parody and critique of the Marxist theories of
immiseration and of revolution. Goldstein/Orwell asserts, like de
Tocqueville, that revolution is more likely in times of prosperity, of
upswings of expectation, not in downswings of hopelessness; and
it is a parody of the labour theory of value—for the surplus from
exploitation of labour need not take the form of profit and capital
accumulation; it can be burned off in war. A parody of Marxism,
certainly with a sash of the Nazi 'Guns Before Butter' thrown in;
but it all now sounds, allowing for Swiftian exaggeration, very
familiar and plausible. We now speak a more restrained language
imputing a slight suspicion that the military and scientific
establishments of the *two* great powers may have a mutually vested
interest in the perpetuation of the armaments race, 'overkill,' and
contination of the Cold War. Some of us feel that we've been in
1984 for many years now.

The suggestion that equality can only rise in times of prosperity
is also unusual and intriguing. Most socialists have taken the view
that poverty creates a desire for equality. But it can be seriously
argued that only rising gross national product can arouse
expectations that equality (or at any rate a radical diminishment
of unjustifiable inequalities) is possible. Did not Marx himself
clearly argue that socialism could only follow the undoubted
achievement of capitalism and would rise on its shoulders, not
pull it down and start again? We are in a fiction, but the argument
is startlingly original and could be intellectually in earnest.

When Winston turns back to Chapter One, he quickly reads that
'as early as the beginning of the twentieth-century, human equality
had become technically feasible with the invention of machine
production.' Yet a 'new aristocracy' had arisen from 'the salaried

middle class and upper grades of the working class .... as compared with their opposite numbers in past ages, they were less avaricious, less tempted by luxury, hungrier for pure power, and, above all, more conscious of what they wre doing and intent on crushing opposition.' And to do that, of course, they had unparalleled technological resources: not merely print and radio, but television with which to watch, so that 'private life came to an end,' and to control, so that 'complete uniformity of opinion ... now existed for the first time.' So it is not a totalitarian ideology that moves them—his is a fabrication to control public opinion— nor the profit motive, but a desire for power over others. This now pure Burnham.

Goldstein tells us who this 'new aristocracy' are: bureaucrats, scientists, technicians, trade-union organisers, publicity experts, sociologists, teachers, journalists and professional politicians.' This makes obvious reference to and use of Burnham's thesis in *The Managerial Revolution* that 'a new class' of 'the managers' would take over the world. Orwell had long shared some of Burnham's key concepts while rejecting his conclusions. When Orwell rashly predicted the coming English revolution in his *The Lion and the Unicorn*, he himself had said that the 'directing brains' for the popular movement 'will come from the new indeterminate class of skilled workers, technical experts, airmen, scientists, architects and journalists, the people who feel at home in the radio and ferro-concrete age.' The last phase betrays his ambivalence towards this revolution even then, despite his special theory (far from implausible, though very irritating to strict Marxists) that the power of the people needed the leadership of altruistic and patriotic elements of the lower middle class to unleash and direct it. What if they weren't altruistic? What if they were Burnham's managers or 'new Machiavellians'? In Goldstein's analysis they are, and all the rest of Oceania's policies follow logically. The people are best controlled by, as it were, 'prolerisation'—keeping them in poverty, ignorance, and corruption; neither ideological indoctrination nor strict regimentation is needed. The concept of totalitarianism only applies to how the Inner Party controls the Outer Party—a situation astonishingly unlike anything that Orwell himself and his readers would have imagined of the real regimes called totalitarian. The treatment of the proles is old autocracy writ large by the debasing effects of modern communications technology: electronic bread and circuses.

Goldstein's testimony really told Winston very little that he did not know already, only that, fearing to have been a 'minority of one' (that is, alone, literally an 'idiot'), he now knew that he was 'not mad.' The account was true. Orwell seems to have intended more of it to be true, or at least speculatively relevant to the dilemmas of our times, than is usually noticed—even if the whole episode somewhat clogs the story and threatens to break the pretence of fiction. The imagined world and the real world becomes confused—an artistic loss, even if politically interesting.

When Winston faces O'Brien revealed, nothing in Goldstein's analysis is rendered implausible, except, of course, that his prophecy of a proletarian uprising is mocked. When O'Brien tells Winston that the Party can do anything, could easily conquer Eurasia and Eastasia if they wished to, Goldstein's logic seems stronger than his. When he launches into his peroration on 'power entirely for its own sake' ('We are not interested in the good of others; we are interested solely in power') this is an impressively plausible stance. We are almost inclined to believe him when he says 'we shall abolish the orgasm'; at least it seems plausible that some regime might try, given the plausibility of sexual repression as a device of political control. But what are we to make of O'Brien's claims that 'our control over matter is absolute,' that 'the earth is the centre of the universe,' and that he could levitate if he wished, just as the Party could reach the stars? They are absurd, as Winston and the reader realise. The good sense of much of Goldstein's testament, at least the congruence of its theories to Winston's solitary perceptions, has sustained Winston's belief in his own sanity, despite his nightmare and his physical and mental isolation. It is O'Brien who is mad. Winston only accepts his mad assertions because of torture and only comes to believe them when destroyed and, as it were, reborn. This cannot possibly be a projection of what total power will come to; rather it is a savage mocking of the pretensions of the power hungry in general. At the height of the imagery of total power, totalitarianism becomes a metaphor for something far more general, more common, and not always as pretentious. O'Brien's reference to the regime holding a Ptolemaic rather than a Copernican cosmology must be intended to make us think of Galileo facing the papal inquisition and reveals a religiosity in O'Brien.

So there is a precise link between what Goldstein has to tell us and the interrogation. There may be some flaws in the execution and writing, but the design is most deliberate and well crafted. Certainly many images suggest the fascination and appeal of sacrifice, cruelty and violence. Orwell had quarreled with H.G. Wells over his assertion that Wells was too much a rationalist ever to understand the appeal of Hitler's irrationality. But the fact that this irrationality did appeal was a descriptive truth; morally he always offered a rational critique of the irrational in politics. His love of oddities and useless things was for private life. So in *Nineteen Eighty-Four* the rational voice (allowing for parody) of Goldstein balances the 'mysticism of cruelty' of O'Brien. Orwell was the craftsman who balanced these two forces for literary effect, not, as Deutscher argued, himself the voice of the 'mysticism and cruelty.'[18]

Consider the structure of Part Three, nearly all inside the windowless Ministry of Love. In the first scene Winston is in a common cell, crowded among other prisoners, and images of degradation abound. The ordinary criminals are all proles; but they treat 'the pupils' with 'uninterested contempt.' An 'enormous wreck' of a drunken woman vomits on the floor. The proles, all 'filthy dirty,' swear at the guards, even scream back at the telescreen, but the guards treat them with a rough forebearance. Party prisoners, however, are beaten brutally if they even talk to each other. Two acquaintances from the office, Ampleforth and Parsons, are marched in, both arrested for thoughtcrime. Ampleforth, producing 'a definitive edition of Kipling' and short of rhymes for *rod*, had left in *God*. (Orwell would certainly have intended the double meaning of humble *rod*, so amid all the horror there is still broad or black humour.) Parsons has been denounced by his little daughter, as he recounts 'with a sort of doleful pride,' for muttering 'Down with Big Brother' in his sleep. (Again, not uncomic.) He uses the lavatory pan in the cell, and 'the cell stank abominably.' Smell and oppression, as well as dirt, are once more linked.

A man comes in whose face looks like a skull. He is starving. Another prisoner, actually given a name, 'Bumstead' (which suggests a decent common man), gives the 'skull-faced man' a crust. He is immediately and savagely beaten up by the guards, his head strikes the lavatory seat, and his dental plate is shattered into halves. There is no humour here, and the dental plate is that kind of precise image of the ordinary that Orwell could invest with such terror, like the prisoner in 'A Hanging' avoiding the puddle before he mounts the scaffold. The skull-faced man is then told he has to go to Room 101. He screams, 'Do anything to me ... Shoot me ... I've got a wife and three children ... cut their throats in front of my eyes, and I'll stand by and watch it. But not room 101!' This, alas, verges on the ludicrous, especially because it unconsciously echoes a silly, sadoerotic schoolboy chant.[19] Perhaps it is one of the passages about room 101 that Orwell's friend Julian Symons found 'melodramatic' and Orwell himself acknowledged as showing 'vulgarity.'

Then O'Brien comes for Winston. ' "They've got you too!" he cried. "They got me a long time ago," said O'Brien with a mild, almost regretful irony.' So at the first moment of truth, the minor motif of the Party as a church and the Inner Party as a priesthood is again sounded: O'Brien must have accepted the rule from early youth. Winston is then beaten by fist and rubber truncheon for a long and indeterminable time, softened up before he is taken to the cell where the interrogation proper, or rather his reconstitution or deconstitution, begins. O'Brien has taken over; he 'asked the questions and suggested the answers'; he controls the electrical machine that causes graduated pain; and he determines when Winston shall have respite, food, or drugs. It is a long process. 'He was the tormentor, he was the protector, he was the inquisitor, he was the friend.' And Winston hears him murmering in his ear: 'Don't worry, Winston; you are in my keeping. For seven years I have watched over you. Now the turning-point has come. I shall save you, I shall make you perfect.' He is almost fatherly, or perhaps it is big brotherly, to Winston.

Obviously it is crassly literal-minded to protest, as some readers do, that this amount of care by O'Brien for one dispensable individual is implausible, either in a possible totalitarian regime or in a fiction. It is, but the satiric point may be that you would have to go to such lengths against 'the last man in Europe' if you were to achieve such results, and if you were so power crazy as to act in this perverse, godlike way. It is a test for O'Brien as well as for Winston. Winston is a difficult case. O'Brien tells Winston that there are three stages in 're-integration': 'There is learning, there is understanding and there is acceptance.' The first stage is fascinating but relatively easy and clear. Winston learns that the past has no real existence, since all records of it can be destroyed. Another copy of the photograph he thought so important is destroyed before his eyes, reduced to 'dust and ashes'—echoing the words of the burial service for the dead in the rites of the Church of England. The Party controls past, present and future. By extreme pain he learns that two and two are not necessarily five, sometimes even four, but always only what the Party says. He is told, to strip down his resistance still further, that there is no hope of martyrdom: 'You must stop imagining that posterity will vindicate you, Winston. Posterity will never hear of you.' The hope of being remembered has indeed sustained free men in dark times throughout history: the Greeks and the Romans, as Machiavelli and the Italian humanists recalled, believed that immortality consisted precisely in being remembered for civic deeds; and Catholic and Protestant martyrs sometimes used martyrdom or hunger strikes for public example or political ends.

Always the stress is on power for its own sake. O'Brien even takes up Goldstein's at first puzzling point that the new regimes are something different from the totalitarian regimes of 'earlier in the century.' 'The command of the old despotisms was "Thou shalt not" The command of the totalitarians was "Thou shalt," Our command is "Thou art".'

It is in the second stage of 'understanding' that O'Brien's famous truth comes out. 'The faint, mad gleam of enthusiasm had come back into O'Brien's face' when he asks Winston to tell him *why* the Party clings to power. Winston, though desperate to please, misreads him: 'You are ruling over us for our own good.'

> That was stupid, Winston ... I will tell you the answer to my question. It is this. The Party seeks power entirely for its own sake. We are not interested in the good of others; we are interested solely in power. Not wealth or luxury or long life or happiness: only power, pure power ... We are different from all the oligarchies of the past, in that we know what we are doing ... The German Nazis and the Russian Communists came very close to us in their methods, but they never had the courage to recognise their motives.

After that he actually declares, 'We are the priests of power' and 'God is power.' Again, certainly there is a satire aimed at totalitarianism, or better the totalitarian mentality; but the greater thrust is not at something that Orwell imagined as going beyond totalitarianism but as something that exists all the time, not necessarily in the form of totalitarianism proper (though in the modern world it helps its growth): power hunger and unprincipled office-holding. Somewhat confusingly, one example of power hunger and hierarchy—the church—which indeed was certainly *not* the most important example in the modern world to Orwell, keeps surfacing in his imagery. Even the name O'Brien, being Irish, may suggest the Catholic.

O'Brien's absurd boast follows. The 'mad gleam' has been noted. Yet despite the imagined power of the Party over the universe and the real total power that O'Brien holds over Winston Smith, the 'last man' still holds out.

'Do you believe in God, Winston?'
'No.'
'Then what is it, this principle that will defeat us?'
'I don't know. The spirit of man.'
'And do you consider yourself a man?'
'Yes.'
'If you are a man, Winston, you are the last man. Your kind is

extinct; we are the inheritors. Do you understand you are *alone?* You are outside history, you are nonexistent.' Indeed, if we had no memory, no history, and no mutual trust, no respect for truth, no aesthetic sense, our humanity could not exist.[29] O'Brien then breaks down utterly this apparent last resistance of Smith's, not by further solipsistic chop-logic or by torture, but by gently showing him in a mirror his own wasted and broken body: a long and ghastly description then follows, obviously taken from the newsreels of Belsen that were shown in London cinemas in ordinary programs open to children, though with a perfunctory warning (I remember vividly). 'Do you see that thing facing you? That is the last man. If you are human, that is your humanity. Now put your clothes on again. 'But satire holds up a mirror, indeed. While the scene is moving and terrible, to look in the mirror the other way is again to show a human being who has held out so far, so very far.

Winston is willing now to accept everything, yet he still says, 'I have not betrayed Julia.' And when O'Brien looks down at him and acknowledges thoughtfully, 'That is perfectly true,' Winston feels a 'peculiar reverence' for O'Brien's intelligence and under-standing. They both knew that he had betrayed everything there was to betray about Julia, and that she had done the same; but they both know that he still loves her. 'You are a difficult case,' says O'Brien. 'But don't give up hope. Everyone is cured sooner or later.'

Then for some time Winston is rested and fed, he even recovers something of his former weight and appearance. He accept everything he has been told and willingly exercises himself in doublethink and crimestop. Only sometimes our dreams betray our deepest feelings: he wakes up crying aloud, 'Julia, my love, Julia.' O'Brien knows, and when challenged by him Winston does not deny his true feelings towards Big Brother.

'I hate him'.

'You must love Big Brother. It is not enough to obey him; you must love him.'

So it seems that he is a jealous god, one can love no other, not even a fellow human being. To love Big Brother is both to love no other person and to lose any proper love for self, for in loving another human being both mutual trust and thus a heightened individual identity are asserted in the face of the Party; and when all capacity to love another is crushed, nothing is left to love except Big Brother.

So then in the room 'where there is no darkness' Winston meets 'the worst thing in the world,' for him a rat, the Prince of Darkness. To Orwell humanity cannot live wholly in the light or wholly in the dark. Both morally and physically we need natural rhythms, not permanent extremes. The good cannot be perfect, and the wicked have some good in them. Imperfect man (here we will all read the parable of 'no darkness' differently; perhaps even Orwell was uncertain) can only be saved by God's mercy or can save each other by fraternal love and mutual aid. But no longer Winston. Even he screams, as the teeth come near to his face, that he must be spared and it must be done to her. He is not offered the choice: he just perfectly understands what O'Brien wants. Then he is lost as a man, for that is a sacrifice that one can only make for another: no one can demand another to lay down their life for oneself. So he is spared, cast out as a loyal but empty shell.

The last section shows him back at some kind of meaningless work, drinking the Victory gin again in the symbolic Chestnut Tree Cafe, and even encountering Julia—an empty, meaningless meeting not even bitter, whose only point is to acknowledge 'that you don't give a damn what they suffer. All you care about is yourself... And after that, you don't feel the same towards any other person again.' If humanity and true individuality are mutual care and trust, Winston and Julia are now both simply the living dead, emptied of humanity.

> Winston, however, looks at the face of Big Brother: Two gin-scented tears trickled down the side of his nose. But it was all right, everything was all right, the struggle was finished. He had won the victory over himself. He loved Big Brother.
> THE END

'THE END' is almost certainly part of the author's text. It is there in the final typescript, it was left by Orwell in the proofs, and was repeated in the later nine-volume Secker and Warburg standard editions of Orwell's books, of which only two others use this device. Bad movies and cheap books used to carry this sign. It is 'the end' if one actually *loves* any Big Brother. And if this could be thought a tenuous argument against all who consider that the book ends on a note of utter despair rather than of black comedy, just consider the comic distancing of those two tell-tale gin-scented tears trickling down poor Winston's nose.

Such great dictators are worthy of such great admirers. For at the end the picture is a comic, grotesque one. And though we must admire Winston Smith for his stubbornness about truth and for holding out so long, he did sell the pass twice. Because of the rat it is easy to understand and forgive his betrayal of Julia. But only God could forgive their mutual willingness to throw sulphuric acid into a child's face, even for rebellion. Rebels who win like that just become the party all over again. Both *Animal Farm* and

*Nineteen Eighty-Four*end in parody transformation scenes. And, anyway, it is not 'THE END'—even that is a little joke. There then follows the delightfully satiric appendix: 'The Principles of Newspeak,' mordantly written in the past tense. The satire is harsh but good-humoured. So the real ending of the book is not on the note of sado-masochistic horror of the scene in Room 101, nor even on the deflating picture of an imaginary dictator being loved by a gin-soaked, broken man, but on the words 'so late a date as 2050.' That is the date for the final translation of everything into Newspeak—quite a long time after 1984, note. What has held up the final solution so long, we are authoritatively told by the *Times*, is 'the difficulty' (that is, the impossibility) of translating the Declaration of Independence and writers like 'Shakespeare, Milton, Swift, Byron and Dickens.' Conjuring with these names, the reader is led to believe that language can *never* become purely a method of control and cease to be imaginative and truthfully communicative. So may clear language and good literature sustain us.

NOTES

1. Quoted in Bernard Crick, *George Orwell: A Life* (Harmondsworth: Penguin, 1982), p. 565. The paperback edition is both revised and corrected, and is to be preferred to the original Secker and Wartburg or Atlantic Press editions.
2. Ibid., p. 569.
3. Ibid., p. 550.
4. Ibid., appendix A, 'The Nineteen Forty-Three Outline of *Nineteen Eighty-Four,*' pp. 582-85.
5. Ibid., p. 546.
6. Julian Symons, Introduction and Appreciation to *Nineteen Eighty-Four*, by George Orwell (London: Heron Books, 1970), pp. xi and 344. Unhappily this excellent essay is little known to critics, since it was written for a book club.
7. Such as George Watson, "Orwell and the Spectrum of European Politics," *Journal of European Studies* I, no. 3 (1971): 191-97 and Norman Podhoretz, 'If Orwell Were Alive Today,' *Harper's*, January 1983. 30-37 (with a proper reply from Christopher Hitchens in the following issue). Even Alex Zwerdling, in his balanced and scholarly *Orwell and the Left* (New Haven, Conn.: Yale University Press, 1974) says that 'the strongly conservative flavour of [his] belief is unmistakable, and the fact that *Nineteen Eighty-Four* was taken up with such enthusiasm by the right is no accident' (p. 110). But he seems to have an ideal image of socialism and confuses conservativism and scepticism about perfectibility (rather than betterment), typical of English socialism, with political conservatism.
8. Kathleen Nott in her *The Good Want Power* (London: Cape, 1977), argues that 'identity ... entails a principle of mutual recognition.' And see my *In Defence of Politics*, 2nd Pelican ed. (Harmondswoth: Penguin, 1982), pp. 234-35.
9. He says so quite explicitly in essays such as 'The Prevention of Literature,' *Collected Essays, Journalism and Letters*, ed. Sonia Orwell and Ian Angus, 4 vols. (London: Secker and Warburg, 1968), 4:64-65, hereafter

cited as *CEJL;* 'Writers and Leviathan,' *CEJL,* 4.407-10; and in his review of *The Totalitarian Enemy,* by Franz Borkenau, *CEJL,* 2-24-26.

10. Quoted by Jeffrey Meyers, *A Reader's Guide to Orwell* (London: Thames and Hudson, 1975), pp. 178-79.

11. *CEJL,* 1:6.

12. Christopher Small, *The Road to Miniluv: George Orwell, the State and God* (London: Gollancz, 1975) argues that Orwell's 'pious atheism' was almost as good as faith itself, and Alan Sandison, *The Last Man in Europe* (London: Macmillan, 1974) shows how deeply Protestant Orwell's assumptions and images were. He may have been closer to Christianity than his nominal humanism suggests, but not to Catholicism: 'Both Communist and Catholic usually believe ... that abstract aesthetic standards are all bunkum and that a book is only a "good" book if it preaches the right sermon' (*CEJL,* 1:257); and 'The Catholic and Communist are alike in assuming that an opponent cannot be both honest and intelligent' (*CEJL,* 4-374). And see Crick, *George Orwell,* pp. 115, 226-29, 254, 273-74, 286; and his introduction to the Clarendon edition of *Nineteen Eighty-Four,* pp. 40-41.

13. In his polemic '1984: The Mysticism of Cruelty,' in his *Heretics and Renegades* (London: Hamish Hamilton, 1955). He offers no examples or evidence. The only parallels (apart from the name) are Trotsky's theory of the emergence in the USSR of a 'bureaucratic caste' ouside normal class relations, and his analysis of Stalinism as 'Bonapartism' (more obviously an influence on *Animal Farm*). Most of Trotsky's book is a detailed attack on and analysis of Stalin's policies on the 1920s and 1930s, of relevance to Goldstein's testament. To say 'paraphrase' is absurd, wholly of a piece with Deutscher's claim that *Nineteen Eighty-Four* is just a crib (see note 14 below) from Zamyatin.

14. Deutscher so dislikes Orwell for writing a book that could be used as an 'ideological super-weapon in the cold war' that he hits him with everything: '*1984* is a document of dark disillusionment not only with Stalin but with every form and shade of socialism. It is a cry from the abyss of despair ... He projected the last spasms of his own suffering into the last pages of his last book' (*Heretics and Renegades,* p. 44). That Orwell had reviewed Zamyatin's *We* became 'a conclusive piece of evidence that Orwell had 'borrowed the idea of *1984,* the plot, the chief characterism the symbols from Zamyatin.' Deutscher exaggerates grossly and has no idea of how extensive Orwell's *other* borrowings were, especially from James Burnham. Cf. William Steinhoff, *George Orwell and the Origins of '1984'* (Ann Arbor: University of Michigan Press, 1975). Steinhoff shows how wilfully Deutscher conflates *We* and *Nineteen Eighty-Four.* See also Mark Reader, 'The Political Critic of George Orwell' (Ph.D. diss., University of Michigan, 1966) for a patient and thorough rebuttal of Deutscher's charges.

15. Steinhoff, *Origins,* chap. 3. 'The Influence of James Burnham.'

16. 'Burnham's geographical picture of the world has turned out to be correct. More and more obviously the surface of the earth is being parcelled off into three great Empires' ('You and the Atom Bomb,' *CEJL,* 2:8-9).

17. Thomas Hobbes, *Leviathan,* pt. 1, chap. 13. Orwell had assumed (cf. 'You and the Atom Bomb'), writing before the hydrogen bomb, that the world could survive nuclear war.

18. Deutscher, *Heretics and Renegades,* takes it for granted that Orwell identifies himself with *both* the masochism of Winston Smith and the sadism of O'Brien. He interprets fiction somewhat literally and, like others, allows Orwell little inventive imagination.

19. Still current in English public school changing rooms as 'Sir Jasper and

the Maiden.' *Sir J.* "*The Whip, the whip!*" *M.* "Anything but the whip!" *Sir J.* "Anything?!?" *M.* "The whip." '

20. Both Small, *The Road to Miniluv,* and Sandison, *The Last Man in Europe,* use this passage to imply Orwell's feeling of helplessness without God. But Orwell says in his essay on Koestler that belief in God is 'the only easy way out,' yet 'the real problem is how to restore a religious attitude while accepting death as final. Men can only be happy when they do not assume the object of life is happiness' (*CEJL,* 4:243-44). By a 'religious attitude' he means something like respecting men and women equally despite their imperfections and respecting nature as if it were a sacred creation.

Twelve

Animal Farm For Schools

Written as 'Background Notes for Teachers and Pupils' for the
National Theatre in 1984 in conjunction with Sir Peter Hall's version
and production of *Animal Farm*.

Animal Farm is one of the most famous political satires ever
written. Almost every British school child reads it, usually far too
early to grasp all its meanings. Almost ten million copies have
been sold in English language versions alone, and it has been
translated into twenty-two foreign languages. Written specifically
against Stalinism and what Orwell saw as the betrayal of
revolutionary principles by the Communist Party of the Soviet
Union, yet it also carries a general meaning of satire of tyranny in
general, and satire at the pretensions of any ruling class to think
they know better than those they rule what is best for them. So
while written forty years ago, it still leaps to life wherever tyranny is
imagined, feared or endured.

In Hungary, before the unseccessful revolt of 1956 against the
Russians, two students, independently and unknown to each
other, translated it and circulated secretly as *samizdat*–illegal typed
or duplicated copies. They compared their versions later in
London. And more recently an Arab journalist emerged from a
prison sentence in Tanzania, having spent his time turning *Animal
Farm* into Swahili. Unfortunately he discovered that someone else
had done it already.

In one part of the world, of course, it has not been received so
well. Only ten years ago, following a BBC broadcast about
Orwell, the *Literary Gazette* of Moscow commented bitterly:

> *Animal Farm* is a malicious caricature of the Russian
> Revolution, which slanderously pictures the revolutionary
> people as a herd of animals. It was written in the days when
> Europe's fate was being decided on the Eastern Front, and
> when even the most hardened Conservative publishers
> could not bring themselves to publish a book that slandered
> their ally in the struggle against Fascism.

This was perhaps Orwell's greatest offence in the eyes not merely
of Communists but of many democratic Socialists in Great Britain

and elsewhere who still hoped that after the war a more democratic regime might emerge in Russia. These so-called 'fellow travellers', who went along with the Soviet Union, some with noble hopes and some with fatuous credulity, denounced *Animal Farm* as an attack on a war-time ally, at the best premature. But to Orwell, with his simple but profound moral vision, 'two wrongs don't make a right', and the fact that Nazism was a greater evil did not condone or pardon Stalin's despotism.

The Origins

What were his reasons for writing when he did? He did not often talk directly about himself (as distinct from using the first person as a narrative device, drawing on his own experience, as in *Down and Out in Paris and London*, but not to be taken as literally true); but in 1947 he agreed to write the Preface to a Ukrainian translation of *Animal Farm*, seeing the need to explain who he was and how the book came to be written so that people of a very different culture could understand it.

I was born in India in 1903. My father was an official in the English administration there. I was educated at Eton, the most costly and snobbish of the English public schools. I went to Burma and joined the Indian Imperial Police. It did not suit me and made me hate imperialism... When on leave in England in 1927, I resigned from the service and decided to become a writer; at first without any especial success. In 1928-29 I lived in Paris and wrote short stories and novels that nobody would print. In the following years I lived mostly from hand to mouth, and went hungry on several occasions. I sometimes lived for months on end amongst the poor and half-criminal elements. At that time I associated with them through lack of money, but later their way of life interested me very much. I spent many months studying conditions of the miners in the north of England. Up until 1930 I did not on the whole look on myself as a socialist. In fact I had as yet no clearly-defined political views. I became pro-socialist more out of disgust with the way the poorer section of the industrial workers were oppressed and neglect than out of any theoretical admiration for a planned society.

In 1936 when the Civil War in Spain broke out, Orwell went with his wife to fight for the Republican Government against the Fascist rebellion led by General Franco. Typically he did not go to attend conferences and political rallies, nor to write for the newspapers, as many Left-Wingers did to show their support for the republic and democracy; he went to fight at the front. Almost by accident he did not join the famous International Brigade, dominated by the Communists, but enlisted in Barcelona with a Catalan militia controlled by POUM (the United Workers' Marxist Party), or 'Spanish Trotskyists,' as he called them somewhat inaccurately. Trotsky claimed to be the true Communist and denounced Stalin as a power-hungry bureaucrat, fleeing the Soviet Union for his life (he was eventually assassinated by Stalin's agents in Mexico in 1940). The POUM, however, were marxists so pure that they had even broken from Trotsky, holding him too to be too dictatorial. And the POUM fought in the line alongside Anarchist contingents, who were at one time the largest party in the province of Catalonia. Orwell described the impact that meeting and fighting alongside these men made in his first fully successful book, *Homage to Catalonia*. 'Successful' is a literary judgement—here first his famous plain, clear style emerged consistently—and an intellectual judgement—that he dealt so honestly with difficult matters that most writers reduce to propaganda; in fact the book was so unpopular that it sold few copies, was commercially very unsuccessful.

> One had been in contact with something strange and valuable. One had been in a community where hope was more normal than apathy or cynicism, where the word 'comrade' stood for comradeship, and not, as in most countries, for humbug. One had breathed the air of equality. In that community where no one was on the make, where there was a shortage of everything but no privilege and no bootlicking, one got perhaps a crude forecast of what the opening stages of Socialism might be like and, after all, instead of disillusioning me, it deeply attracted me.

The parallelism between this warmth and Manor Farm *just after* the expulsion of Mr Jones and his men is obvious. The revolution was a time of hope. Orwell saw all the difficulties in hoping to achieve freedom through revolution, but he did not think that violent events necessarily taint the actions that follow—only that they give opportunities to the power hungry ('the pigs') who exist in any society. For the first time, he wrote to his friend Cyril Connolly, he really *believed* in socialism, saw it, felt it, experienced it, which previously had only been an intellectual speculation to him. But his optimism and euphoria did not last long. The Communist Party hated the POUM quite as much as they hated Franco and Fascism. Orwell, wounded in the throat by a fascist bullet, which missed his jugular vein by an eighth of an inch, was sent to Barcelona to convalesce, and there he saw his anarchist friends being hunted down, shot or imprisoned by the

Communists. He himself was in danger, and only escaped through the great courage of his wife, Eileen. The effect on him was profound, as he told his Ukrainian readers:

These man-hunts in Spain went on at the same time as the great purges in the USSR and were a sort of supplement to them. In Spain as well as in Russia, the nature of the accusations (namely conspiracy with the Fascists) was the same and as far as Spain was concerned, I had every reason to believe that the accusations were false. To experience all this was a valuable object lesson: it taught me how easily totalitarian propaganda can control the opinion of enlightened people in democratic countries. My wife and I saw innocent people being thrown into prison merely because they were suspected of unorthodoxy. Yet on our return to England we found numerous sensible and well-informed observers believing the most fantastic accounts of conspiracy, treachery and sabotage, from the Moscow trials.

From then on he was convinced that if the democratic Socialist movement was to be revived it was essential to achieve, he told his Ukranian readers, 'the destruction of the Soviet myth'. By 'Soviet myth' he seemed to mean both the myth that the Soviet Union was a truly socialist country and the myth of Soviet power—that there was no alternative way for socialists. But the tide seemed to be going against him, especially when after Stalin's brief attempt in 1939 to reach an understanding with Hitler, the USSR was invaded by Germany in 1941 and became an ally of the West. These sudden changes of front revolted Orwell with his memories of the lies and the treachery in the Spanish War. Many ordinary people thought that any regime attacked by Hitler must be perfect, lacking the cynicism of Winston Churchill, a very strong anti-Communist but who remarked that if Hitler were to invade Hell he would make a speech in the House of Commons the next day complimentary to the Devil. 'One could not have', said Orwell, 'a better example of the shallowness of our time, than the fact that we are all more or less pro-Stalin. This disgusting murderer is temporarily on our side, and so the purges etc. are forgotten'.

The war continued and admiration and gratitude for the Russians' resistance to the Nazis mounted in the West, but Orwell's views never changed. In December 1943, Churchill, Roosevelt and Stalin met at Tehran, nominally to discuss military strategy, but rumours abounded that they also discussed a division of the world between the Great Powers into spheres of influence. Tehran was to furnish both the satiric scene in *Animal Farm* when the pigs and the men meet and become allies, and the basis of the imaginary history of *Nineteen Eighty-Four*, the division of the world between three rival powers, nominally hostile but in fact only pursuing a desultory cold war aimed at subjugating their own populations not at conquering the nominal enemy. In that same December the first explicit reference to *Animal Farm* occurs in a letter Orwell wrote to an American scholar, Gleb Struve, then living in London and who, like himself, was a socialist but firmly anti-Communist:

> Please forgive me for not writing earlier to thank you for the very kind gift of your book *Twenty-Five Years of Russian Literature*. I am writing a little squib which might amuse you when it comes out, but is not so O.K. politically that I feel certain in advance that anyone will publish it. Perhaps that gives you a hint of its subject.

And in that same Preface to the Ukrainian translation he revealed a little more about the origins of the book:

> On my return from Spain, I thought of exposing the Soviet myth in a story that could be easily understood by almost anyone and which could be easily translated into other languages. However, the actual details of the story did not come to me for some time until one day, in a small village, I saw a little boy, perhaps ten years old, driving a huge cart-horse along a narrow path, whipping it whenever it tried to turn. It struck me that if only such animals became aware of their strength we should have no power over them, and that men exploit animals in much the same way as the rich exploit the proletariat. I proceeded to analyse Marx's theory from the animals' point of view.

The Story

Old Major, the Berkshire hog who was the prophet of the revolution to come, advances the fruits of that analysis:

> Comrades, what is the nature of this life of ours? Let us face it: our lives are miserable, laborious and short. We are born, we are given just as much food as will keep the breath in our bodies, and those of us who are capable of it are forced to work to the last atom of our strength; and the very moment that our usefulness has come to an end we are slaughtered with hideous cruelty. No animal in England knows the meaning of happiness or leisure after he is a year old. No animal in England is free. The life of an animal is misery and slavery: that is the plain truth. . . . Why then do we continue in this miserable condition? Because nearly the whole of the produce of our labour is stolen from us by human beings. . . .

Remove Man from the scene, and the root cause of hunger and overwork is removed for ever.

Man is the only creature that consumes without producing. He does not give milk, he does not lay eggs, he is too weak to pull the plough, he cannot run fast enough to catch rabbits. Yet he is lord of the animals. He sets them to work, and he gives back to them the bare minimum which will prevent them from starving, and the rest he keeps for himself.... You, cows—what has happened to that milk which should have been breeding sturdy calves . . .? And you, Clover, where are those four foals you bore, who should have been the support and pleasure of your old age . . .? You young porkers who are sitting in front of me, every one of you will scream your lives out in the block within a year. To that horror all must come. You, Boxer, the very day that those great muscles of your lose their power, Jones will sell you to the knacker, who will cut your throat and boil you down for the foxhounds.... What then must we do? Why, work night and day, body and soul, for the overthrow of the human race. That is my message to you, comrades: Rebellion!

And Old Major composed and taught them the great song, 'Beasts of England':

Beasts of England, beasts of Ireland.
Beasts of every land and clime,
Harken to my joyful tidings
Of the golden future time . . .

Soon or late the day is coming
Tyrant man shall be o'erthrown,
And the fruitful fields of England
Shall be trod by beasts alone.

Rings shall vanish from our noses
And the harness from our back,
Bit and spur shall rust for ever,
Cruel whips no more shall crack.

Whatever happens afterwards in the story, the nobility of the aspiration towards a classless, egalitarian society seems undoubted in the power, humour and beauty of Orwell's writing. Those who read the book as a satire on the possibility and principles of socialism in general rather than a satire on its power-hungry betrayers, must be deaf to the power of the above passages. A reader may think that Orwell's socialism is misguided or foolish, but the author's intention is quite clear. Yet he knew quite well that this vision had not been realised; indeed he was attacking those

who claimed that the Soviet Union was something like Old
Major's (or old Marx's) vision, but not attacking the vision
itself.

The sequence of events that follows in the story is broadly
similar to what happened in Russia. The animals escape from the
tyranny of man (or the Czarist regime), only to fall under the
tyranny of the pigs (the Commissars). Far from creating a classless
society, 'the pigs' become a new ruling class. Like every ruling class
they profess to be more intelligent and to know what is best for the
others, whether the others like it or not. After Old Major's death,
Napoleon (the Stalin figure) and Snowball (the Trotsky figure)
worked together for a time, in seeming fraternal amity. But then
Napoleon, hungry for absolute powerm chased Snowball out on
trumped-up charges, and with an unexpected and terrifying
display of power.

> There was a terrible baying sound outside, and nine
> enormous dogs wearing brass-studded collars came
> bounding into the barn. They dashed straight for Snowball,
> who only sprang from his place just in time to escape their
> snapping jaws. In a moment he was out of the door and they
> were after him. Too amazed and frightened to speak, all the
> animals crowded through the door to watch the chase.
> Snowball was racing acorss the long pasture that led to the
> road. He was running as only a pig can run, but the dogs were
> close on his heels. Suddenly he slipped and it seemed certain
> that they had him. Then he was up again, running faster than
> ever, then the dogs were gaining on him again. One of them
> all but closed his jaws on Snowball's tail, but Snowball
> whisked it free just in time. Then he put on an extra spurt
> and, with a few inches to spare, slipped through a hole in the
> hedge and was seen no more.
>
> Silent and terrified, the animals crept back into the barn.
> In a moment the dogs came bounding back. At first no one
> had been able to imagine where these creatures came from,
> but the problem was soon solved: they were the puppies
> whom Napoleon had taken away from their mothers and
> reared privately. Though not yet fully-grown, they were huge
> dogs, and as fierce-looking as wolves. They kept close to
> Napoleon. It was noticed that they wagged their tails to him
> in the same way as the other dogs had been used to do to Mr
> Jones.

As man exploits man, so animal exploits animal. But that wasn't
the worst of it. For it wasn't, in Orwell's eyes, a case of Stalin bad
and Lenin (who does not figure in the story) or Trotsky good.

'Snowball' gains our sympathy, but only relatively. He was no pure idealist destroyed by the power-hungry and brutal Napoleon. For as Orwell saw it, Trotsky was just as much guilty as Stalin of selling the pass, helping the Communist Party to become a dictatorship. True, Trotsky wanted democracy within the Party and opposed Stalin's autocracy; but he indeed meant the Communist Party when he talked, like Lenin, about the need for a temporary and transitional (so they said!) 'dictatorship of the proletariat', he did not mean the common people. Orwell explained to a friend that a key passage in the book is when the pigs secretly had the cow's milk added to their own mash—the crucial betrayal of egalitarian revolutionary idealism! Snowball consented to this first act of inequality. And notice that the pigs also expropriate the apples—some echo of that first great betrayal in Eden? Snowball is not as bad as Napoleon, but he is pig enough. Napoleon's public relation's man, Squealer, explains all this to the trusting animals; and Squealer is a compound of every Party or Government 'official spokesman' there ever was.

> 'Comrades!' he cried. 'You do not imagine, I hope, that we pigs are doing this in a spirit of selfishness and privilege? Many of us actually dislike milk and apples. I dislike them myself. Our sole object in taking these things is to preserve our health. Milk and apples (this has been proved by Sciences, comrades) contain substances absolutely necessary to the well-being of a pig. We pigs are brain-workers. The whole management and organisation of this farm depend on us. Day and night we are watching over your welfare. It is for *your* sake that we drink that milk and eat those apples. Do you know what would happen if we pigs failed in our duty? Jones would come back! Yes, Jones would come back! Surely, comrades,' cried Squealer almost pleadingly, skipping from side to side and whisking his tail, 'surely there is no one among you who wants to see Jones come back?

Because that was the last thing the animals wanted, they accepted Squealer's specious explanation. 'This has been proved by science' was, indeed, a catch-phrase of Communist propaganda in the 1930s when marxism claimed to be 'scientific', indeed that its philosophical dogmas were more scientific than empirical science. And from then on, in the story, the great principles of Old Major's 'Animalism' (cf. humanism) become diluted and corrupted by the pig elite to justify their own indulgence and power hunger at the expense of the others.

Old Major had said, 'No animal shall sleep in a bed' but Squealer amends, 'No animal shall sleep in a bed with sheets.'

'No animal shall drink alcohol.' 'No animal shall drink alcohol to excess.' 'No animal shall kill another animal.' No animal shall kill another animal without cause.'

These last words were added when, in an episode that recalled the great purges and show trials of the 1930s when Stalin framed and executed *nearly all* the surviving fellow leaders of the 1917 revolution, some of the young pigs were tried on a charge of having secretly helped the exiled Snowball.

> The four pigs waited, trembling, with guilt written on every line of their countenances. Napoleon now called upon them to confess their crimes. They were the same four pigs as had protested when Napoleon abolished the Sunday Meetings. Without any further prompting they confessed that they had been secretly in touch with Snowball ever since his expulsion, that they had collaborated with him in destroying the windmill, and that they had entered into an agreement with him to hand over Animal Farm to Mr Frederick. They added that Snowball had privately admitted to them that he had been Jones's secret agent for years past. When they had finished their confession, the dogs promptly tore their throats out, and in a terrible voice Napoleon demanded whether any other animal had anything to confess.
>
> The three hens who had been the ringleaders in the attempted rebellion over the eggs now came forward and stated that Snowball had appeared to them in a dream and incited them to disobey Napoleon's orders. They, too, were slaughtered. Then a goose came forward and confessed to having urinated in the drinking pool—urged to do this, so she said, by Snowball—and two other sheep confessed to having murdered an old ram, an especially devoted follower of Napoleon, by chasing him round and round a bonfire when he was suffering from a cough. They were all slain on the spot. And so the tale of confessions and executions went on, until there was a pile of corpses lying before Napoleon's feet and the air was heavy with the smell of blood, which had been unknown there since the expulsion of Jones.

After that the pigs can move to amend the greatest of Old Major's commandments: 'All animals are equal.' 'All animals are equal but some animals are more equal than others.' (This famous phrase Orwell took, whether consciously or unconsciously, from a short story by Philip Guedella called 'A Russian Fairy Tale' in a volume, *The Missing Muse,* of 1929. In it there is a Good Fairy 'who believed that all fairies were equal before the law, but held strongly that some fairies were more equal than others.' Orwell was a

magpie more than an inventor; as in *Nineteen Eighty-Four*, there are
many borrowings—as in Shakespeare, one might add; but the use
he makes of them is the point to create a coherent imagined world).

The tone of the writing can embrace harsh satire, as in the above
'pile of corpses lying before Napoleon's feet'; great humour, as in
the debate between the animals on whether 'rats are comrades'
and the cat's rather self-interested role in the 'Wild Comrades Re-
education Committee' (the old Communist Party was prodigal
with such 'front' organisations); and a profound tenderness—as
above all shown in the characters of Clover and Boxer.

As Clover looked down the hillside her eyes filled with
tears. If she could have spoken her thoughts, it would have
been to say that this was not what they had aimed at when
they had set themselves years ago to work for the overthrow
of the human race. These scenes of terror and slaughter were
not what they had looked forward to on that night when old
Major first stirred them to rebellion. If she herself had had
any picture of the future, it had been the of a society of
animals set free from hunger and the whip, all equal, each
working according to his capacity, the strong protecting the
weak, as she had protected the lost brood of ducklings with
her foreleg on the night of Major's speech. Instead—she did
not know why—they had come to a time when no one dared
speak his mind, when fierce, growling dogs roamed everywhere, and when you had to watch your comrades torn to
pieces after confessing to shocking crimes. There was no
thought of rebellion or disobedience in her mind. She knew
that, even as things were, they were far better off than they
had been in the days of Jones, and that before all else it was
needful to prevent the return of the human beings. Whatever
happened she would remain faithful, work hard, carry out
the orders that were given to her, and accept the leadership of
Napoleon. But still, it was not for this that she and all the
other animals had hoped and toiled. It was not for this that
they had built the windmill and faced the bullets of Jones's
gun. Such were her thoughts, though she lacked the words to
express them.

Stylistically, it is a great achievement: the words and the tone are
almost perfectly matched. It is Orwell's famous plain style at its
best. But the ease with which he uses it conceals much previous
trial *and* error on his part, and the pain of careful writing and
rewriting—so much writing is rewriting. The style appears to be
natural, but of course there is no such thing as natural style. Orwell
deliberately chose a form of rhetoric first used by Daniel Defoe

and prominent among Jonathan Swift's armoury of styles: plain and simple monosyllabic words to create the impression of honest, simple direct to ordinary people. One needs to remind oneself, however, despite what Orwell implied in several notable essays on language ('The Prevention of Literature', 'Politics and the English Language', 'Politics vs. Literature' and 'Writers and Leviathan'–all in the fourth volume of the Pelican *The Collected Essays, Journalism and Letters of George Orwell* or in the one volume *The Penguin Esays of George Orwell*) that the devil can lie in monosyllables just as God may speak in polysyllables and may sometimes be hard to understand. Orwell's style is a great achievement and a good model, but it is not the only way to write English, nor a style for all purposes and seasons. Yes, we should distrust obscure and sententious official utterances, but there is no way whatever of deriving the truth of a proposition or assertion from the structure of a sentence—for example 'this lovely world of ours is flat'. Write plainly and clearly but also tell the truth—Orwell wanted both.

The predominant tone is, however, not harsh satire, but tenderness and pity. We pity great Boxer, we do not sneer at his simplicity. No one worked harder than Boxer. The technological achievements of Animal Farm, that is the creation of the windmill that can generate *electricity* ('Communism', Stalin had said, 'is socialism plus electricity'), could not have been possible without him. He symbolises every socialist's belief that modern economies depend, in the last analysis, on the toil of the individual worker. He is portrayed as a 'Stakhanovite' or Hero of Soviet Labour, after a real or mythical fellow who always worked twice as hard as the official norm. Yet when age and over-work robbed Boxer of his power and usefulness, and he fell ill, his end was just as Old Major had prophesised, he was sent to the knackerman for his flesh to be cut up for dog meat and his bones melted down for glue; but he was sent not by Jones the farmer but by his fellow animals, the pigs. They have no pity. At worst, we think that they know only self-interest; or at best we think that they put the interests of collective survival before individual morality—a common and terrible human dilemma to which only anarchists have an easy answer.

> For the next two days Boxer remained in his stall. The pigs had sent out a large bottle of pink medicine which they had found in the medicine chest in the bathroom, and Clover administered it to Boxer twice a day after meals. In the evenings she lay in his stall and talked to him, while Benjamin kept the flies off him. Boxer professed not to be

sorry for what had happened. If he made a good recovery, he
might expect to live another three years, and he looked
forward to the peaceful days that he would spend in the
corner of the big pasture. It would be the first time that he had
had leisure to study and improve his mind. He intended, he
said, to devote the rest of this life to learning the remaining
twenty-two letters of the alphabet.

However, Benjamin and Clover could only be with Boxer
after working hours, and it was in the middle of the day when
the van came to take away. The animals were all at work
weeding turnips under the supervision of a pig, when they
were astonished to see Benjamin come galloping from the
direction of the farm buildings, braying at the top of his
voice. It was the first time that they had ever seen Benjamin–
indeed, it was the first time that anyone had seen him gallop.
'Quick, quick!' he shouted. 'Come at once! They're taking
Boxer away!' Without waiting for orders from the pig, the
animals broke off work and raced back to the farm building.
Sure enough, there in the yard was a large closed van, drawn
by two horses, with lettering on its side and a sly-looking man
in a low-crowned bowler hat sitting on the driver's seat. And
Boxer's stall was empty.

The animals crowded round the van. 'Good-bye, Boxer!'
they chorused, 'good-bye!'

'Fools! Fools!' shouted Benjamin, prancing round them
and stamping the earth with his small hoofs. 'Fools! Do you
not see that is written on the side of that van?'

That gave the animals pause and there was a hush. Muriel
began to spell out the words. But Benjamin pushed her aside
and in the midst of a deadly silence he read:

' "Alfred Simmonds, Horse Slaughterer and Glue Boiler,
Willingdon. Dealer in Hides and Bone-Meal. Kennels
Supplied." Do you not understand what that means? They
are taking Boxer to the knacker's!'

A cry of horror burst from all the animals. At this moment
the man on the box whipped up his horses and the van
moved out of the yard at a smart trot . . . Too late, someone
thought of racing ahead and shutting the five-barred gate;
but in another moment the van was through it an rapidly
disappearing down the road. Boxer was never seen again.

Thus did the revolution, in the classical phrase, 'devour its own
children.' That is a beautifully written passage. The mixture of
terror and tenderness is effective. The homely language and
incidents obviously have a wider symbolic meaning, but it is not

necessary to tie this meaning too narrowly to events in Soviet history—Stalin's purge of the peasant small-holders, for instance, and the compulsory and bloody collectivisation of agriculture after 1928. The tale of Boxer getting his unjust reward can stand for any group of autocrats betraying the common people on whose backs they have risen to power and enjoy the fruits of privilege. Orwell would have appreciated the irony that *Animal Farm* on account of its Good English is used to teach English in language schools in ever so many African, Central and South American and South East Asian dictatorships, simply because censors see its main meaning, anti-Stalinism or anti-Communism, as its only meaning—which is far from the case. The reader is meant to take seriously the egalitarian and libertarian principles of Old Major's uncorrupted 'Animalism'. Literature may often escape the tunnel-vision of political censors simply because it is, even when seemingly simple, more complex in meaning than it at first appears.

The official version of Boxer's death is that he died happily in hospital urging with his last breath, 'Napoleon is always right'; and that the knackerman's sign was on the van that drove Boxer away only by mistake, an oversight. Such explanations are given in totalitarian or autocratic regimes everytime leaders or celebrities popular with the people are purged.

The last stage of the story moves on remorsely and quickly. The pigs have long ago taken up residence in the farm house and begun acting like humans, just as Stalin began to takeover many of the attributes of Czardom, even of a demigod. They finally reinstitute trade with men, then invite the men to visit them: the party, the drinking, the quarrelling...

> But as the animals outside gazed at the scene, it seemed to them that some strange thing was happening. What was it that had altered in the faces of the pigs? Clover's old dim eyes flitted from one fact to another. Some of them had five chins, some had four, some had three. But what was that seemed to be melting and changing? ... No question, now, what had happened to the faces of the pigs. The creatures outside looked from pig to man, and from man to pig, and from pig to man again; but already it was impossible to say which was which.

The revolution was finally betrayed. 'All power corrupts', wrote Lord Acton, 'and absolute power corrupts absolutely'. And power had replaced ideology: the principles of the animals and the principles of the men (seem as socialism and capitalism originally) had emerged into a common passion for power. Both *Animal Farm* and *Nineteen Eighty-Four* end in transformation scenes: animals and men in the one case, and Winston ceasing to be a human being and loving Big Brother like a Zombie on the other. Both books satirise absolute power—indeed any pretentions to exercise power on behalf of other people without consulting them. ('Teacher *always* knows best'). There are Napoleons and Big Brothers in everyday life, in schools and homes, not merely in party headquarters and on thrones. Indeed despite the very different form that Orwell chooses for the two books, the very different size and the very different tone, they are intellectually fully consistent with each other—so long as one realises that they are both satires of power, not despondent prophecies. *Animal Farm* is the story of the revolution betrayed, and *Nineteen Eighty-Four* the story of what would happen for ever afterwards. The moral is not simply to love liberty and strive for human equality, but it is to rebel long before the Pigs and Big Brother become entrenched in power. The time to do this, Orwell suggests (rather as Roman republicans would have urged), is at the first public breach of principle—the stealing of the milk and apples—not to wait to see if things may get better, or worse. By then it is usually too late.

Publication Difficulties

There is a long cold war among literary critics between those who will look only at the text and those more sociologically minded who insist on looking first at the *context*. I say quite simply, always begin with the text! But to understand a text fully it may be necessary to look at the context—to what issues of the time was it addressed, what did key concepts mean at the time, what assumptions was the author making about his audience (all particularly important in reading satire). So begin with the text, then turn to the context, yet finally come back to the text. Something about the challenge and contentiousness of the text can be appreciated by knowing something of Orwell's great difficulties in getting it published at all—not just politics in literature but the politics of literature, indeed.

Orwell wrote as a socialist, but one of that peculiarly English breed of socialists, secular, left-wing, egalitarian but also libertarian and anti-Communist. If he was not always as anti-Marxist as often supported, yet he was always far more moralistic then typical Marxists and unimpressed by their attempts to show that all individual actions are really class actions, determined by the economic structure of society. In a word, he was a *Tribune* socialist. Indeed by the time he wrote *Animal Farm*, in the winter of 1943-4, he was actually literary editor of the *Tribune* magazine, then edited by

Aneurin Bevan (to be succeeded by Michael Foot). He wrote a
weekly column called 'As I Please' which roamed through politics
and literature, always provocative, thoughtful, often funny matter;
and above all he enjoyed rubbing the fur of his fellow socialists the
wrong way. He seemed to set himself up as a self-appointed
conscience of the Left, spending more time trying to keep the
commitment to liberty of egalitarians up to scratch than in
attacking the enemy. He was almost as difficult to have as a
political friend as an enemy. He was a bit like those lads with loud
voices who stand on the terraces shouting 'What a load of rubbish'
and 'Sell 'em!' and turn out to be, on inquiry, supporters of the
team they thus familiarly address. Many of his fellow-socialists
have wished him to go away and support someone else, being
experts in a tactic called 'Closing the ranks' and 'No criticism in
public'; but Orwell almost made it a test of liberty to force people to
hear things they did not want to hear—such as that the Soviet
Union, 'our glorious war-time ally', was not a model of socialism
but a case of its betrayal or failure.

   Not merely socialists might object to publishing *Animal Farm* in
1944. In early 1944 the Red Army was still locked in uncertain
conflict with the German army. They had defended the homeland,
could they carry the war into Germany itself? In Britian the tense
and tremendous build up for the launching of the Second Front
was underway, amid rumours that Hitler had some kind of secret
weapon in hand (the rockets and guided missiles). The end of the
war was not exactly in sight, but much thought was being given to
post-war reconstruction which needed, to reestablish international
trade and lay the basis for a lasting peace, co-operation between
the allies. This was hardly the time, some 'responsible people'
thought, to launch a bitter attack on a wartime ally, particularly
one so sensitive and so powerful. Leading British Conservative
politicians were then very practical people: they detested the
Soviet system, would try to prevent its extension; but recognised its
realities and instinctively adopted an attitude of 'live and let live',
what people do in their own houses is their own concern.

   So Jonathan Cape, then one of the greatest literary publishers in
London, to whom Orwell sent the manuscript, turned it down on
second thoughts, after initial enthusiasm. Cape explained why in a
letter to Orwell's agent:

                                                    19 June 1944

   My Dear Moore,
   Since our conversation the other morning about George
   Orwell, I have considered the matter carefully and I have
   come to the conclusion that, unless the arrangement that

exists whereby our author has to offer two works of fiction to another publisher can be waived, it would be unwise for us to enter into a contract for his future work. However, it does not seem to me unlikely that some compromise could be reached with Gollancz so far as this matter is concerned.

I mentioned the reaction that I had had from an important official in the Ministry of Information with regard to *Animal Farm*. I must confess that this expression of opinion has given me seriously to think. My reading of the manuscript gave me considerable personal enjoyment and satisfaction, but I can see now that it might be regarded as something which it was highly ill-advised to publish at the present time. If the fable were addressed generally to dictators and dictatorships at large then publication would be all right, but the fable does follow, as I see now, so completely the progress and development of the Russian Soviets and their two dictators, that it can apply only to Russia, to the exclusion of other dictatorships. Another thing: it would be less offensive if the predominant caste in the fable were not pigs. I think the choice of pigs as the ruling caste will no doubt give offence to many people, and particularly to anyone who is a bit touchy, as undoubtedly the Russians are ... I think it is best to send back to you the typescript of *Animal Farm* and let the matter lie on the table as far as we are concerned ...

Yours sincerely,

Jonathan Cape

In the margin of that letter in Orwell's hand, against the reference to pigs, is the terse, rude word 'balls'. When there was no official censorship, Orwell was particularly angry at a publisher putting themselves voluntarily into censorship, as it were, by consulting the Ministry of Information. (Billeted in the Senate House tower of London University—which was to be described in *Nineteen Eighty-Four* as the Ministry of Truth, interiors from the B.B.C., certainly, as often said; but the exterior can only be Senate House in caricature. Thus he worked off old scores).

Next he sent it to the equally prestigious publishing house, Faber & Faber—for once he had no doubt about the merit of his product and at first, for reasons that are not at all clear, forsook his usual non-fiction publisher, Secker & Warburg. T.S. Eliot was a director of Faber's, and to him fell the task of writing one of the most remarkable turndowns ever penned.

... I know that you wanted a quick decision about *Animal Farm* but the minimum is two directors' opinions, and that can't be done under a week. But for the importance of speed,

I should have asked the Chairman to look as it as well. But the other director is in agreement with me on the main points. We agree it is a distinguished piece of writing; that the fable is very skilfully handled, and that the narrative keeps one's interest on its own plane—and that is something very few authors have achieved since Gulliver.

On the other hand, we have no conviction (and I am sure none of the other directors would have) that this is the right point of view from which to criticise the political situation at the present time. It is certainly the duty of any publishing firm which pretends to other interests and motives than mere commercial prosperity, to publish books which go against the current of the moment; but in each instance that demands that at least one member of the firm should have the conviction that this is the thing that needs saying at the moment. I can't see any reason of prudence or caution to prevent anybody from publishing this book—if he believed in what it stands for.

Now I think my own dissatisfaction with this apologue is that the effect is simply one of negation. It ought to excite some sympathy with what the author wants, as well as sympathy with his objections to something: and the positive point of view, which I take to be generally Trotskyite, is not convincing. I think you split your vote, without getting any compensation strong adhesion from either party—i.e., those who criticise Russian tendencies from the point of view of a purer communism and those who, from a very different point of view, are alarmed about the future of small nations. And after all, your pigs are far more intelligent that the other animals and therefore the best qualified to run the farm—in fact, there couldn't have been an *Animal Farm* at all without them: so that what was needed (someone might argue) was not more communism but more public-spirited pigs.

I am very sorry because whoever published this will naturally have the opportunity of publishing your future work; and I have a regard for your work, because it is good writing of fundamental integrity . . .

Now it is fair to enough for any publisher with a political conviction not to want to publish books plainly of another conviction (Eliot also said that Orwell's book seemed written from a 'Trotskyite' perspective—perhaps the only label that Elio could find for a revolutionary Left-winger who was not a Communist). But from a literary point of view to compare a book favourably to Swift's *Gulliver* (as did many reviewers when it at last appeared) and then not to publish it, is fairly odd, shows that political judgements can be very strong even among the nominally literary.

The publisher of Orwell's fiction and all his early books, Victor Gollancz, had also turned it down. But Orwell had wanted him to turn it down. As he was bound by contract, he sent it to Gollancz with a short note attached that he was sure he wouldn't like it, since it was 'rude to your friend Stalin'. Gollancz replied indignantly that he was not a fellow traveller, but then almost overnight read it and returned it with a short note saying that Orwell was right, he couldn't possibly publish it. Afterwards Gollancz was to say that he never regretted the decision, even though had he published *Animal Farm* he would also have had *Nineteen Eighty-Four* and between them could have become rich.

Then Orwell tried to borrow money from his friend David Astor to publish it himself as a pamphlet at two shillings. Astor dissuaded him. But Orwell then took up the offer of Paul Potts, a Canadian poet living in London who sold broadsheets of his own poetry in pubs and occasionally published booklets. Paul Potts wrote in his strange autobiographical essays, *Dante Called Me Beatrice*:

> At one point I nearly became the publisher of *Animal Farm* which only means that we were going to bring it out ourselves. Orwell was going to pay the printer using the paper to which the Whitman Press (his broadsheets) was entitled. We had actually started to do so. I had been down to Bedford with manuscript to see the printer twice. The birthplace of John Bunyan seemed like a happy omen. Orwell had talked about adding a Preface to it on the freedom of the Press.

Either few people read Potts or nobody believed a poet. But he was right. In 1972 this lost Preface, called indeed 'The Freedom of the Press', was found and published (*Times Literary Supplement,* 15 September, 1972).

In it Orwell attacked violently the attitudes of the publishers who had turned down the book. No official censorship could have done worse, he said, than what they did themselves.

> ... But now to come back to this book of mine. The reaction towards it of most English intellectuals will be quite simple: 'It oughtn't to have been published'. Naturally, those reviewers who understand the art of denigration will not attack it on political grounds but on literary ones. They will say that it is a dull, silly book and a disgraceful waste of paper. This may well be true, but it is obviously not the whole of the story. One does not say that a book 'ought not to have been published' merely because it is a bad book. After all,

acres of rubbish are printed daily and no one bothers. The English intelligentsia, or most of them, will object to this book because it traduces their Leader and (as they see it) does harm to the cause of progress. If it did the opposite they would have nothing to say against it, even if its literary faults were ten times as glaring as they are. The success of, for instance, the Left Book Club over a period of four or five years shows how willing they are to tolerate both scurrility and slipshod writing, provided that it tells them what they want to hear.

The issue involved here is quite a simple one: Is every opinion, however unpopular—however foolish, even—entitled to a hearing? Put it in that form and nearly any English intellectual will feel that he ought to say 'Yes'. But give it a concrete shape, and ask, 'How about an attack on Stalin? Is *that* entitled to a hearing?' and the answer more often than not will be 'No'. In that case the current orthodoxy happens to be challenged, and so the principle of free speech lapses. Now, when one demands liberty of speech and of the press, one is not demanding absolute liberty. There always must be, or at any rate there always will be, some degree of censorship, so long as organised societies endure. But freedom, as Rosa Luxemburg said, is 'freedom for the other fellow'.

For a quite a decade past I have believed that the existing Russian regime is a mainly evil thing, and I claim the right to say so, in spite of the fact that we are allies with the USSR in a war which I want to see won. If I had to choose a text to justify myself, I should choose the line from Milton:

'By the known rules of ancient liberty'.

The word *ancient* emphasises the fact that intellectual freedom is a deep-rooted tradition without which our characteristic western culture could only doubtfully exist. From that tradition many of our intellectuals are visibly turning away. They have accepted the principle that a book should be published or suppressed, praised or damned, not on its merits but according to political expediency. And others who do not actually hold this view assent to it from sheer cowardice. An example of this is the failure of the numerous and vocal English pacifists to raise their voices against the prevalent worship of Russian militarism. According to these pacifists, all violence is evil, and they have urged us at every stage of the war to give in or at least to make a compromise peace. But how many of them have ever suggested that war is also evil when it is waged by the Red Army? Apparently the Russians have a right to defend themselves, whereas for us to do is a deadly sin. One can only explain this contradiction in one way: that is, by a cowardly desire to keep in with the bulk of the intelligentsia, whose patriotism is directed towards the USSR rather than towards Britain.

I know that the English intelligentsia have plenty of reason for their timidity and dishonesty, indeed I know by heart the arguments by which they justify themselves. But at least let us have no more nonsense about defending liberty against Fascism. If liberty means anything at all it means the right to tell people what they do not want to hear. The common people still vaguely subscribe to that doctrine and act on it. In our country–it is not the same in all countries: it was not so in Republican France, and it is not so in the United States today–it is the liberals who fear liberty and the intellectuals who want to do dirt on the intellect: it is to draw attention to that fact that I have written this preface.

Perhaps it is as well that this 'Preface' was not published with the book. It sounded intemperate and would have spoiled the satiric pretence of the sub-title (so often omitted): 'A Fairy Story'. And in any case, it was not needed. He went to Fredric Warburg of Secker & Warburg. Warburg afterwards would say that Orwell had brought it to him first, but that he had used up all his paper ration. This sounds unlikely. But at any rate when Orwell went back to him, he had paper and was personally eager, not without some dissent in his firm, to publish the book. But it did not appear until 17 August, 1945, three months after the end of the ar in Europe, two days after the Japanese capitulated following Hiroshima, and also after the British General Election. Orwell believed (without any evidence) that his *Tribune* colleagues had put pressure on Warburg not to publish before the General Election for fear of damaging Labour. This is probably untrue, but the time it spent in the press was extraordinarily long for those days, especially for such a short book. After the three or four turndowns, small wonder that Orwell seemed slightly paranoid about the book's progress and reception.

Reviewers were greatly divided about its merits, as well as its political relevance and timelessness. *The Times Literary Supplement* (25 August 1945) reviewed it as if he was a socialist who had blurted out something really rather Tory:

Animals, as Swift well knew, make admirable interpreters of the satiric intention, and Mr George Orwell has turned his farm into a persuasive demonstration of the peculiar trick which the whip wrested from the hands of a tyrant has of turning itself into a lash of scorpions and attaching itself to a new authority.

Labour Action of New York had this to say (30 September, 1946):

When one has read the book, he is still at a loss as to precisely how the whole thing is meant, what he is to understand by it all. It lies in the general confusion of Orwell, and we believe in the fact that he really does not himself know what to conclude from his tale, therefore his inability to write a true parable. Actually, what is Orwell saying? Many have interpreted it as a rejection of the conception that it is possible to build a socialist, egalitarian community in this world: that the degeneration into Napoleon/Stalin's pig-collective state was a natural and inevitable process.

But the British anarchists had praised it to the skys in their *Freedom* (25 August, 1945):

It is related of Jonathan Swift that, at the end of his life, on being handed a copy of the 'Tale of a Tub' he remarked, 'Good God! What a genius I had when I wrote that book'. Likewise I am prepared to claim in behalf of Mr Orwell's *Animal Farm* that it is of far greater significance than its unassuming title would suggest. *Animal Farm* may well prove to be an excellent First Primer in the hands of the Political Child of our Times, the member of any one of Father Stalin's Innocents' Clubs; the moral is grim–one which anarchists have been repeating to a hitherto deaf world for many decades: power corrupts all who succeed in achieving it, and no one with power in his hands escapes its taint.

The Adelphi in London looked down its nose at him (January 1946):

Orwell seems to have constructed a Disney piece where animals make and eventually betray a revolution, so that he can stress that deeds are often less commendable than good intentions. The analogies are naive. For all Orwell's sincerity, this allegory misses the mark. It falls short of great literature and may not survive much longer than its topical value and the polemic it has evoked.

But a Left-wing journal in New York, *New Leader* (September 1946) must have said what Orwell wanted to hear:

Orwell cast this book into the form of a fable because temperamentally he is not one just to make a diatribe against the Soviet Union. His message is so much larger than of the present ruler of that unhappy land and yet very simple—

larger because it involves other lands and simpler because it involves the basic truths about democracy. He possessed that first requisite of the satirist, a positive point of view from which to criticise.

The British Communist *Daily Worker* kept on coming back to the attack. On 3 January 1947 it noted that: 'In response to a magnificent gesture by the Soviet Union, Lord Montgomery is going there as a guest of the Red Army. Is this why the Third Programme is busily preparing to broadcast that anti-Soviet farrago: George Orwell's *Animal Farm?*'

Whatever the reviewers thought of it, the book was an instant and astonishing success. In March 1946, Orwell could write to a friend: 'a month or two back, the Queen sent to Warburg's for a copy, and as there was not a single one left, the Royal Messenger had to go down to the Anarchist Bookshop for a copy. However, now a second edition of 10,000 has come out, also a lot of translations are being done.'

Its success was no mere accident, simply a bye-product of some other activity or a piece of lucky timing. In an article called 'Why I Write', published in 1946, Orwell reflected on his own work:

What I have most wanted to do throughout the past ten years is to make political writing into an art. My starting point is always a feeling of partisanship, a sense of injustice. When I sit down to write a book, I do not say to myself, 'I am going to produce a work of art'. I write it because there is some lie that I want to expose, some facts to which I want to draw attention, and my initial concern is to get a hearing. But I could not do the work of writing a book, or even a long magazine article, if it were not also an aesthetic experience. Anyone who cares to examine my work will see that even when it is downright propaganda it contains much that a full-time politician would consider irrelevant. I am not able, and I do not want, completely to abandon the world-view that I acquired in childhood. So long as I remain alive and well I shall continue to feel strongly about prose style, to love the surface of the earth, and to take pleasure in solid objects and scraps of useless information. It is no use trying to suppress that side of myself.

The job is to reconcile my ingrained likes and dislikes with the essentially public, non-individual activities that this age forces on all of us . . . *Animal Farm* was the first book in which I tried, with full consciousness of what I was doing, to fuse political purpose and artistic purpose into one whole. I have not written a novel for seven years, but I hope to write another fairly soon. It is bound to be a failure, every book is a failure, but I know with some clarity what kind of book I want to write.

Animal Farm brought Orwell fame, money and constant demands to write. But by then this rugged, civilised, angry, kindly, secretive, friendly, socialistic, traditional, very paradoxical man had retired to a bleak, small farm on the northern tip of the isolated island of Jura in the Hebrides: to devote himself to writing *Nineteen Eighty-Four* which he saw as a major work and had begun to plan even before he wrote *Animal farm*. And he had not long to live. His recurrent tuberculosis grew worse. Perhaps he would have lived a bit longer had it not been for the physical as much as the mental effort of writing *Nineteen Eighty-Four*. He regarded it as a warning of what could happen not a prophecy of what would happen; and as a satire on the power hungry, not a cry of despair; he is mocking all the Big Brothers of this world, not accepting their inevitability. He dictated some angry rebuttals late in 1947 from what was, in hindsight, to prove his death bed, attacking reviewers who had (especially in the United States) hailed it as a repudiation of all possible kinds of socialism—just as some 'thickheads', as he said to a friend, had read *Animal Farm* as anti-socialist, as a lament for the old order rather than a lament for socialism betrayed. As he wrote in his 'Why I Write' of 1946: Every line of serious work that I have written since the Spanish War has been written, directly or indirectly, *against* totalitarianism and *for* democratic Socialism, as I understand it.'

And with what exact pedantry did Orwell write a lower-case 'd' and an upper-case 'S'—a detail missed in some slovenly reprints. Among the very last words he scribbled in his hospital notebook was the strange epigram: 'At fifty everyone has the face he deserves'. And talking of faces, he had written ten years before in his famous essay on Dickens a description of Dickens which has often, and understandably, been taken as a self-portrait:

I see a face which is not quite the face of Dickens' photgraphs, though it resembles it. It is the face of a man of about forty, with a small beard and a high colour. He is laughing, with a touch of anger in his laughter, but no triumph, no malignity. It is the face of a man who is always fighting against something, but who fights in the open and is not frightened, the face of a man who is *generously angry*—in other words, òf a nineteenth-century liberal, a free intelligence, a type hated with equal hatred by all the smelly little orthodoxies which are now contending for our souls.

How can *Animal Farm* be read in any other way than would follow the sincerity of the words Orwell puts into Old Major's wide mouth?

> That is my message to you, comrades: 'Rebellion'. I do not know when the Rebellion will come, it might be in a week or in a hundred years, but I know, as surely as I see this straw beneath my feet, that sooner or later justice will be done. Fix your eyes on that, comrades, throughout the short remainder of your lives.' And above all, pass on this message of mine to those who come after you, so that future generations sh.all carry on the struggle until it is victorious.

Literature and writing are, however, curious things. Imagination, in the hands of a great writer, does not run riot, but it is hard to control strictly. And satires can be read rather differently according to the different assumptions of different audiences, and according to their degree of knowledge or ignorance of what the tongue-in-cheek author really believes in.

A fellow author and critic, anarchist indeed, Herbert Read, had written to him:

> Thank you very much indeed for *Animal Farm*. I read it through at a sitting with enormous enjoyment. My boy of seven and a half then spotted it, and I tried Chapter One on him. He has insisted on my reading it, chapter by chapter, every evening since, and he enjoys it innocently as much as I enjoy it maliciously. It thus stands the test that only classics of satire like *Gulliver* survive.
>
> What seems to me to be its rare quality is its completeness. The cap fits all round the head: everything is there and yet there is no forcing of the story—it is all completely natural and inevitable. I do most heartily congratulate you.

So here are two levels of meaning aptly described, both compatible with the text. But also levels of misunderstanding. His friend, the poet William Empson, wrote to him a more worried but also wise letter:

> My Dear George,
> Thanks very much for giving me *Animal Farm*—it is a most impressive object, with the range of feeling and the economy of method, and the beautiful limpid prose style. I read it with great excitement. And then, thinking it over, and especially on showing it to other people, one realises that the danger of this kind of perfection is that it means very different things to different readers. Our Mr Julian [his son] the child Tory was delighted with it; he said it was very strong Tory propaganda.

Your point of view of course is that the animals ought to have gone on sharing Animal Farm. But the effect of the farmyard, with its unescapable racial differences, is to suggest that the Russian scene had unescapable social differences too—so the metaphor suggests that the Russian revolution was always a pathetically impossible attempt. To be sure, this is denied by the story because the pigs can turn into men, but the story is far from making one feel that any of the other animals could have turned into men...

I certainly don't mean that that is a fault in the allegory; it is a form that has to be set down and allowed to grow like a separate creature, and I think you let it do that with honesty and restraint. But I thought it worth warning you (while thanking you very heartily) that you must expect to be 'misunderstood' on a large scale about this book; it is a form that inherently means more than the author means, when it is handled sufficiently well.

Bill Empson

So in the end any work of literature and imagination must be open-ended and ambiguous to some degree.

The Longman's school text of *Animal Farm* has an introduction in which the editor states unequivocally that the text seeks to prove that all revolutions are incompatible with liberty. And in an appendix specimen examination questions invite the student to show how this is so. For myself, I think this interpretation is wrong, both by Orwell's known intentions and the text itself (though as a general point of principle, the argument is, of course, open). But such a misinterpretation, if such it is, matters far less than the incitement to teach such a text as if there is only one true possible meaning. This demeans both literature and politics. Literature has a great political message even when its context is not explicitly political: there is always more than one way from A to B, even when you want to get to B and think you are for sure at A. Orwell was a political writer, indeed; but an open-minded and speculative writer. Imagination and politics are not antithetical, politics needs imagination and literature cannot avoid politics—dilemmas as well as values.

In a rich text people can discover and stress different things. Sir Peter Hall's National Theatre production seems to stress less the Communist versus democratic Socialist debate than a concept of defending 'the green' of nature and the countryside against man. Much of this is in Adrian Mitchell's lyrics, far less in Orwell's words. They have used the text to preach a contemporary environmentalist, almost Green Party, sermon. There is *something* of this in Orwell's text, I grant, although I read it very differently to them. But it is infinitely discussable, and any work of art, however seeming simple, is more complex than it looks; and will carry different meanings to different generations, especially when translated from the printed page to the theatre. All the commercial 'cribs' and Readers' Guides to *Animal farm* try to close down and tightly define true meanings (differing true meanings, usually). I hope I have, like a good teacher, opened up dilemmas, which seems to me one of the purposes of literature as well as education.

Thirteen

Orwell and English Socialism

A version of this was delivered as, rather oddly, the Second Marx Memorial Lecture in Sheffield City Hall, 1984. There is the text as printed in Peter Buitenhuis, ed, *George Orwell: a reassessment* (Macmillan, London: 1988)

In 1946 in the essay 'Why I Write' Orwell wrote: 'What I have most wanted to do throughout the past ten years is to make political writing into an art.' And he might well have added into a popular art, for I believe that he developed his famous clear, plain, simple, colloquial and forceful style precisely in order to reach what he was more apt to call 'the common man' than the working class. His debt to Swift has often been noted, especially for the strategies of his two major satires, but his deliberate choice of rhetoric, his adopted style and conscious persona as a writer, may owe more to Daniel Defoe, and he wrote for much the same kind of audience.

Orwell's pre-war novels had all been written to catch the attention of the public for whom Charles Dickens and H.G. Wells had written, a public composed of both working class and lower middle class who used and depended upon the free public library and had, like Orwell himself, missed the over-rated advantages of full-time higher education. From his own experience he deeply believed in the potential moral superiority of the self-taught over the institutionally educated (there is at least this parallel between Orwell and Rousseau!). But as his sales showed, he singularly failed to reach this audience until he became literary editor and a columnist for the left-wing newspaper *Tribune*, which enjoyed a large readership, and until he wrote *Animal Farm* and *Nineteen Eighty-Four*. Yet their very success played a trick with his reputation. Many on the Left held that it is never timely to tell salutory truths about the home team. Many on the Right accepted his fierce libertarianism but either ignored his egalitarianism or dismissed it as silly and superficial. And perhaps ordinary readers who did not know where Orwell stood already might be forgiven for thinking that the two satires are just about the Soviet Union and not also all forms of power hunger and rational hierarchy. Indeed I have met whole school classes who regularly skip

'Goldstein's testimony' and so are not aware that at the heart of *Nineteen Eighty-Four* is a satire on the useless manufacture of atomic warheads: they are manufactured, remember, simply to 'burn off surplus value' which otherwise would be spent on welfare, thus undermining the basic conditions of an hierachial society.

In that same essay, 'Why I Write', he remarked that 'every line of serious work that I have written since 1936 has been written, directly or indirectly, against totalitarianism and for democratic Socialism, as I understand it.' The last phrase, whether honest or evasive, is not accidental. I want to try to clarify what he did understand it to be. And I will conclude that, if we ignore some famous detractors on the Left and some infamous bodysnatchers on the Right, while charitably allowing that he did say some intemperate and ill-defined things in the heat of polemic and that he was not a systematic political thinker (he was a writer), so that he is open to honest misunderstanding (it has not always been honest) if one goes into him only on a particular occasion or at a particular stage of his rapid but by no means unilinear development, yet that at the end of the day he is a pretty typical English Left-wing socialist in the tradition of Morris, Blatchford, Carpenter, Cole, Tawney, Laski, Bevan and Foot, and quite as influential as the last three. I say 'English socialism' for once, not 'British' for there is in 'Scottish democracy' a harsher republican and populist tradition, and in Welsh socialism, however secular it tries to be as on the rhetoric of Aneurin Bevan and his disciple, Neil Kinnock, the language of evangelism and 'New Jerusalem' keeps breaking through. '*Tribune* socialism' might convey more: egalitarian, libertarian, environmental, individualistic in practice if not in theory, highly principled but somehow untheoretical, or if tinged with Marxism, then only in its broadest and most libertarian forms, and very much divided among itself about distrust of using the central state—a municipal social and quasi-communitarian strand—and a desire to nationalise and control 'the commanding heights' of industry.

Orwell's path towards socialism was slow and unsure—as Peter Sedgwick pointed out in an essay of 1969 in the journal *International Socialist* which did much to restore Orwell's image among the new Left. His first published novel, *Burmese Days*, is certainly anti-imperialist.

> You see louts straight from school kicking grey-haired servants. The time comes when you burn with hatred of your own countrymen, when you long for a native rising to drown their Empire in blood. And in this there is nothing

honourable, hardly even any sincerity . . . You are a creature
of the despotism, a pukka sahib, tied tighter than a monk or a
savage to an unbreakable system of tabus.[1]
But beware of hindsight and myopia. Others besides socialists
have hated imperialism. At this time, Orwell was aware of socialist
doctrines but did not claim to be a socialist. When shortly after
leaving Burma another young writer asked him sententiously
'where he stood', Orwell replied that he was a 'Tory anarchist'.
There is more in this than a joke. Some old high Tories (or 'Little
Englanders') took their individualism so seriously that they held
strong views against imposing moral and cultural values on
others. Almost as much as Mr Doolittle, they disliked middle class
morality, especially its imposition. They could accept the military
necessity of Empire, but everywhere favoured 'indirect rule',
respecting, often studying and preserving native cultures. Some of
them even 'went native', at least lived between two worlds. They
opposed the missionaries, European secondary education and the
moral prejudices of white wives. They had no hope or desire for
progress, believing the subject peoples were incapable of self-
government, but they were tolerant and indulgent.

Even *Down and Out in Paris and London* is not specifically
socialist. Its tone is melancholy and descriptive. Orwell simply
went among tramps to see if we treated our natives as we treated
those in the Empire, and on the whole he concluded that we did. It
is not the book of a stirrer, as yet, rather of—in Victor Pritchett's
famous phrase—'a man who went native in his own country.' But it
meant that when the time came when he did speak as a socialist, he
knew more about poverty than most middle class socialists.

When Orwell first declares clearly that he is a socialist, in *The
Road to Wigan Pier*, he straight away adopts his persona of the
teller of home truths. He attacks socialists for worshipping the
Soviet Union simply on account of its power and for allowing the
movement to become invested with 'cranks'. It would be a thin-
skinned comrade who could not laugh at the comic exaggeration
of the famous passage: 'One sometimes gets the impression that
the mere words 'Socialism' and 'Communism' draw towards them
with magnetic force every fruit-juice drinker, nudist, sandal-
wearer, sex-maniac, Quaker, 'Nature Cure' quack, pacifist and
feminist in England . . .' But one would have to be abnormally
thick-skinned not to take offence at the picture of those who come
'flocking towards the smell of "progress" like bluebottles to a dead
cat.'[2] The voice of the supporter on the terraces cries, 'What a load
of rubbish! Sell 'em!' Orwell's tone is uncertain at times. See how a
rather laboured sarcasm precedes a noble peroration:

It is usual to speak of the Fascist objective as the 'beehive state', which does a grave injustice to bees. A world of rabbits ruled by stoats is nearer the mark. It is against this beastly possibility that we have to combine. The only thing for which we can combine is the underlying ideal of Socialism; justice and liberty. It is almost completely forgotten. It has been buried beneath layer after layer of doctrinaire prigishness, party squabbles and half-baked 'progressivism' until it is like a diamond hidden under a mountain of dung. The job of the Socialist is to get it out again. Justice and liberty! *Those* are the words that have got to ring like a bugle across the world.[3]

Indeed, but one does not have to be a very hard dialectician to ask quite what these two words mean. And if one must rant and bang the portable, what is wrong with good old 'Liberty, Equality, Fraternity'?[4] But he does make a very serious point about the image of Socialism in relation to those who need to be won over.

The Road to Wigan Pier is his remorselessly honest account of class relationships not an abstract account, but one disturbingly specific. He was by birth, he said, a member of 'the lower-upper middle class' which was, he helpfully explained, 'the upper middle class without money'. They were a special section of the middle class, and in his opinion a specially dangerous one. He tells us that he was brought up to believe that 'the lower classes smell' and he gives that as an example of a belief, however false one knows it to be, that it is hard to be sure, if one is honest, that one can never fully shake off. He takes for granted that socialism aims at a classless society, but he warns us, in a tone of comic pessimism, that it is not easy to achieve—there is much self-deception and what we would now call 'tokenism'.

> Many people . . . imagine that they can abolish class distinctions without making any uncomfortable change in their own habits and 'ideology'. Hence the eager class-breaking activities which one can see in progress on all sides. Everywhere there are people of good will who quite honestly believe that they are working for the overthrow of class-distinction. The middle class socialist enthuses over the proletariat and runs 'summer schools' where the proletarian and the repentant bourgeois are supposed to fall upon one another's necks and be brothers for ever; and the bourgeois visitors come away saying how wonderful and inspiring it all has been (the proletarian ones come away saying something

different). And there is the outer-suburban creeping Jesus, a
hangover from the William Morris period, but still surprisingly common, who goes about saying 'Why must we
level *down*? Why not level *up*?' and proposes to level the
working class 'up' (up to his standard) by means of hygiene,
fruit-juice, birth-control, poetry, etc. Even the Duke of York
(now King George VI) runs a yearly camp where public
schoolboys and boys from the slums are supposed to mix on
exactly equal terms, and do mix for the time being, rather like
animals in one of those 'Happy Family' cages where a dog, a
cat, two ferrets, a rabbit and three canaries preserve an armed
truce while the showman's eye is one of them.[5]

Note that the humour only consists in its being true and specific in
contexts usually inhabited by abstract generalisations—instead of
the customary 'alliance of workers by hand and workers by brain'
we have the middle class socialists meeting the workers most
intensely at—where else?—summer schools.

What he actually argues for is a most interesting sociological
theory, that a working class movement depends for its leadership
upon members of the lower middle class, or what he sometimes
calls 'the sinking middle class' or the 'rising working class' (my
hypothetical class of the public library educated). This class must
be wooed not alienated. This class, he says, could turn to Fascism,
or to Socialism: it is essential 'for the moment . . . to go easy and
not frighten more people than can be helped.' Perhaps it is just an
urban version of the old myth of the yeomanry beloved of the
Victorian radicals and the early socialists; but it also anticipates a
key concept in post-war historical and sociological accounts of the
rise of European Fascism and Nazism. In specific terms he looks
to the kind of people who make the corporals and the sergeants,
the ward secretaries and the shop stewards, neither the rankers by
themselves, nor the traditional officers, nor renegade gentlemen
adventurers like himself. Several times he talks about the growth
of a new 'intermediate class'.

A fierce egalitarianism only emerges in *Homage to Catalonia*, his
account of what happened when he went to Spain to fight Fascism
and save the Republic. 'I have seen wonderful things and at last
really believe in Socialism, which I never did before.' The stress in
this sentence must be on 'really' and on 'believe', as if before he
saw the anarchist and the independent Marxist militias (the quasi-
Trotskyist P.O.U.M.) in Catalonia, his socialism had been celebral
or intellectual, perhaps even just anti-capitalist and little else: the
Catalans had made him feel a socialist and convinced him that an
egalitarian society was possible. 'The essential point of the system',

he recalled, 'was social equality between officers and men. Everyone ... mingled on terms of complete equality ... Of course there was not perfect equality, but there was a nearer approach to it than I had ever seen or than I would have thought conceivable in time of war ... I was breathing the air of equality, and', he admitted, 'I was simple enought to imagine that it existed all over Spain. I did not realise that more or less by chance I was isolated among the most revolutionary section of the Spanish working class.'[6] There was a deep feeling for justice in *The Road to Wigan Pier*, only the egalitarianism was lacking. But egalitarianism by itself is not English socialism, nor necessarily democratic. The values of *moral individualism* and *honesty* transfuse both books. It was he who told us in *The Road to Wigan Pier*, not his critics, 'that you do not solve the class problem by making friends with tramps', and that at that time 'I had carried my hatred of oppression to extraordinary lengths. At that time failure seemed to me the only virtue'; and that it took him a long time to get away from 'the simple theory that the oppressed are always right and the oppressor always wrong.' Some of us never have. How much the public might respond to such shattering honesty from party leaders rather than so many easy lies, half-truths and evasions.

Another characteristic of English socialism that is so Orwell-like is the attempt to strike a balance between the interests of humanity in nature and in manufacture, or between town and country. His novel of 1939, *Coming Up For Air,* shows a warm love of a traditional England of the 1900s that is being gradually destroyed by urban development, and will shortly be utterly destroyed by the bombing planes in a meaningless war—he links two themes that come together today in the strange alliance between British environmentalists and the CND. But Orwell is careful not to resurrect the pastoral utopianism of William Morris. Indeed he mocks it. His character 'George Bowling' has an excess of nostalgia which pulls him backwards from what he dimly senses needs to be done. Orwell sees that industry alone can create the higher standard of living needed for the health and well-being of the people, not simply for the meaningless accumulation of goods or 'the worship of the money god'. He seeks some balance, which is sensible if banal: the kind of thinking that lay behind the Town and Country Planning Act of 1947, to control the growth of housing and industrial.

But beneath this lies something deeper. In his own lifestyle Orwell clearly shows that he believes that a person who loses touch with the activities and rhymes of the countryside becomes less human. In the novel *Nineteen Eighty-Four* there is the vision of the 'golden country', but also the symbol of the final torture chamber as the place where it is never dark. Mankind, he is saying, cannot live at extremes of light or dark, goodness or evil, nor all in the natural country nor all in the built town. This believe that there is something deeply moral in attachment, however part-time, to the land, even minimally to gardening or allotments, is a characteristic both of Orwell and English socialism. Every working man wanted a small house of his own with a patch of land. Orwell sensed a deep cultural dislike for purely urban, terrace or apartment living. And he had an almost pietistic love of ordinary solid things and actions, of natural substances and do-it-yourself.

Orwell's experience in Spain led him to join the Independent Labour Party. He later wrote that a writer 'cannot be a loyal member of a political party'—the stress must have been on 'loyal'. The I.L.P. regarded itself as to the Left of the Labour Party, an arguable proposition domestically, depending on which section of the Labour Party one considered; but in foreign policy the difference was clear. The I.L.P. in foreign affairs had a position hard to distinguish from that of Trotsky. A war was coming, an imperialistic war, British, French and German rivalry for the control of markets. As late as July 1939 Orwell published an article with the sardonic title, 'Not Counting Niggers', which mocked the preparations for war, a war that was purely in the interests of the governing class, and reminded readers 'that the overwhelming bulk of the British proletariat does not live in Britain, but in Asia and Africa.' They are never counted. 'Nothing is likely to save us except the emergence in the next two years of a real mass party', he asserted, 'whose first pledges are to refuse war and right imperial injustice.' He adopted the stance of a revolutionary socialist opposed to all capitalist wars.

When the war broke out, he changed his mind almost overnight. Chamberlain's England, even, was preferable to Nazi Germany and Nazi conquest. And, furthermore, the war could only be won if there was a social and political revolution. He argued in *The Lion and Unicorn* that not merely had the old order got us into this Dunkirk mess, but that it had to be swept away if the country was to survive. He convinced himself, for a while, that 'the English revolution started several years ago, and it began to gather momentum when the troops came back from Dunkirk'.[7] He briskly synthesised his Catalan revolutionary fervour with a Left-wing version of civic patriotism.

Patriotism has nothing to do with conservativism. It is
devotion to something that is changing but is felt to be
mystically the same ... To be loyal both to Chamberlain's
England and to the England of tomorrow might seem an
impossibility, if one did not know it to be an everyday
phenomenon. Only revolution can save England, that has
been obvious for years, but now the revolution has started
and it may proceed quite quickly if only we can keep Hitler
out. Within two years, maybe a year, if only we can hang on,
we shall see changes that will surprise the idiots who have no
foresight. I dare say the London gutters will have to run with
blood. All right, let them, if it is necessary. But when the red
militias are billeted in the Ritz I shall still feel that the
England I was taught to love so long ago and for such
different reasons is still persisting.[8]

Patriotism and traditionalism are characteristics of English
socialists. Their world did not begin in 1789 and 1917 but in 'the
long revolution' of the peasant revolts, the English Civil War,
agrarian riots and Chartism. The proles in Oceania, it will be
remembered, ' ... had stayed human. They had not became
hardened inside. They had held onto the primitive emotions
which he himself had to relearn by conscious effort.' Indeed
Orwell implies, both in *The Lion* ... and in *Nineteen Eighty-Four*,
that the common people had retained a sociability, a mutual
helpfulness or 'decency' which the middle classes, power hungry
and economically competitive, rivalling each other, had lost. True
individualism is mutual recognition or sociability, not competitive.

The image of the family as the primary social group is thus
important to Orwell. He cannot begin to imagine why some way-
out socialist theorists 'reject' the family as inherently inegalitarian.
Orwell sees it as a natural institution and as the source of morality
and sociability—hence 'the Party' in 1984 has to destroy the family
and get children to denounce parents in order to remove the very
source of individuality. But families are not all of a kind.
'[England] is a family in which the young are generally thwarted
and most of the power is in the hands of irresponsible uncles and
bedridden aunts. Still, it is a family. It has its private language and
its common memories', he says, 'and at the approach of an enemy,
it closes its ranks. A family with the wrong members in control—
that is, perhaps, as near as one can come to describing England in
a phrase.'[9]

How a writer rather than a theorist works can be seen when,
almost as an aside in a typical peroration in *The Lion* ... he

advances a most challenging social theory which found academic support only long after the end of the war.

> The inefficiency of private capitalism has been proved all over Europe. Its unjustice has been proved in the East End of London. Patriotism, against which the Socialists fought so long, has become a tremendous lever in their hands. People who at any other time would cling like glue to their miserable scraps of privilege, will surrender them fast enough when their country is in danger. War is the greatest of all agents of change. It speeds up all processes, wipes out major distractions, brings realities to the surface. Above all war brings it home to the individual that he is not altogether an individual.[10]

'War is the greatest of all agents of social change', a dark thought for a socialist; but most post-war histories of the British welfare state, while they trace the ideas back much earlier, see its actual emergence in the conditions of the war not simply in the post-war legislation. Orwell was original and thoughtful, but not a systematic theorist; yet he throws out, almost as asides, more important, speculative generalisations, of that kind, than many famous social theorists ever possessed.

He is fully aware that his advocacy of revolution, on the one hand, and of traditional values on the other, appear to some as contradictory. He is fully aware of the Marxist position, that all values are a product of bourgeois property relations; but regards it as so foolish as to be unworthy of explicit refutation. He adopts the position, with an almost perverse commonsense, that we know instinctively what values to pursue, liberty, equality and fraternity (or 'decency' or sociability). They have been known in the past, but suppressed in extent by greed and property relations: they do not need to be 'subsumed' or 'transformed', but simply made general and liberated from constraints.

> An English Socialist government will transform the nation from top to bottom, but it will still bear all over it the unmistakable marks of our own civilization ...
>
> It will not be doctrinaire, nor even logical. It will abolish the House of Lords, but quite probably will not abolish the Monarchy. It will leave anachronisms and loose ends everywhere ... It will not set up any explicit class dictatorship. It will group itself around the old Labour Party and its mass following will be in the Trade Unions, but it will draw into it most of the middle class and many of the younger sons of the bourgeoise. Most of its directing brains will come from the new indeterminate class of skilled workers, technical

experts, airmen, scientists, architects and journalists, the people who feel at home in the radio and ferro-concrete age. But it will never loose touch with the tradition of compromise and the belief in a law that is above the State. It will shoot traitors, but it will give them a solemn trial beforehand and occasionally it will acquit them. It will crush any open revolt promptly and cruelly, but it will interfere very little with the spoken and written word... It will show a power of assimilating the past which will shock foreign observers and sometimes make them doubt whether any revolution has happened.

But all the same it will have done the essential thing. It will have nationalised industry, scaled down incomes, set up a classless education system.[11]

Orwell never changed his values after 1936. There is no bio-graphical evidence that his socialism waned; *Animal Farm* is a democratic socialist polemic against Soviet Communism; and *Nineteen Eighty-Four*, when read as a Swiftian satire, is compatible with this same position. Orwell had consistently said, since his first commitment in *The Road to Wigan Pier,* that totalitarianism could come from the Left as well as the Right. This does not make him anti-socialist, it makes him anti-Communist. But what did change, between the writing of *The Lion and the Unicorn* and the publication of *Animal Farm*, was the wild hope that he had from 1936 onwards that 'the revolution', albeit a relatively benign 'English revolution', was around the corner. He was not alone in hoping that 1945 would see the beginning of 'the Republic', but he was quicker than many to see that Mr Attlee's Government was not embarked on a revolution process, yet could be defended, much as he had defended 'Chamberlain's England' in 1940, as a relative good.[12] He did not cease to believe in 'the Republic' but, like many, he grew more realistic in considering time-scales. The creation of an egalitarian Britain would be a task for generations: 'revolution' became a process, not an event. He no longer seriously hoped to see a socialist Britain in his life-time. This seems to me a sensible and realistic perspective, neither a sign of changing ideology nor of abnormal pessimism.

Everything else found *The Lion and the Unicorn* remained: his traditionalism, belief in the moral superiority of the common people, his pietism towards nature, and above all his belief that liberty and equality were not merely not antithetical, but that more liberties could actually be exercised in an egalitarian society: they were conditions of each other. He had a very positive sense of freedom: liberties were to be exercised not simply enjoyed, and the results could be turbulent. In some ways Orwell's ideas of civic freedom owes as much to the Roman and the French Jacobin traditions as they do to nineteenth century English liberalism: hence his desire to be 'in on the action', his belief in direct participation and also his tough-guy talk about shooting traitors after 'a solemn trial' and crushing 'open revolt promptly and cruelly'—not the Orwell most often quoted by his liberal admirers.

He is clear about the best possible outcome. But he is realistic about the post-war world and says quite explicitly that he would prefer to live under the relative tolerance of American capitalism than under Soviet power. Yet these alternatives exclude a middle position which he continued to believe (which took some optimism) was both preferable and realistic: a United Socialist States of Europe.[13] What is remarkable about Orwell as a practical political thinker is that he is both idealistic about best-possible outcomes and realistic about second-bests, a curious mixture of optimism and pessimism, of rhetoric and plain honesty. He believes in the basic decency of human nature and that we *could* attain 'the Republic', but he does not believe in inevitable progress and recognises that things could go terribly wrong again, as they did under Stalinism and Hitlerism and imperialism. The outcome depends not on 'impersonal forces', 'economic formations' or 'determining social structures' but on a collective aggregation of individual will power and morality.

Thus Orwell is an ethical socialist. Consider this well known review of Hayek's *The Road to Serfdom:*

> In the negative part of Professor Hayek's thesis there is a great deal of truth. It cannot be said too often ... that collectivism is not inherently democratic, but, on the contrary, gives a tyrannical minority such powers as the Spanish Inquisitors never dreamed of.
>
> Professor Hayek is also probably right in saying that in this country the intellectuals are more totalitarian-minded than the common people. But he does not see, or will not admit, that a return to 'free' competition means for the great mass of people a tyranny probably worse, because more irresponsible, than that of the State. The trouble with competitions is that somebody wins them. Professor Hayek denies that free competition necessarily leads to monopoly, but in practice that is where it had led, and since the vast majority of the people would rather have State regimentation than slums and unemployment, the drift towards collectivism is bound to continue if popular opinion has any say in the matter ...

Between them these two books sum up our present predicament. Capitalism leads to dole queues, the scramble for markets, and war. Collectivism leads to concentration camps, leader worship, and war. There is no way out of this unless a planned economy can somehow be combined with the freedom of the intellect, which can only happen if the concept of right and wrong is restored to politics.[14]

The implication is that freedom of the intellect must be qualified by morality. Presumably we should exercise our freedom with responsibility towards others. And Orwell also seems to believe that there are some things that the State can do which it should not do. Interests may attach to groups but they should not override certain rights attaching to individuals. There are, indeed, philosophical difficulties in this position; but such is his position.

Orwell's socialism is libertarian. As *Animal Farm* shows, he has a speculative sympathy for anarchism—indeed personal sympathies too. But he is too tough-minded to adopt that position philosophically. He sees the State as a necessary evil, acknowledges its function in general but distrusts it in all its particular actions. This was characteristic of the old *Tribune* Left: in theory a demand to nationalise nearly everything and the seize control of the 'commanding heights', but in practice an intense suspicion of leadership and a rooted belief that all power tends to corrupt. In the *Lion and the Unicorn*, even, Orwell had warned:

> Centralised leadership has very little meaning unless the mass of people are living roughly upon an equal level, and have some kind of control over the government. 'The State' may come to mean no more than a self-elected political party, and privilege can return, based on power rather than on money.

Thus in commonsense terms, but perfectly clearly, he is one of the first socialist thinkers to say that class structure can be a product of power-hunger and office-holding, not simply of economic exploitation. He rejects Marxism as too simplistic rather than as wholly false. I read the sociology of the 'Outer Party' in the novel *Nineteen Eighty-Four* as a savage satire on bureaucracy: intellectuals deserting their, to him, historic task of 'education and agitation' among the masses, for the comfort and security (or so it seemed at first) of desks and departments. The concept of 'bureaucratisation' has caused almost as much trouble to orthodox Marxism (I mean has proved as 'problematic') as nationalism. Orwell, in essays and asides, was onto this before my colleagues, the high-brow polysyllabic neo-Marxists. Dislike of bureaucracy links to his concern with immediate experience, rather than abstract benefits, to place him firmly in the small-group, decentralist tradition of socialism rather than either the Fabian or the Marxist versions of *etatism*.

His libertarianism is also typical of English socialism in his undisciplined commitment to free speech and truth. In the famous essays on censorship, propaganda and the control of literature he not merely restates a classic liberal argument that the dangers of censorship are always greater than its benefits, but tries to establish that plain language speaks the truth whereas polysyllabic neologisms are either obfustications or lies. Well, it isn't as simple as that. Syntactically there is no way of telling whether plain words lie or not. But it is a good rule of thumb. And one is for ever grateful to him for pointing out that a phrase like 'ideologically correct' simply means ' a lie for the party'. He has the robust commonsense to believe that a good cause can afford to admit errors and mistakes. And if the guardians of the cause will not make these admitions themselves, then he will: 'liberty is telling people what they do not want to hear'. Such men are always happier in opposition.

A characteristic of English socialism, in contrast to Marxian socialism, has been to recognise that there are some areas of life which have to be preserved from politics. A good politics even sets up barriers of laws, institutions and customs against itself; and similarly to recognise that while economic factors condition and limit everything to some extent, yet they determine nothing. Only an English socialist could talk, as Morris, Tawney and Orwell did, about the importance of privacy in the good life. But to Orwell the most important of these 'reservations' was literature itself. He had said that above all else he wanted to make 'Political writing into an art'. He saw that his best writing was political, but it was his best because it was good writing or art, not for the truth or relevance of the message.

He recognised a tension: 'My book about the Spanish civil war . . . is, of course, a frankly political book, but in the main it is written with a certain detachment and regard for form. I did try very hard in it to tell the whole truth without violating my literary instincts.'[16] And he recognised the peculiar problems of his times: 'Any writer or journalist who wants to retain his integrity finds himself thwarted by the general drift of society rather than by active persecution . . . Everything in our age conspires to turn the writer . . . into a minor official, working on themes handed to him from above and never telling twhat seems to him the whole of the truth.'[17] He may be forced by the state, or even by his conscience, into writing propaganda, but then:

> ... he should do so as a citizen, as a human being, but *not as a writer*. ... To suggest that a creative writer, in a time of conflict, must split his life into two compartments, may seem defeatist or frivolous: yet in practice I do not see what else he can do ... To yield subjectively, not merely to a party machine, but even to a group ideology is to destroy oneself as a writer.[18]

Indeed destroy not merely oneself, but any distance between politics and culture. He is quite happy to say that a culture can be thoroughly political, both good politics and bad politics; but not wholly and exclusively political. If it does, it becomes both bad writing and actually anti-political—while politics is the medium of freedom. Thus Orwell's position is essentially dualistic. Moral and aesthetic judgements are not the same. He is not saying *'l'art pour l'art'*, he is saying 'culture for humanity'; but part of that humanity is this very dualism, not merely that a good man can be a bad writer, but that an evil man, say Ezra Pound, can be a great poet. What contempt he has for those socialist theorists who cannot allow a class enemy to be a good writer nor a class hero to be a bad one.

Any kind of socialism contains a systematic critique of society as it is and a prophecy of society as it could and—most advocates try to argue—will be. Marxian socialism has tried to brush aside moral dilemmas and awkward thoughts (such as that economic oppression is not the only kind of oppression) by claiming to be scientific, deterministic, historical, certain—at least in broad terms—about the stages and direction of social change. But Orwell's critique of society as it is, would be true, in his perspective, even if there was no future. What should be done should be done, we can never be quite sure of the consequences; and to do evil for the sake of the future is always either a bad excuse or a self-deception. We do not act freely for the sake of future happiness, but because it is good to act freely. We cannot be sure of the future. He did have a vision of the future, but it was both perennial and long term. When socialist writings, precisely because it is commited both to critique and prophecy, is commonly so rhetorical, Orwell's mixture of a short-term pessimism with a long-term optimism is peculiar, and salutary.

In 1946 he reviewed a group of books under the heading, 'What Is Socialism?' It was a particularly revealing piece and a particularly unfortunate ommission from the familiar four volume *Collected Essays:*

> ... a Socialist or a Communist ... is a person who believes the 'earthy paradise' to be possible. Socialism is in the last

analysis an optimistic creed and not easy to square with the
doctrine of original sin ... At this moment it is difficult for
Utopianism to take shape in a definite political movement.
The masses everywhere want security much more than they
want equality, and do not generally realise that freedom of
speech and of the Press are of urgent importance in
themselves. But the desire for an earthly paradise has a very
long history behind it.

If one studied the genealogy of ideas for which writers like
Koestler and Silone stand, one would find it leading back
through Utopian dreamers like William Morris and the
mystical democrats like Walt Whitman, through Rousseau,
through the English Diggers and Levellers, through the
peasant revolts of the Middle Ages, and back to the early
Christians and the slave revolts of antiquity. The pamphlets
of Gerrard Winstanley, the Digger from Wigan, whose
experiments of primitive communism were crushed by
Cromwell, are in some ways strangely close to modern Left
Wing literature.

The 'earthly paradise' has never been realised, but as an
idea it never seems to perish, despite the ease with which it
can be debunked ... Underneath it lies the belief that human
nature is fairly decent to start with, and is capable of
indefinite development. This belief has been the main
driving force of the Socialist movement, including the
underground sects who prepared the way for the Russian
revolution, and it could be claimed that the Utopians, at
present a scattered minority, are the true upholders of
Socialist tradition.[19]

But does he really mean that utopians are a 'scattered minority',
and not rather that there must be a touch of utopianism in every
socialist thinker and writer, even in a realist like himself? The
categories are not exclusive they exist on different levels of
experience and on different time-scales. Intense optimism and
intense pessimism can go side by side in the socialist mind, and
certainly do in Orwell's. That 'optimistic' passage was written
when he was beginning to compose *Nineteen Eighty-Four*, his
allegedly totally pessimistic novel.

Now consider a very black and pessimistic passage (until the
very end) written in 1943 when he was still in his revolutionary
phase. He devoted most of a *Tribune* column to 'reactionary
writers' (few socialists have written so fairly and sensibly about
their enemies):

The danger of ignoring the neo-pessimists lies in the fact

that up to a point they are right. So long as one thinks in short periods it is wise not to be too hopeful about the future . . . .

The real answer is to disassociate Socialism from Utopianism. Nearly all neo-pessimist apologetics consist in putting up a man of straw and knocking him down again . . . Socialists are accused of believing that society can be—and indeed, after the establishment of Socialism, will be—completely perfect; also that progress is inevitable . . . .

The answer is . . . that socialism is not perfectionist, perhaps not even hedonistic. Socialists don't claim to be able to make the world perfect: they claim to be able to make it better. And any thinking Socialist will concede to the Catholic that when economic injustice has been righted, the fundamental problem of man's place in the universe will remain. But what the Socialist does claim is that the problem cannot be dealt with while the average human being's preoccupations are necessarily economic. It is all summed up in Marx's saying that after Socialism has arrived, human history can begin.[20]

That is, indeed, a curious way of dissociating oneself from utopianism; to which, in any case, in a modified or speculative way, he returned. The logical contradiction is fairly obvious, except again it may be a question of time-scales, whether he is thinking in 'short periods' or the longest possible term of human history. But what is as interesting is the psychological ambivalence, again typical of 'English socialism': on the other hand a sensibility and perception that is close to observable experience and intensely practical, but on the other hand Pilgrim with his eyes raised towards Zion, head-in-the-air while feet necessarily tramp through the Slough of Despond and Vanity Fair. But perhaps only the latter sustains the former through the hard work and daily disappointment that gradualism is heir to.

NOTES

1. *Burmese Days,* p. 69 (all my references, unless otherwise noted, are taken from the Secker & Warburg 'Uniform Edition').
2. *The Road to Wigan Pier*, pp. 173-4 and 182.
3. *Ibid.,* p. 214.
4. Bernard Crick, *Socialist Values and Time,* Fabian Tract 495 (London, 1984).
5. *The Road to Wigan Pier*, pp. 162-3.
6. *Homage to Catalonia*, pp. 26-7 and 69-70.
7. *The Lion and the Unicorn*, p. 67.
8. 'My Country Right or Left', *Collected Essays, Journalism & Letters of George Orwell*, ed. Sonia Orwell and Ian Angus (Secker & Warburg, London 1968), Vol. 1, pp. 539-40 (hereinafter referred to as *Collected Essays*). This essay was originally published in the Penguin *Folios of New Writing* (Autumn, 1940), of which whole sections were reused in *The Lion and the Unicorn*, see pp. 87-8 for example.

9.   *The Lion and the Unicorn,* pp. 28-9.
10.   *Ibid.,* pp. 73-4.
11.   *Ibid.,* pp. 85-6. A fuller discussion of *The Lion and the Unicorn* can be found in this author's introduction to the Penguin edition of 1982.
12.   As he did in writing for an American audience in 'Britain's Struggle for Survival', *Commentary* (New York, Oct. 1948), then a Left-wing journal. Orwell's own title was 'The Labour Government After Three Years'. This is another of those annoying ommissions from the *Collected Essays* which create in the last volume the illusion that he 'went off' socialist writing while composing *Nineteen Eighty-Four.*(Professor Peter Davidson's *The Complete Works of George Orwell* is now slowly but surely repairing all such damage).

Fourteen

On the Orwell Trail

From *Granta*, January 1985.

Thank you, Mr Chairman, for your kind words. I'm delighted, I really am, to be making my first visit to Grand Rapids, and, no, I can never tire of talking about Orwell.

God but am I tired and saddlesore. What a year. I just kept on talking through all that media razzmatazz and ideological bodysnatching. For mental self-protection I tried to vary my standard *'Nineteen Eighty-Four* in 1984' lecture with an occasional 'Little Eric and the Bodysnatchers' or 'The Other Orwell'; but market forces went for the standard product—thirty-one times in this country alone. And in North America, Grand Rapids, Akron, Chicago, Cleveland, Ann Arbor, Montreal, Boston, New York—all in January. Then back in the spring for Albion, Michigan; Syracuse, New York; Portland, Maine; Rosemont, Pennsylvania; Wake Forest, Guildford, Charlotte, Wilmington Beach, Greenboro, Laurinburg, Chapel Hill, Raleigh—all in North Carolina; Boulder, Denver, Fort Collins, Pueblo, Colorado Springs, Grand Junction— all in Colorado. Then the great Library of Congress Orwell experts' shoot-out in Washington and the Institute of Humanities at NYU to end, not forgetting, or forgetting, as the case may be, half a dozen High Schools along the trail.

Tired and saddlesore. Now there is only one more Orwell conference in Vancouver where I'll do 'Orwell's Socialism', a more academic version of Sheffield Town Hall back in March (the second Marx Memorial Lecture); and one more special lecture, 'Orwell and Englishness' at Bangor, North Wales. But the gods punished me only yesterday. A seven-hour train journey from Edinburgh to Cardiff was two hours late, in time to see the last of the Historical Association fading down the lane. And to think that in April I had driven myself through a blizzard across the Rockies from Colorado Springs to get to Grand Junction in time. British Rail is the pits.

*I must admit to feeling a little nervous here at Albion College when I see
so crowded a hall and so many of you clutching, or pleasantly sharing a
text. I feel like that proverbial lion thrown into a den of Daniels.*

On the trail in the States, it could make such a difference if the
audience actually had a copy of the text. *Nineteen Eighty-Four* acted
as a catalyst for discussion of any high matters that were worrying
people, but was it *Nineteen Eighty-Four* or 1984? Some questions
revealed that it was not only dear Julia who fell asleep during
Goldstein's testimony. I began to realise that even the virtuous
who had read the text could be completely defeated or brain-
washed by the media's preoccupation.

The year began briskly. On 2 January, *The Times* reported: 'Mrs
Margaret Thatcher in a buoyant New Year message to the
Conservative Party yesterday said that George Orwell was wrong
and she promised that 1984 would be a year of hope and liberty.' I
checked my lecture script against my notes in a motel somewhere
in North Carolina in April and found that I had been smuggling in
the word 'prosperity' after 'hope'. I amended. But it was bad
enough. Her speech-writers—all educated Oxford men, nary a girl—
should have known a satire from a prophecy. But at least they
didn't claim Orwell for themselves. In the same paper, on New
Year's Eve, Neil Kinnock had already tried to restore Orwell to
socialism: it *was* a satire and mainly from a *democratic Socialist*
point of view) someone[1] had schooled Neil that Orwell always used
the holy phrase with a lower-case *d* and an upper-case *S*), for
which Conor Cruise O'Brien gave Kinnock a drubbing on 8
January in the *Observer*. O'Brien had already had a go at me in a
full-page blast-off on 18 December. In my 'otherwise admirable'
biography, I had been so obtuse as to say that *Nineteen Eighty-Four*
was anti-totalitarian in general, whereas it was obviously about
'something which can only be Communism, as it developed in the
Soviet Union . . . If *Nineteen Eighty-Four* is even partially any kind
of satire on our Western way of life, I'm a Chinaman.' Amazing
how old street-fighters stop moving and lower their guards: 'If
Nineteen Eighty-Four is even partially any kind . . .' I often read that
passage on the more intelectual campuses, and they rolled in the
aisles. But it isn't in the least funny if you don't know about
O'Brien and his Left-Right late development. I can *just* see that if
you had grown up in the darkest mid-West, or in a Communist cell
totally isolated from the rest of British society, and knew nothing
about Orwell's other writings, you *could*, I admit, read the texts of
Animal Farm and *Nineteen Eighty-Four* as purely an attack on the

Soviet Union, and not even partially as any kind of satire on our Western way of life.

The worst atrocity was in the *Daily Mail*, which printed doctored extracts from the book throughout the first week in January. The guardian of the text is the literary agent Mark Hamilton, head of A.M. Heath Ltd, who is in the tricky position of being both agent to the estate (which now benefits the adopted son Richard Blair) and Sonia Orwell's literary executor. His decisions are usually better than that: each *Mail* page had a box by Professor John Vincent pointing out the anti-Soviet and anti-social implications of each altered extract, in case the *Mail's* readers were very, very thick. Hitherto, I'd only thought them thick. And not merely a grossly shortened text, but a simplified diction too: real Newspeak sub-editing. Nothing remained, for instance, of Goldstein's remarks about the useless manufacture of atomic bombs and the institutionalising of the 'cold war' (the earliest use of the phrase I know is Orwell's in 'You and the Atom Bomb' of 1945): a device, Goldstein explains, to burn off 'surplus value', frustrate equality and maintain hierarchy. Nor were the *Mail* readers given the passage that spells out all that went on in sweet Julia's section of Minitrue:

> Lower down there was a whole chain of separate departments dealing with proletarian literature, music, drama and entertainment generally. Here was produced rubbishy newspapers containing almost nothing except sport, crime and astrology, sensational five-cent novelettes, films oozing with sex, and sentimental songs which were composed entirely by mechanical means on a special kind of kaleido-scope called versificator. There was even a whole section . . . engaged in producing the lowest kind of pornography.

I share Orwell's view that the masses are controlled—or that people are massified—by prolefeed. We've no idea whether that is what they 'really want', for that is all they are *given*. A large part of his book was a great cry of rage that the Education Acts, the Reform Bills and cheap printing should have resulted in—the popular press. The disparity between formal literacy and the content of print does chill the bones: and that it should be done to Orwell himself!

Television and radio did better. I did scores of interviews in November and December: with the French, Swiss, Swedish, Dutch, American, German, Spanish (and Catalan), Australian and Japanese. In television and radio, words can be left out, but they cannot be deliberately written to suit editorial policy. But the producers usually cut when I said that the date 1984 was just a joke

on George Orwell's part. On the whole, though, I was able to get
them off the psuedo-question, 'Is 1984 going to be anything like
Orwell prophesised?' and on to the, I think, better one: 'Of the
things he was attacking in 1948, what should still worry us today?'
What a difference it made when, not so often, the interviewers *had
read the book*. The best moment was when a great Japanese literary
journalist, who had come over specially, had trouble with his
English; the hired cameraman had filmed me the week before for
the Swiss, and had gone away and read the book: and so he asked
the questions, and did so well. Such small extramural triumphs
are rare but worth whole seminars.

I didn't see the ninety-minute life, *The Road to 1984,* with James
Fox as Orwell, produced for Granada Television by David
Wheatley. But I read the script. Everything violent, sadistic,
deathwishywashy, with flashbacks within flashbacks till the mind
boggled, as I'm told the eye did too. No sign of the gentle, pastoral
Orwell. I was sent the script because someone anonymous and
friendly in the organisation thought that I might be interested to
see that every quotation from Orwell's own words could be found
in my book. A massively simply research effort on someone's part.
As was *Time* magazine's. *Time* boasted of putting a Reporter-
Researcher on the project, their London correspondents inter-
viewing Orwell's old friends and colleagues, before 'Senior Staff
Writer Gray pondered the Orwell legacy.' Now either this tip-top
Time team didn't get beyond Dillon's Bookshop or everyone they
interviewed used the identical words they had used for me some
years before. But there's no copyright in research, and they could
have gone to the sources and reached exactly the same conclusions.
That is possible. I used to find that some distinguished literary
men prepared for being interviewed by me for the biography by
closely rereading their old interview and articles. How wise not to
trust their memories. Most people's memories are a compost of
what they recall about a famous friend at the time and what they
have subsequently read. 'I knew Orwell, Professor, ever since we
both came back from Spain at the beginning of the thirties,' said
Stephen Spender.

BBC Arena's five programmes, 'Orwell Remembered', produced
by Nigel Williams, were well received and got in just before the
invasion of Grenada and the turn of the year. But I was a bit
disappointed: Nigel Williams had come to me two years before
with a lot of interesting talk about the unreliability of memory
(from my 'Introduction' to the *Life*), and wanting to do a
programme that didn't sin by confusing the photographic
authenticity of old people's remembrances with truth, but would

instead cross-cut and juxtapose conflicting viewpoints and testimony. But it didn't really work out except in the Spanish war sequence. Elsewhere it proved too difficult. Old people talking were so compelling as images that the quest for truth soon went out of the window. Still 'Orwell Remembered' was fascinating visually, even though it was inexcusable for Nigel Williams to read his well-chosen Orwell passages himself. Williams has the would-be classless, flat-vowelled, modern South London accent, invented by Paul Scofield, popularised by Peter Hall in Pinter productions, and affected since 1968 by the sixth forms of London Public Schools to show their classlessness and annoy their parents and teachers. Orwell spoke in an upper-class military accent, the inflectionless tone of people who have had to read without comment (as in his Burmah days) reports about trivialities, massacres and monumental cock-ups regardless.

I'm sure there was a comic if morally rather impressive disjunction between the military tone of Orwell's voice and many of the radical things he said (and an alienation effect indeed, positively forcing the reader/listener to think): 'We cannot win the war without introducing Socialism, nor establish Socialism without winning the war.' Strange that we don't have any recording of his voice, when he worked for the war-time BBC writing scripts even after *Animal Farm* had made him internationally famous. Probably the truth is that his BBC colleagues regarded 'Old George' as one of the boys, and what a joke that one of his books had become a bestseller. Hope for everyone! Most unsuccessful authors deeply believe that it is all luck what isn't influence. But Ronald Pickup in 'Orwell on Jura'—a brilliantly successful, gentle and elegaic low-cost film from BBC Scotland, written by Alan Painter, produced by Norman McCandlish, directed by John Glennister—got the voice exactly. And the mannerisms and character. Old Orwell friends who saw it, and the two nieces and the nephews portrayed in it, were awed at the exactness of the impersonation. What a first rate actor can do! I think he got Orwell's character better than I did (but then, I don't think biographies should be about 'character'—Dr Johnson misled us and still more did Boswell). My only contribution was the simple suggestion that they listen to tapes of Avril Blair reminiscing about her brother.

'Mr Chairman, I know the lecture has been on Nineteen Eighty-Four *as a work of fiction, and the lecture has made his point. But nevertheless would he mind telling us why, despite Orwell's own express prohibition in his will, did he write a biography at all?'*

'Well, thank you for asking that. It may relieve the gloom and boredom. I found that no problem [not quite true]. That was a problem for his widow Sonia. When I first heard of his wish that no biography should be written, years before Sonia approached me or I thought of doing a life at all, I remember thinking, "that's either a very arrogant or a very modest fellow." I imagine that he thought biography meant that Lytton Strachey had made it mean: the reduction of a public achievement to some private "hidden wound". Some reviewers thought the worse of me that I didn't find one, or else they didn't notice that I had. But I think that that's a pretty odd way to approach giving a clear account of someone's actual life. "Inspector, I've discovered that he had a very unhappy infancy." "Cut the shit, Sergeant, I want the record not the explanation!" '

I may have had a second drink before that lecture, or on the other hand, the second drink may have been wearing off, leaving me tired and irritable. I could see the year coming a mile off and realised that I was getting sucked back into Orwell and away from my romantic hope of being totally absorbed in a work on the nations of these islands. But I decided to lie back and enjoy it.

There's an apocryphal story that Sir Alan Bulloock set 1 May 1963 as an arbitrary cut-off date for his life of Hitler, and if on 2 May evidence was discovered from captured archives that Hitler had Jewish parents on both sides, it would have to wait for the second edition. In my book, I had a deadline thrust on me. But I never reckoned on the afterbirth. And when the 'Great Year' began, I just lost control and my First of May became New Year's day 1985. I couldn't resist Barcelona or Jerusalem, or Holland and South Germany for the British Council. Old students, whose careers seemed to hinge on my coming to the school, multiplied. I was asked to the Council of Europe's three days on '1984 and the Future', but was pledged to Pennsylvania at the time. I was not asked in September to the American Freedom Foundation's Orwell Conference at Peterhouse, where the princes of the radical Right gathered like Mormons to rewrite history and re-baptize the departed soul of Orwell as Rightist. They claimed that many old friends of Orwell attended. I could offer a list of those who didn't. Saint Malcolm Muggeridge did, who is of the opinion that had Orwell lived he would be a Conservative and a Catholic; and his closer old friend, Tosco Fyvel, who is convinced, he told the *Hampstead and Highgate Express*, that had Orwell lived he, like Fyvel, would have joined the SDP. I find it (sorry, Tosco) an odd kind of friendship that amends the views of a dead friend.

Some friends said, 'Bernard, you were clever to get your book out in 1980, then in paperback in time for the Great Year.' Again hindsight. I got it out then because a contract was signed in 1973 between Mrs Orwell and myself. I demanded unrestricted access to everything *and* an unrestricted right to quote from copyright anything he wrote, even if she didn't like the result; and the right to take the manuscript elsewhere if the publisher to the Orwell estate, Secker & Warburg, turned it down. And she countered, very sensibly, by saying that I must deliver within five years a publishable manuscript. When I delivered it, she had, predictably, changed her mind about the whole commission. The first version was not publishable, but Tom Rosenthal, then head of Secker & Warburg, pretended it was—held out desperately, as if at Verdum, against Sonia's attacks, and gave me time to regroup and rewrite helped by excellent readers. Harcourt, Brace Jovanovich in New York did not hold out; indeed Jovanovich himself needed little urging to drop it since on reading it he discovered that Orwell was a socialist, or that I persisted in foolishly thinking so. He lost a BIG non-returnable advance; I admire a man of principle. But by then Rosenthal was too shattered to celebrate Jovanovich's benefaction. Sonia gave Rosenthal no peace. But she wasn't in a good position: she had actually lost the contract, her agent had never seen it, and she had had to ring me up to get a copy to take advice on how to break it; so the threat wasn't as seriously as it sounded. And my small solicitor (Mr Peter Kingshill of Gray's Inn) had done his work well. It withstood the scrutiny of the big boys. 'It makes a change from conveyancing and divorces.'

Sonia was, I would say to questioners, really very magnificent and scatty. She read one review I wrote in the *New Statesman* (8 October 1971) of a volume of essays on Orwell edited by her friend Miriam Gross. I praised the book, called him a giant with warts; but ended by saying that 'the time may not be far off when there can be a full biography and a proper critical appraisal, not the strident attacks or warm justifications which dominate the Orwell market before these present essays.' I noted that she had asked Saint Muggeridge to do it, but that he had backed off:

> A thousand pities that, with her obvious fears of enemies, Orwell's widow presented the biography to such an Impossibly Busy Person and entrusted mainly to herself the Secker & Warburg so-called *Collected Essays, Journalism and Letters of George Orwell:* the best one can say is that it is a good amateur job, but incomplete, and is now an obstacle to a genuine collected works. Perhaps the excellence of the present essays may convince her that it is wrong to defend her late husband's reputaion, papers and writing so jealously.

She rang up Tom Rosenthal and said, 'That's the man, who is he?'

Never so cast-up and cast-down in one sentence. Sonia didn't know me, even though I was then writing signed articles monthly on the leader page of the *Observer*, being one of David Astor's last promising 'young men' (touching forty, still some promise left); Sonia, instead, had been reading the literary pages line by line to see if her proteges were being puffed, or to plan punishments for their detractors. She spent her fortune entertaining the great or fattening young lions in the hope they would grow into big, mainly male cubs of the kind towards whom Orwell (to his discredit) was not particularly tolerant–the 'pansy poets' and 'the nancy boys of literature' (usually from Cambridge). David Plante bit the hand that fed him in his portrait of Sonia in *Difficult Women*—witty, 'insightful' as they say, but nasty.

Of course she was impressed by the genius of my review. But I think it was a mixture of my luck and her guile. The luck, for me (since I instantly wanted to do it), was that that very week she had realised she could not stop Stansky and Abrahams' *The Unknown Orwell* from appearing, albeit she stopped them from quoting anything. Her guile was that I think she knew no more of me than that I was a professor of politics who could plainly write in English and not socialsciencese; so by choosing me, first, she would disappoint all her friends, those who had candidates or wanted to do it themselves (but that none could say she had acted irresponsibly—a professor, after all); second, by the same token she wouldn't actually lose any friends; and third, she probably believed I'd write a pretty flat, boring, wholly political account and not go too deep into anyone's motives, hers or his.

She was a strange mixture of sophistication and simplicity. And a very tough lady, but also a vacillating one, capable of great indecision as well as wild decisiveness. Tom Rosenthal wanted a press release announcing that there was at last to be an authorised biography. But I rang him up two days before and again the morning before our deadline. Virtually the same conversation: 'Tom, she hasn't signed the contract. I'm going to say to the first journalist who gets hold of me that there's been an awful misunderstanding, that she hasn't met the only conditions which I think are possible for a scholarly biography with a living widow.' 'Don't worry, I'll talk to her.' I went to bed that night at about 11.30. My then wife said to me 'Are you very upset?' I said that I was terribly disappointed but not upset. I knew what I needed to know. If she wouldn't sign, the whole project was impossible. 'I don't want to waste five years of my life and then have colossal quarrels and end up with a manuscript I cannot publish. I wasted two years with that damned Rowntree toleration project because nothing was put on paper.' Then as in a fairy story or a Le Carre novel, the bell rang and there was a taxi driver who had brought the signed contract from Chelsea to Hampstead. A little note was attached: 'I've signed your bloody piece of paper. Let's have lunch some time.'

The contract with Secker & Warburg had a secret clause. I insisted on deeding the British volume rights to a charitable trust to help young writers of the kind that Orwell would have helped had he lived. I told David Astor of this and he promised, being one of Orwell's friends, to match my first year's contribution. Rosenthal was very worried. He saw beyond my philanthropy. My philanthropy was genuine enough. I disliked the idea of making a lot of money out of a socialist; Sonia had already told me that she had torn up three or four thousand pounds of IOUs from 'poor writers' on Orwell's death; and I disliked the fact that after that good act she had made no charitable use whatsoever of her growing fortune. But my scheme was also intended to blackmail the widow. I would approach her shortly before publication—say, the day before—tell her that my fund with some support from others was about to go public, and invite her to head the subscription list. But never try blackmail. By the time the book was being printed, she was dying from cancer, and obsessed with dislike of the book and with self-reproach for breaking Orwell's expressed wish. And she and I had not spoken for eighteen months. It all went very sad and sour.

I delayed the announcement of the trust for a decent two years, and the trustees have now made the third annual award to a poor writer.

So that's the tale of how I got on to the Orwell trail.

'Where would George Orwell have stood had he been alive today?'

'He would have stood with difficulty on either one or two sticks, being eighty-one. God knows. It is difficult enough to explain what did happen, quite impossible to explain what did happen. I know that the good Mr Norman Podhoretz has written an article called 'If Orwell Were Alive Today' in Harper's Magazine *in January 1983, and that he says that Orwell would now certainly be a neo-conservative. He says that I only make him a socialist because I am a socialist. And I suppose ditto for Mr Michael Foot who is convinced that if his old* Tribune *colleague were still alive today and walking with him in Hampstead Heath he would still be an old style* Tribune *socialist. Foot may reach this conclusion for very much the same reasons as Podhoretz: an ideological perspective, comrades. But it does by chance coincide with the only possible scholarly rule: to locate somebody at their last known address on this earth. I wonder what Professor Zwerdling thinks?'*

'That sounds good to me, Bernard. Could I have a question, one on the text?'

American academic conferences on Orwell—there have been none in Britain (except for a University of London Extramural Department summer school)—tended to produce too many papers prepared in advance, over-long and remorselessly read: all written for publication, somewhere—perhaps. The art of the stimulating lecture is in decline. Idiot questions from the audience are usually ignored, and the discussion period is often token. But being used to extramural and political platforms, I'd usually take the questions and make something of them, or use them as an excuse to say something else that at least makes the questioner sit down feeling less of an idiot.

None of the campuses was in the least like those in Kingsley Amis, Malcolm Bradbury and David Lodge novels. As regards sex, I was never out of the sight of people called Deans, often 'Deans of Chapel'; and as regards booze, they've certainly cut down in the last decade. I remember as a young man first lecturing in the States and being tongue-tied by alcohol at free-flowing parties afterwards, frequently even before. Now so many people are munching fibre and drinking spring-water out of sterilized bottles. But it may be that a ghost is haunting the trail, particularly in departments of English Literature; the ghost of Dylan Thomas. Some plainly think that they killed him. I think he killed himself. Sensibly most American academic hosts now try and size up their guest a little, sometimes even ask him, before giving him the California wine equivalent of the old Martini treatment. The Martini is now almost as archaic as the cinema organ, the Atlantic liner, the kibbutzim and the LSE.

At Rosemont College, the good teaching sisters of the Holy Child of Jesus voted me an awfully good sport to stay the whole weekend. I thought that that was what I was being paid for, not just an in-and-out job; besides, some of the other papers were interesting, and the audience was fascinating. Indeed in most conferences, the bigshots tended to come in, give their paper and go. One moment there was Christopher Lasch, and the next even the grin was gone. After his talk, an old friend Sheldon Wolin, perhaps the best, hard punching light heavy-weight political philosopher, looked wistfully at me as if he wanted to talk, even suggested that I rode out to the airport in his cab. I stuck with the troops. Or, for the hour or so that they did stay, the bigshots would only talk to me or to each other. I suppose they have had enough of students all the time, and are bit uncertain how to handle odd members of the public. Orwell certainly attracts odd members of the public.

The very mixed nature of the audiences in the United States made one of my points for me. Even though these audiences were very different from the 'common man' for whom Orwell thought he was writing—the old Wellsian public library-using lower middle class—many of the non-university Americans who attended the campus lectures represented some kind of equivalent. They were not worried, unlike our dandy princes of the *New Left Review*, about Orwell's incorrect theoretical stance, or lack of one: they loved him for the irreverence of his radicalism, especially those who had got past—yes, perhaps in some way the stumbing blocks of—*Nineteen Eighty-Four* and *Animal Farm* into the essays and the better of the earlier books. And many people turned up only having read, or heard of, *Nineteen Eighty-Four* to talk about war and peace. Several conferences almost turned into 'nuclear freeze' rallies, and the old militant Right did not picket. Perhaps it took 'em by surprise. Such discussions got far away from the text, but I had a private feeling that Orwell would have relished them. Satire is, after all, essentially negative, meant to discredit some established position and open up new thought and new perspectives. I don't say that the new thoughts would have been his thoughts, but he triggers them off. His books are very good for adult political education, much better than the humourless polysyllabic didacticism of many fellow socialists.

I certainly saw in the large numbers of non-university people who came to the campus Orwell occasions an America that is not represented by President Regan, however large his recent election margin. Many people were deeply worried by the nuclear arms race and the growth of state surveillance. On every occasion there was plenty of evidence that the Podhoretz body-snatching had not worked. Most people laughed at it. An almost definitive refutation was written by Gordon Beadle in the winter number of *Dissent* for 1984. Mark you, Podhoretz is a clever man. There's no street fighter more cunning than an old Trot turned radical Right. The aforementioned January 1983 article in *Harper's* was not mistiming or jumping the gun, but was just the inevitable dreary preliminary, written with a minimal reference to the facts, to the cheerful. vulgar mass version that appeared later in the January 1984 *Reader's Digest:* Orwell as unequivocally a friend of free enterprise and an enemy of all socialism. But I doubt if such rubbish does anything more than titillate the saved-already, or please Mr Podhoretz's rich friends.

Some of the ambiguities have arisen because almost from the beginning people typecast Orwell as a simple, straightforward man who happened to write simple, straightforward books. It should be obvious that Nineteen Eighty-Four *is anything but straightforward: it is a highly complex text. So it is then thought that Orwell was over-reaching himself, or was in a kind of inspired depression. I simply assume, however, that Orwell was a highly self-conscious literary artist who deliberately achieved the effects he did achieve.*

In the end Orwell fully succeeded in his deepest ambition, to be a popular novelist. Indeed he is almost all that is left of our common culture, as regards the printed word rather than the broadcast media: he is still read for pleasure and instruction by audience almost as wide as once read Dickens, Mark Twain and H.G. Wells, writers on whom he modelled himself. The plain style he developed was to reach the common man, not fellow intellectuals.

The further I got down the trail the more I realised that the references to Dickens and Wells did not mean much to the non-Eng. Lit. members of the audience—the majority. Thus I slipped in Mark Twain. But as it stands, that is a bit of half-thought-out word-processing, for Orwell did not model himself on Twain. He was rather like Twain, both in the audience he addressed and as a pessimistic humourist: 'God damn the Jews,' said the Yankee, 'they are as bad as the rest of us.' And I'd never been able to make much of Orwell's unsuccessful request in 1934 to Chatto and Windus to write a short life of Mark Twain. It needs more thought. I'm good at throwing up ideas in lectures, a bit lazy about following them up. So many, so many.

I was saying all this, and more, about Orwell's 'I' often being a literary device. I couldn't care less whether he shot an actual elephant or saw an actual hanging. In the biography I cast some doubt on both incidents. Sonia's amanuensis scrawled in my manuscript's margin, 'He said he shot a bloody elephant, why doubt his word!!!' It is not that his achievement would actually be greater if it was proven to be a fiction, then to be classified under 'Stories, short' rather than 'Elephants, shooting of'; but simply that the achievement is, in any case, a stylistic and, I think, a moral one (David Lodge has written so well on the stylistic achievement in his *The Modes of Modern Writing*). And here I had trouble with general audiences. Devoted Orwellians demanded that I should not shake their faith by doubting anything Orwell said. I would reply that I had greater faith than they in his ability as a creative writer But he does figure in a kind of secular cult of 'the honest and straightforward man'. I didn't want to feed that, however worthy its adepts.

Then I learned something on the trail, hearing a lecture by
Hugh Kenner on 'The Politics of the Plain Style'. Kenner's politics
are not mine. But I found his argument very convincing. He
locates Orwell's style in Defoe more than Swift, and he points out
that plain style is as much a rhetoric device, to inspire trust, as is
high style, to inspire respect. And the divide between fact and
fiction is crossed freely by both men. *The Story of Robinson Crusoe,
by Himself* said the original title page. Originally many people were
confused, and it took some time to realise that the book was by
Defoe, the Grub Street hack. And his *Journal of the Plague Year* is
vivid with accurate and true detail, but Defoe was five at the time,
so the 'I' was a storyteller's eye—though one who had obviously
'interviewed' or talked at length to many adult eye-witnesses of the
horror.

The great trick of satire, Kenner said, is to create confusion
about the genre. I had already been quoting Abraham Lincoln's
remark that 'Honest Abe is very useful to Abraham Lincoln' as a
way of confusing the too literally-minded common Orwellians:
Lincoln, another god of the political cult of the common man,
could be highly self-conscious about his projected image, and it
fitted him well. As did Orwell fit Blair.

One trouble with Orwell's common style and populist stance is
that they embarrass some academic literary critics. They are more
comfortable with either the traditional novel or the modern, post-
futurist one. They don't know what standards to apply to Orwell,
and in Britain are still not sure that he is 'in the canon'. There has
been a notable holding-off from any critical reappraisal of Orwell
or reviews of books about him in both the *Times Literary
Supplement* and the *London Review of Books*. Odd. Also, British
literary editors are, I suspect, offended by the 'Is this 1984?'
razzmatazz of the media. There's still a good deal of the
'Literature' with a capital *L* around, and if the mob get hold of the
wrong end of the stick then the stick is polluted. As a political
philosopher I've never handled a clean stick in my life.

The contrary was true in America. Some pretentious rubbish
has been writen, but also very much good criticism, either already
published or in the pipeline from some of the conferences.
American journalists and universities actually like the interdisciplinary nature, as they see it, of Orwell's achievement. In
Britain, it is an embarrassment when so much intellectual activity
in universities is either demarcation disputes, or the markings of
territory with ritual droppings. Some Eng. Lit. teachers made me
quite (but quietly) angry by complimenting me publicly on the fact
that I could read a text closely and write English. This was often

plain arrogance, but in Britain it was also curricular isolation. They haven't got a clue what goes on in other subjects and pick up nothing, unlike their counterparts in the States, from their over-speciaised students.

At the end of the day I prefer American middle-brow civic earnestness to our habitual extremes of indifferent high intellectualism or the cynical provision of prolefeed: the dismembering of the common man and the common reader. Orwell proves, on the demand side, that more common men can be common readers than literary editors imagine. But on the supply side, I'm puzzled. The frequent question, 'Are there any people writing like Orwell today, and if not, why not?' always stumped me. No pat answer. I could only go off into a reflective ramble.

'Orwellian' conveys gloom and pessimism; but 'Orwell-like' conveys simplicity, straightforwardness and a love of both nature and naturalness. For a man who prided himself on simplicity of expression, the varying interpretations of Nineteen Eighty-Four *both now and at the time of publication are extraordinary.*

In England the non-university Orwell evenings—especially a memorable Adult Education weekend in Highnam Hall near Cockermouth–attracted the already convinced Orwellians. They were rather like old Wellsians, all radical in sympathies, but loving and exemplifying the non-political values: home-brewers and country lovers to a man and a woman, not the urban intellectual socialists who politicize everything. But they were all-too uncritical of him, and mostly pretty cool about *Nineteen Eighty-Four*. Even if they saw it was satire, they didn't like its savage tone. They didn't like 'that sort of book'. 'What sort of book?' 'Too modern and violent.' Many different worlds exist side by side. Both literary and political culture are pluralistic. In America popular audiences were inclined to read *Nineteen Eighty-Four* very literally, almost to forget it was a novel. And when I said 'Swiftian', as the original jackets had said, it didn't always ring a bell. It probably didn't even back then in 1949 to all common readers. I had to work on that.

Swift in Gulliver's Travels *lashed the follies of mankind, almost as if he despaired of them: the darkness was part of a grim or black humour. And Swift worked by gross and savage caricature—like some of our 'sick' cartoonists today. We do not believe that there are giants in a place called Brobdingnag, but we do believe that mankind can be monstrously cruel and also careless: some of the power-hungry like tramping on us, others do it by accident because they simply do not notice people of our size. We do not believe that there are dwarves in a placed called Lilliput, but we do believe that mankind can be small, petty, pompous and parochial. Orwell similarly works by gross and comic—if your stomach is strong—exaggeration to mock the power-hungry of all kinds, whether totalitarian or domestic.*

That became in a sense the key passage in my little defence of *Nineteen Eighty-Four* as a thoughtful novel against '1984' as a media event, an event that confused rather than focused real public worries. By dismissing, like the Prime Minister, a literal-minded reading of the text, the inference was drawn that everything in the garden is still lovely—for those of us still in jobs and with a deep shelter. Podhoretz and O'Brien (the Chinaman, not the Oceanian Inner Party member) play the same game: if Orwell was an anti-Soviet communist, as indeed he was, then he must be really, truly, at heart, for unrestricted free-enterprise, tax cuts and greater military expenditure. Most of us dwell somewhere in between—as he himself often said.

Nevertheless, so many miss its satire. Perhaps it was too difficult to write a novel on two levels which would appeal equally to the common reader and the intellectual.

> He gazed up at the enormous face. Forty years it had taken him to learn what kind of smile was hidden beneath the dark moustache. O cruel, needless misunderstanding! O stubborn, self-willed exile from the loving breast! Two gin-scented tears trickled down the side of his nose. But it was all right, everything was all right, the struggle was finished. He had won the victory over himself. He loved Big Brother.

Orwell had scrawled a random sentence in his last notebook: 'The big cannibal critics that lurk in the deeper waters of American quarterly reviews.' Ever so many of them have gone on about the despair, pessimism, even nihilism in this last passage of the novel; and most ordinary readers agree. Leave aside that it is *not* the last passage (the last passage tells us about the failure to translate the classics of English literature into Newspeak, and shows us that Newspeak had been abandoned). Just read that passage slowly, sorry. It is so familiar. I would sometimes read it twice, once in a tragic, serious voice, once in Mr Polly's kind of voice. Could Orwell possibly, had he meant to be pessimistic, have written such an awful, grotesque, inflated passage? 'O cruel, needless misunder-standing. O stubborn, self-willed exile from the loving breast.' This is deliberately the language of bad romantic popular novels. Then the early-Wellsian, ludicrous 'gin-scented tears', followed by two sentences lifted straight out of the stock language of street-corner evangelicalism and the temperance movement: 'the struggle was finished' and 'the victory over myself'. This is not pessimism, it is mockery. Big Brother can break little brothers, but then look what they get: not Aryan man, Soviet man, still less *citoyen,* but a broken pathetic little drunk. They can break, but they cannot make. Hannah Arendt is right.

An old Southern story someone told me helped get the point across. The well-fed, clean-uniformed Federal cavalryman rides down and catches a filthy, limping rebel foot-soldier with a broken musket. 'Johnnie Reb, I got yer.' 'Yep, and a hell of a git you've got.'

Laughter is a great enemy of tyranny. Historians and social scientists have concerned themselves with two modes of controlling absolute power: the first is to put power against power—checks and balances, defence, even rebellion; the second is reason, persuasion, some might add prayer; but there is a third, much practised by both writers and ordinary people who have to live under tyranny, or even under elected governments whose politics they detest but cannot change; and this third dimension if often ignored by historians and social scientists, or only studies by students of literature as a genre, not for its content or social force—satire. Orwell mocks the power-hungry and offers Nineteen Eighty-Four *as both a mocking text and a weapon in all such struggles.*

But as one climbs down from the podium (I hope I can readjust to a fixed desk), the real world is still there and one almost looks forward to 1985. But these are just notes towards an interpretation of the Orwell phenomenon, which he would have hated.

NOTES
1.   Me.

Fifteen

Wedekind's 'Spring Awakening'

From the *Times Higher Education Supplement*, 21 June 1974.

WENDLA: Why have you made my dress so long, mother?
FRAU BERGMANN: You're fourteen today.
WENDLA: I'd rather not have been fourteen, if I'd known you'd
make my dress so long.
FRAU BERGMANN: Your dress isn't too long, Wendla.
What next. Can I help it if my child is four inches taller every
spring? A grown child can't still go around dressed like a little
princess.

If I were Ronald Butt, the good Lord Longford or Mrs Mary
Whitehouse, I would be out there picketing the National Theatre
Company for staging the first uncut version in English of Frank
Wedekind's *Spring Awakening*. For it is surely the worst thing that
has happened, from their point of view, since the abolition of
censorship in the British theatre.

The English Stage Society gave it two Sunday club performances
in 1963 in Tom Osborn's translation, and after two years of
negotiations the Lord Chamberlain granted it a licence for public
performance on condition that 'there was no kissing, embracing or
caressing' between two schoolboys in the vineyard scene, nor use
of the words 'penis' or 'vagina', and that an alternative was found
to a scene of group masturbation in a boys' reformatory—one
wonders that he allowed the girl's death at the hands of an
abortionist (but, after all, it was tactfully off-stage and she did die).
At that time, in 1965, the National Theatre turned it down—a
spokesman is said to have said, 'all right for some poky
experimental theatre in Sloane Square' (not mentioned in its
otherwise totally emancipated programme notes); but now they
have made great amends to a great play, and in a new translation
by Edward Bond.

By dragging up the ghost of the Lord Chamberlain, I have
contrived to mention every superficial aspect of the play which
attracts both the censorious and the half-liberated salacious. In

fact, the group masturbation scene is perfectly fitting in this work of art when 'taken as a whole', as the law on obscenity now sensibly says. But even without these things, it is a play which would upset the three good people I've mentioned. For as long ago as 1890, when he wrote it, or 1906 when its premiere was directed by Max Rheinhardt in Berlin, Wedekind had turned their charges of corruption upside down, had accused with with, delicacy and deadly insight, the sexually censorious of themselves creating the very troubles and perversions that they attacked. Brecht called Wedekind 'one of the great educators of modern Europe', and Wedekind is the great link between the theatre of Buchner and of Brecht.

The play is about sexual repression, both in a political and a psychological sense, and also about the repression of youth by school and family. The fourteen year-old Wandla dies because, practically speaking, her mother is too embarrassed to tell her the facts of life; but more profoundly she dies because her 'innocence' is a common artificially imposed by adults in which absence of real knowledge makes sweet spontaneous irrationally explosive. The nineteen-year-old, Moritz Stiefel, kills himself because, practically speaking, he thinks he has failed the exams upon which *everything,* family and school drum into him, depends. But more profoundly he kills himself because an adult, his best friend's mother, who like a tolerant and enlightened woman has played at treating him as an equal human being, utterly refuses to help in his hour of need; and she refuses with honeyed, self-deceiving words.

Wedekind puts the two themes of repression side by side, sex and school. He shows how they can relate to each other. But he is not saying that they are the same, as the silly, ideological programme notes would have us believe, by printing first a huge chunk of Wilhelm Reich's *The Sexual Revolution:* then a horror tale of real teaching today in an East End school; and finally the usual (sorry, a tasteless remark) photographs of a Nazi rally and of war dead. All this to get us in the mood presumably—the wrong mood. The play transcends this nonsense. Wedekind is against *both* the repression of sexuality *and* the examination ladder-of-success system. He does not, like Reich and Marcuse, ingeniously equate them as all part of capitalist system. It is the adults who believe that Moritz kills himself because he has been deranged and corrupted by a dirty writing that is found after his death—an account of copulation, with diagrams, pedantically written out for him by his best friend at his request. The best friend, Melchior Gabor, is expelled and sent to reformatory. This dirty writing must be the explanation, say school parents. But the explanation is plain in the very first scene between the boys:

> MELCHIOR: I'd like to know exactly what we're in this world for!
>
> MORITZ: School makes me wish I was a cart horse! What do we go to school for? We go to school to be examined! And why are we examined? So we can fail. Seven have got to fail simply because the next classroom is only big enough for sixty. I've felt so odd since Christmas . . .

When Melchior's father wishes to send him to reformatory because of the dirty writing, at first his mother refuses: the fault is not so great and 'a decent nature will be made criminal' in such an institution (it is no new thought that prisons create criminals). But then for all her 'imaginative methods of rearing children'—and she is dressed like a *fin de siecle* woman of advanced principles— she gives way, indeed screams that he must go into the reformatory when her husband produces a letter Melchior has written to the now fifteen-year-old Wendla explaining that his conduct gives him no peace, that he has wronged her, but will stand by her, she is not to worry even if she suspects consequences and he is already taking steps to find help. The mother can defend the word but not the deed. She is as repressed as the rest of them. And poor Wendla did not know what it meant at all.

> WENDLA: Oh mother, why didn't you tell me everything?
>
> FRAU BERGMANN: Child, child, don't let's make each other more unhappy. Keep calm. Don't give up hope, my dear . . . if only we don't become timid now . . . God's love will not abandon us. *Be brave, be brave, Wendla . . .* Why are you shaking?
>
> WENDLA: Someone knocked.
>
> FRAE BERGMANN: I didn't hear anything, my precious. [Goes to the door and opens it].
>
> WENDLA: Oh, I heard it so clearly. Who's outside?
>
> FRAU BERGMANN: No one. Mrs Schmidt's mother from Garden Street. You're just in time, Mrs Schmidt.

Mrs Schmidt is the abortionist. Mrs Schmidt is death.

Actually, the first half of the play is lyrically tender. Gloriously the production rises far above the harsh, trendy programme-notes all about the Third Reich or Wilhelm Reich. It is tender and beautiful. Wedekind, who lived by writing soup advertisements, sang cabaret songs in Munich, and wrote for *Simplicissimus*, is witty and compassionate; and the producer, Bill Bryden, aids and abets magnificently. One imagines it could be played more harshly and the text would allow it, but this production brings out the sadness of Wedekind's attack on the older generations—he is not blinded with rage like his boring successors today. Wendla's mother played with a marvellous restraint by Beryl Reid (yes!), is not harsh—on the contrary, she is loving and warm, but just totally shy and incapable, even when she tries bravely to tell Wendla that it is not the stork. They both agree that it is not the stork. But no further than that. Melchior's mother finally joins the repressive state when literature, her worldly wise indulgence at the boys' reading the seduction scene in *Faust*, becomes life. But at first she is perceptive and tolerant— up to a point.

Contrast this with the dreadfully silly caricature of autocracy that the Aldwych, with Peter Barnes's *The Bewitched*, have landed themselves with. Wedekind sees the plausibility of repression, even when he shows savagely its consequences. Only the schoolmasters are portrayed and acted in harsh and unmotivated caricatures of tyranny and are given crazy names: Gutgrinder and Bonebrakers as translated.

He catches marvellously the knowing ignorance, the gawky self-assurance of adolescence. Peter Firth as Melchior catches this perfectly, as he did a very different adolescent man in *Equus* recently; he has a plausible Romeo in him, and we haven't seen that for years. Michael Kitchen plays equally well the worried and eccentric Moritz, with all those sudden changes of mood that makes adolescence like English summer weather: storms, showers, chills and scorchings all cheek by jowl. What a test for actors. An actress having to make plausible a fourteen-year-old girl who does not know where babies come from, as Veronica Quilligan does with a graceful intensity, and other young actors, besides the principles, having to play German youths of nineteen in a classical *Gymnasium*, hence terribly erudite, terribly manly, but also terribly arrested psychologically—anxiously exchanging views on how it is done, piecing together information from the classics, enclyclopaedias, nature and rumours of what Rilow's English governess showed him. Children don't come like that any more. Is that how the aggressive anti-permissives want them? But the actors made them fully plausible. Enough is still in common. Or much of it. Much, even among the students, is talk, so the surveys tell us. A mood of nostalgia covered the middle-income, mainly middle-aged audience. We too had been adolescents. We too were parents.

And there was a glow of genuine youthful eroticism. Real eroticism. They fold into each other's arms in the hay. but the curtain wall closes sensibly: the vision surpasses the reality. Actors acting copulation debase not elevate sexuality. Wedekind and this producer know that. And death is there too. The adolescents talk about it a lot. Symbolic premonitions of death, in the best Ibsen manner, were built in rather heavily, but so was light and fruitful dialogue, the wandering talk of adolescents through religion, sex, death, what to wear and the evening's homework.

Real eroticism in the theatre, as in Wedekind, is so rare and was missed so entirely in John Elsom's recent book which, even if called *Erotic Theatre* (Secker and Warburg, 1973) was in fact partly about mere nudity in the theatre (which is a great bore as a compulsory badge of progress. and better pictures can be seen elsewhere nowadays), or else about pornography and some kind of celebration or justification thereof. But pornography as such is quite extraneous to the needs of theatricality. So often now it is just another miserable and conceited ideology trying to use the theatre. Certainly the theatre can use it—if the plot really calls for it and if over-use does not defeat what is, after all, only a device to get a reaction from the audience of a particular kind. No more than anything else can either pornography or the erotic break down those barriers between actors and audience, the very essence of theatre which some muddled lads today deplore.

The genuinely erotic, however, unlike the pornographic, arouses in a natural way, that is in a way directly familiar to us, and is, by its nature, highly theatrical. For it is the long enacted stage of expectation before explicit acts of sex; and once that last boundary is crossed, illusion fails. Art is not life—it can only suggest, comment, celebrate or point towards. The eroticism of Wedekind is not obscene (poor people that might think so, he makes this point) and is fully acceptable: or perhaps we now accept, for his original audiences must have been bitterly divided over the eroticism of the two boys, two other boys, kissing in the vineyard all on a long spring evening. Not perversion. So natural. Only the prison perverts, and the school represses.

After the suicide of one boy and the imprisonment of the other, the play loses, abandons, its naturalistic style and changes abruptly to heavy symbolism. When Melchior escapes from the hell of the reformatory, he meets the ghost of Moritz in a graveyard, who tempts him to find peace and rest, until a masked stranger—somewhere between Ibsen's Buttonmolder and Goethe's Mephistophilis playing the Masterbuilder—draws him into 'the world'—presumably of *Sturm und Drang,* challenge and response, the quest for self and unknown sins. Moritz chooses Life not Death, but quite what he chooses is, if vibrant, yet vague. The play could as well end with the imprisonment and the death of the girl. The condemnation of the old order is strong and precise but the affirmation of the new is both weak and woolly. Yet it is a great play, intelligently acted and sensitively produced. Compared to the liberation dramas that have followed, it is so much more literate, sensible and wise—it knew its enemy, it did not have to invent one. And it used the 'obscene' devices so deliberately and with so much telling restraint. It did not make a meal of them. It preached eroticism against the pornography which arises from oppression. And it looked forward not to the abandonment of the great tradition of German philosophy and letters in education in favour of pure self-expression but to the teaching of it in a humane way. This play belongs to the Enlightenment.

Sixteen

Horvath's 'Tales From the Vienna Woods'

From *The New Review*, March 1977.

In a monthly periodical, the theatre critic can either get the best of both worlds or fall between two stools with a thud. If he writes for, as it were, a potential theatre-goer, seeking to influence before the event, then the plays that he can write about are limited to those likely to run for several months, hence to our two national theatres, that's to say, the National itself and the RSC at the Aldwych and in Stratford. So he misses both the excellence of theatre in the provinces (which one hopes the National will bring to London) and the stimulus of much of the short, lively and sometimes alternative in London (which one hopes the National will not kill with kindness, or socialise by offering them licensed happenings on the site). Could the marvellous short frolic that the Bush did just before Christmas, a version of Bill Tidy's *Fosdyke Saga,* spoofing committed proletarian theatre, have possibly survived the official embrace? (But if you missed it, five volumes have been published, funnier than Clive James so, no need to read *The Daily Mirror* daily or at all.) But a monthly does have a bit of precious time and space to keep a stern and serious eye on programmes, policies and actual developments of our major theatrical institutions, not just talk up or down a play. One thing the critic *can* do for an individual play in a monthly, however, is to take time to read the text, obviously a rare luxury for the daily and weekly professionals. And another odd thing he can do is read (a wicked liberty) those other fellows too—before he writes but only after he has been and seen.

Certainly the National's recent production of Odon von Horvath's *Tales From the Vienna Woods* proved an astonishing trap for and caused havoc among the professionals under pressure. For Horvath has never been performed before on a British stage. This play had its premiere in November 1931 in Berlin, earning some of the last free applause that was to be heard for many years.

In that same year, Carl Zuckmayer had presented Horvath with the great Kleist Prize, perhaps the most prestigious of German literary awards, already held by Bertolt Brecht and Robert Musil. The Nazi press howled with anger at Zuckmayer ('the half-Jew'), himself the author of one of the greatest satires on the Kaiserreich, *Captain from Kopenick,* for making an award to the author of the recent *Italienische Nacht,* satirical of the Nazis. Horvard hung on in Vienna until 1938, his comic vein becoming blacker and blacker, and fewer and fewer theatres willing to perform him; so that, even before he fled into exile, he had turned from drama to the novel. Reaching Amsterdam he consulted, being superstitious, a clairvoyant who told him in great excitement that he must go to Paris at once. He went. And only a week later and at the age of thirty-six, he sheltered from a thunderstorm under a tree in the Champs Élysées opposite the Theatre Marigny and was killed by a falling bough.

His plays sank into obscurity until towards the end of the 1950s, as Christopher Hampton tells us in the introduction to his translation (Faber Paperbacks). They then began to reappear in German theatres and producers look back to what appeared almost a golden, if agonised, era of German stage and film. By the 1970-71 season, there were twenty-five major productions of his plays in German theatres. Many young playwrights began to model themselves on him, consciously and explicitly. To quote Christopher Hampton:

> Peter Handke . . . writing in 1968 on Horvath, took the opportunity to launch a broadside against Brecht, contrasting his simple solutions 'which for me are nothing more than a *bon mot* or an aphorism', with the much richer texture and far more ambiguous effects of Horvath, who has the ability, 'elsewhere only found in Chekhov or Shakespeare', to write a line, often banal in itself, but so dislocating as to suggest and contain an infinite variety of response.

By a nice irony, the foyer of the National contains at the moment, a bit lost amid all the timetables of spontaneous happenings, a rather good if pious exhibition on 'Bertolt Brecht in Britain' compiled and edited by Nicholas Jacobs and Prudence Ohlsen (who have also composed a still better catalogue). No one could be so uncritical about Horvath as the old Unity Theatre crowd and the young Marxists are about Brecht; but one could wish for a lot more Horvath about, whereas both audiences and producers could do with a brief rest from Brechtomania.

Tales From the Vienna Woods comes out of a tradition of middlebrow theatre that we are not at all familiar with, the nineteenth-century Austrian comedies of Nestroy and Raimund. They were comic, bitter-sweet, episodic, lower-middle-class, anecdotal and broad Jack Tinker in the *Daily Mail* did well to head his review 'Coronation Strasse', and he continued 'the soap-opera is pure carbolic, unscented by kindness, hope or optimism. Though we are on the edge of the Blue Danube, the tramp of the jackboot is never far behind the lilt of the endless mocking music.' For within the *Volksstuck* form, Horvath found that political satire could be inserted and even the kind of symbolism of Ibsen and Wedekind. What seemed still to be folksy panoramas on the surface became very different underneath. And yet, he stayed in character. Unlike in Brecht, there are no 'happy endings'—for, of course, if Brecht mocks 'happy endings' in the *Threepenny Opera*, it is only because he had a far happier and compulsory one. He had history and dialectical necessity on his side, not mere dramaturgy. And I often sadly muse, as the record gets put on again, that 'Pirate Jenny's' song prophesied revolution indeed, but the wrong bloody one: the Nazis inherited the collapse of the bourgeois republic, not the Communists. Horvath's ordinary characters show the hollowness of things, but also the humanity, yet don't see easy or any solutions. The bottom has fallen out of things; there is an expectation of collapse; but, after all, we may still be able to muddle along individually. It may be that for some individuals things would be settled by happening to win the lottery. Every morning the poorly pensioned Captain asks the buxom tobacconist about the lottery results. Other things may be settled by a falling tree. I'm not really an apostle of blind accident, but it does militate against the purely theatrical inevitabilities of Brecht's stage Marxism.

A cast of fifty and a cafe orchestra playing sick waltzes— certainly the Olivier Theatre of the National looked giddy with success as the great revolve turned endlessly, too restlessly for my taste. If they want spectacle and fully-kitted-out scenes like that, the guest director Maximillian Schell might just as well have made one of his films of it. But that's another question.

Superficially the plot is straightforward and melodramatic. Three shops stand side by side: a butcher's, a toy and magic shop and a tobacconist's. That's something in itself. For the year is 1931 (but he wrote it in that year, so no hindsight). The oafish, Catholic reactionary, but really decent enough butcher, Oskar (Warren Clarke) is about to marry the girl next door, the toy shop owner's daughter. Marianne (marvellously played by Kate Nelligan) is simple, hardworking, but idealistic. The engagement party is intruded upon by the horrible young Alfred (Stephen Rea) who is the boyfriend or kept fancy-man of the lusty, fifty-year-old Valerie (Elizabeth Spriggs), the tobacco shop owner. Many other characters flit in and out, particularly Alfred's peasant mother and domineering, hateful, hating and grimly religious old Gran. Alfred seduces Marianne, she believing that it is true love, even he a bit, just for a season, affected. A baby comes. The *Zauberkonig*, her father (Paul Rogers), that is the 'king of magic', the toy shop owner, cuts her out of his life utterly. No magic left there. He and the butcher cover her memory with good Catholic curses. Alfred deserts. Marianne ends up in a strip club. Father on a drunken outing finds her there. But no instant reconcilliation, despite efforts from the poor Captain (Nicholas Selby) and Valerie-with-the-heart-of-gold. It takes another scene. Then they are all reconciled to each other. Valerie having seen off her chain-smoking young Nazi (Struan Rodger), who when drunk keeps control by shouting orders to himself, and taken back Albert. They all dash off to the country to unite Marianne with her baby, who was left with Albert's Mum. But Grannie hates baby for being a bastard and has left him in a draught, killing him dead. Marianne is just restrained from killing Gran with her own zither and curses God. But good Catholic butcher forgives her, and takes a living corpse off the stage in his decent but blundering arms, with the ghastly curtain lines: 'And now everything's been put right like this. I once told you Marianne, you wouldn't escape my love.'

Well, that's the surface of it anyway. But the regulars broke ranks on whether there was anything underneath. I happen to have read thirteen reviews, eight strongly for and five strongly against. The apparent majority is less significant than the lack of anything in the middle. They went one way or the other, with a commendable lack of hedging.

Michael Billington in *The Guardian* called the production 'a triumph ... to savour and see again; ... it shows the National superbly colonising a major piece of foreign drama.' And John Barber was as strong in *The Daily Telegraph*: 'The first English production of a European masterpiece as theatrical as it is profound, as funny as it is cruel, and as perceptive as it is passionate.' Whereas Milton Schulman hammered it down: 'Horvath is a minor talent who happens to be riding a crest of sentimentality about a period that the Germans recall with a mixture of guilt and envy.' (That packs a lot of power in one right swing.) Robert Cushman in *The Observer* hailed Horvath warmly and would 'advise you to go to the woods at the earliest opportunity (there may be crowds but persevere): you will, though, be sure of more than the regulation big surprises.' Yet Herbert Kretzmer in *The Daily Express* 'found Odon von Horvath's old war-horse of a play a lumbering, heavyfooted soap opera, distinctly inferior to the loving directorial skills that Schell has lavished upon it.'

Frank Marcus in *The Sunday Telegraph* said that 'The National Theatre can be proud of having introduced a seminal dramatist to English audiences'; and Jack Tinker in *The Daily Mail* similarly tried to wash salt from sore wounds (if giants feel anything) by saying that 'It is not every day of the year one feels impelled to rush from the National bearing anything approximating to glad tidings.' But he did, briefly but well. Yet Felix Barker, equally breathless (or spaceless), told readers of *The Evening News* that 'what we saw last night was bad. Terribly bad. The whole thing came over as a sub-Brechtian comic strip, a melodrama with banal dialogue that would have shamed East Lynne'.

Irving Wardle in *The Times* committed himself the least, but plainly found it a tremendously interesting social document on an Austrian society 'reeling from inflation and beset by the not-so-distant tom-toms of National Socialism . . . But if this is a play for the 1970s, it is because Horvath did not know what was coming' (a good point). And yet John Walker in the *International Herald Tribune* saw it as a mere period piece, 'firmly stuck in a theatrical mode that has little to commend it'.

Finally, B.A. Young in *The Financial Times* vainly cried that 'the production is a triumph for the National Theatre, and may do something to quiet the carping criticism they are subject to'. For the Prince of Carps who can never be quiet, now reigning in the *Sunday Times* too, said that it was 'not quite so unendurably dreadful as "Counting the Ways" or "Force of Habit", but it is thin, trite and unsatisfying, and the long awaited turning of the tide beneath Waterloo Bridge must wait a little longer.' And Bernard Levin added pontifically: 'It gives me no pleasure to write about the National Theatre, month after month, like this. But the dawn had better come.'

Such extreme divisions on the merits of a play must be rare. What had caused it? What are its merits? I think the trouble is unfamiliarity and that the merits are considerable, but not quite as stated.

Unfamiliarity can breed contempt. For the professional critic, working at great speed, anything off the beaten track is likely to be treated not as a relief from boredom, but as a trap, an unwelcome unseen examination. Why unseen? The text was on sale, but not a line was quoted by anyone. I'd sometimes ask for an unpublished text or acting copy: usually lent, provided one could be spared, though with some surprise at the unusualness of the request. Also, Horvath wrote in German, and though the German post-war theatre and our own have had considerable effect on each other, few critics seem at all sure of what is happening in Germany—or of German. Foreign is still French.

I admit that one cannot learn, say, Japanese in forty-eight hours in order to attend a Noh Play without earphones, but one can bone up a bit on the background and usually the text. Speed may be the enemy. But if both the National and the RSC now show their plays for several nights before the official 'first' or critics' night, why cannot this kind of embargo be pushed a bit further? Why not embargo press reports until, say, three days after even the official 'first night'? Consider book reviewing: books go out three or four weeks in advance. True, theatres have to be filled. But the two national companies both fill the early days of any new production by post and by their regulars. Good or bad reviews only affect whether it will be a middling or a long run. So why not take more time all round? Wouldn't the professionals welcome this themselves?

Should theatre call for instant judgments? There is a simple case, after all, that it should: for most people will only go once and take it as it comes. But here the critic's role is important in giving a prior hint of what to listen for and too look for. Those critics who saw *Tales From the Vienna Woods* as simply a saccharine melodrama plainly had missed a lot themselves, so could hardly suggest that the banalities, as in Pinter, are often pregnant and are to be listened to closely. But in Pinter we are now ready for it, and don't expect clear plots. Yet what an intellectual theatre his has to be, only the illusion of commonness! Are we shocked or just disorientated when something with a well-made plot, that could just jerk the tears and provoke a moral discussion if it got to (or better still started from) Leatherhead or Shaftesbury Avenue, cuts deeper?

The King of Magic is dressing to go to a Requiem Mass for his much-hated old wife. He has lost his suspenders, the old fool. As ever, he blames his daughter. The poor Captain courteously offers to lend his own, having garters as well.

> ZAUBERKONIG: How very kind of you, *enchante*, but we must have order. Marianne will just have to use her magic touch to find them again.

'We must have order.' And whose 'magic touch' would it be? One thinks of Thomas Mann's short story, *Mario and the Magician*. And isn't there something symbolic as well as comic in the well-dressed military man having, as it were, both belt and braces? And so dependent on his daughter? His type will survive.

A lady orders toy soldiers for her little darling: 'I'll go over it again, shall I, just to make sure everything's clear. That's three boxes of seriously wounded and two boxes of dead ... It's his birthday on Friday and he's been wanting to play doctor for ages.' Grown-ups who play doctors commonly kill and maim a lot of people.

Marianne tells Alfred, 'the best thing about you is that you're not stupid'. At first one laughs at how just the remark is, in that her fiance, the butcher, her father, and indeed nearly everyone else we've seen, is just that: plain stupid. But we remember that Alfred is a crook. What happens to idealistic people when to escape from mundane stupidity they trust to the clever? We forgot that there were idealistic and clever Fascists. So the remark surely has a double irony? 'Stupid bitch', says her father much later, 'she thought she could change the world.' Not just her. The simple phrase needed pointing, was pointed and Horvath plainly meant it to be.

One could go on. But the examples of metaphysical terror contained in ordinary phrases in banal contexts do not, in fact, add up to anything very specific or coherent, despite the surface naturalism of the play. One does not look for an ideology in Pinter. Just that always under the surface of the ordinary something terrible could happen. Or, there again, the most terrible thing is that people may just carry on living like that endlesslv. Perhaps the stupid are, after all, right to see what Albert will never accept and what Marianne once ignored, that ordinary work has to be done. Marianne (Austria and *Mittel Europa* too, in one sense), totally defeated, is dragged off to be part of someone else's idea of living, not allowed to die decently in her own way.

Yet nearly all the critics, whether pro or con, perhaps prompted by the one annoying part of an otherwise very fine production, find the play's meaning in a premonition of Nazism. That is, indeed, a theme. But I doubt if it is the main theme. B.A. Young in *The Financial Times*, almost alone, saw this: 'Only incidentally is it an anti-Nazi play. It is an anti-hypocrisy play.' John Barber in *The Daily Telegraph* went further:

> I would only question one strand in the brilliant production ...: the emphasis, in Brechtian captions, on the Nazi background. Horvath is not here writing about politics. With Chekhovian detachment, he is concerned with the malice, the latent blood-lust, and the rotten sentimentality of the Viennese, qualities he relishes and ridicules ...

I think Barber is very right to object to the captions, newspaper headlines that the characters all stand in line to stare up at (not in the author's stage directions at all). But I am not sure that he is right to deny that Horvath is writing about politics. The play is satire on a whole society, so has a great deal of political analysis. It is only not politics if politics simply means pursuing some doctrinaire solutions. Yet politics also means understanding the dilemma of a political situation, that is conflicts of values and of interests.

Yet all the critics missed the clearest piece of politics in the whole play: his bitter scorn of the Catholic Church. This was, after all, Austria. A butcher and a *Zauberkonig,* no less, are presented as the good Catholic laymen. And the terrible old grandmother, so indulgent to her wicked grandson (being legitimate), so full of hate to his innocent son (being illegitimate), she is a 'good Catholic' too. The most powerful scene in the whole play, which only one of my critics' coven mentioned, is a scene where Marianne is turned away from the confessional because she will not repent having had her child. The church is dark and threatening and the litany is sung with a kind of mechanical savagery. The priest is half asleep, bored, morally rigid and only irritated, not in the least touched with care or pity, by Marianne's persistence in seeking spiritual help. She was a fool to have woken him up.

In the last scene, moreover, when they tell Marianne that her baby is dead, her father drops a rattle that he has bought for it. Granny picks it up as if it is a holy-water sprinkler; and with her long skirts and suddenly priest-like appearance, she does a savage little dance before she trots away from them all carrying her absurd zither, her ritual music. Then Marianne publicly curses God before being forgiven by the lumpish Oskar and imprisoned by him in utterly the wrong love. Not since the RSC performed O'Casey's *Silver Tassie* have I seen such vivid symbols of hatred for the superstition and for the tolerance of tyranny of the Catholic Church. Odd that all that was utterly missed by the critics. Is this secular blindness or a fear of arousing fierce and irrelevant controversy?

All right, an extravagant production. A smaller cast might have pointed it better. But this is exactly what a national theatre should be doing, introducing us to an unknown foreign master, just as the other national theatre ('What's in a name?') has currently revived a long forgotten and joyful native classic, John O'Keeffe's *Wild Oats*.

Seventeen

Pinter's 'No Man's Land'

From the *Times Higher Education Supplement,* 9 May 1975.

'He asked me the way to Bolsover Street. I told him Bolsover Street was in the middle of an intricate one-way system. It was a one-way system easy enough to get into. The only trouble was that, once in, you couldn't get out. I told him to take the first left, first right, second right, third on the left, keep his eye open for a hardware shop, go right round the square, keeping to the inside lane, take the second Mews on the right and then stop. He will find himself facing a very tall office block, with a crescent courtyard. He can take advantage of this office block. He can go round the crescent, come out the other way, follow the arrows, go straight past two sets of traffic lights and take the next left indicated by the first green filter he comes across. He's got the Post Office Tower in his vision the whole time. All he's got to do is to reverse into the underground car park, change gear, go straight on, and he'll find himself in Bolsover Street with no trouble at all. I did warn him, though, that he'd still be faced with the problem, having found Bolsover Street, of losing it. I told him I knew one or two people who'd been wandering up and down Bolsover Street for years. They'd wasted their bloody youths there. The people who live there, their faces are grey, they're in a state of despair, but nobody pays any attention, you see. All people are worried about is their illgotten gains. I wrote to *The Times* about it. Life At A Dead End, I called it. Went for nothing...'

We have all come a long way since the first London performance in 1958 of *The Birthday Party* at the old Lyric Theatre, Hammersmith, collapsed after a week, hammered by the critics. Now almost every critic agrees that Pinter is the best playwright writing in the English language. What once seemed so obscure now seems so resonant.

What once seemed inconsequential now seems precisely how people do go on. He has taught us to accept that we usually come in on the middle of any story, happening, event or other person's

239

life; we learn more if we do not hold things up by sending the script back to be written so that we will be told at the beginning precisely who everyone is and what has happened before we came in (as if we ever know); and we no longer expect, of course, happy endings, or even clear and resolved ones.

Our relationships with other people's worlds are largely accidental, but this does not render them meaningless. Consider a street accident (the metaphor is Pinter's own): the situation creates certain relationships; we can see, clearly or less clearly, what probably happened and what is happening, may even guess at certain outcomes; but we can take all this in, be affected and moved without demanding a biography of everyone involved, and we may linger without any guarantee of knowing, perhaps without the least desire to know, what happens to them all afterwards.

Pinter has created a new sensibility. We say 'Pinteresque' when some ordinary, inconsequential cliche appears to carry some deeper import than its literal meaning, or when a colloquial meaning is suddenly taken very disturbingly literally. Each of his major plays has contained at least one sustained flight of cliche turned fantastical, like Mick's hopeful vision of the aformosia teak veneer penthouse in *The Caretaker* or Duff's of the perfectly kept beer barrel in *Landscape;* but now in *No Man's Land,* only the equal morbidity of either trying to reach or to leave Bolsover Street.

Far from his old obscurity, a Pinter play is now a major event. Socially he did not desert his former actor mates, indeed he married one of them, the superb Pinter actress, Vivien Merchant, but now the grandest actors in the land show their paces in his plays. Ralph Richardson and John Gielgud play the leading parts and do show, it has to be said, that they are extraordinary actors in that they can come down to Pinter's middle earth, dropping all hints of high rhetoric, but equally not plunging into symbolist mannerisms.

My high praise is slightly ungracious: they did it so well and yet did not overbalance the play. Peter Hall, who is so sensitive to the pace and to all the push and pull of a Pinter text, has run a risk and no harm came of it. But why run the risk? Surely the National Theatre would be filled for a new full-length play by Pinter without star appeal? Perfect ensemble playing is not always achieved by the great.

However, the reasonably clear plot of *No Man's Land* allows scope for two heavyweights. In a large rich house in Hampstead lives Hirst, a famous literary man in his sixties, with his two handlers/servants/retainers, for he is alcoholic and plainly near to death. Richardson gives him some of the mannerisms and morals of H.G. Wells and he is dressed like Osbert Lancaster. One of his 'servants', Foster (Michael Feast), is in his early thirties, a nasty beautiful youth, who has been out East as a sailor.

The other, Briggs (Terence Rigby), a man in his forties, is completely without attributed identity, but is thick-set, thick-looking yet no fool and, as ever, menacing. Into this menage intrides Spooner, also in his sixties, also a literary man, *probaby* an Oxford man too, but a seedy failure.

On the handlers' night out. Hirst has gone to Jack Straw's Castle and picked him up—it first appears, but then it seems more probable that Hirst was completely sloshed and Spooner helped him home, hoping to be let in for a glimpse of comfort and even some literary talk.

We are treated to some marvellously observed and frightentingly comic old Hampstead bohemian pseudish talk, with a bit of Blooms bury and parody-Eliot thrown in (as Hirst crawls out of the room, after collapsing paralytic with drink. Spooner intones: 'I have known this before. The exit through the door, by way of belly and floor'—that did not happen in the *Cocktail Party*).

At first, Spooner, just like the tramp in *The Caretaker,* thinks his luck will not last, so he savages his host, probing obvious wounds of either impotence, marital failure, or both. But instead of being thrown out in the morning for the 'servants' do not exactly take to him, his host appears to recognize him as an old friend, or mistakes him for someone else, but in either case to accept him as one of the family—for such it seems.

Indeed, Spooner seeks to supplant Foster as Hirst's secretary, but his pathetic boasts of how his literary talents will make him the perfect feudal servant are unanswered. Hirst dreams of death: 'I saw a body drowning, but I am mistaken. There is nothing there.' Spooner replies: 'No you are in no man's land. Which never moves, which never changes, which never grows older, but which remains forever, icy and silent'. And that is all. Either Hirst is about to die or, miserably, he will live on a while longer but knowing that he has never lived.

As ever with Pinter's full length plays a clear and simple story or anecdote binds it all together: somebody opened the door, came in and ... mystery and tension, comedy and terror. There is a plot and it is not obscure. What *happens* is perfectly clear. But what it all means can never be fully clear.

In one sense, the house itself is the no man's land—a sterile, blasted and unliveable landscape, but none the less one in which men have to survive. In another sense, no man's land is the all too brief interval between birth and death. And if Eliot's Sweeney said:

'There's nothing in life but three things', that third—copulation—is not going to help Hirst's household, all of whom, Spooner included, despite his boasting of a gracious wife and two daughters, are almost certainly childless and probably sterile.

So it is no woman's land either. Hirst and Spooner boast sadistically that they seduced each other's genteel wives and horsey true-loves, but it all sounds most improbable. And Spooner's biggest boast is the rather sad one: to have had 'a form of affair' with Hirst's Arabella. 'She had no wish for full consummation. She was content with her particular predilection. Consuming the male member.' Consuming indeed.

The wildly comic in Pinter has always had its agonizing point. Hirst's household is a loveless one.

> SPOONER:'I have never been loved. From this I derive my strength. Have you? Ever? Been Loved?'
> HIRST: 'Oh, I don't suppose so.'
> SPOONER: 'I looked up one into my mother's face. What I saw there was nothing less than pure malevolence. I was fortunate to escape with my life. Yo will want to know what I had done to provoke such hatred in my own mother.'
> HIRST: 'You'd pissed yourself.'
> SPOONER: 'Quite right. How old do you think I was at the time?'
> HIRST: 'Twenty-Eight.'
> SPOONER: 'Quite right. However, I left home soon after.'

It is very funny and very, very painful.

Women are not even allowed their peculiar honours, and male sterility must be allowed bonorific compensation. Hirst remembers that in his village church the beams were hung with garlands for young women who died virgin, 'indeed in all who died unmarried, wearing the white flower of a blameless life'. Spooner asks pointedly: 'And the old men of the parish who also died maiden are so garlanded?' 'Certainly', Hirst replies; and a garland is, after all, what true poets desire above all else.

Hirst's home or habitat is utterly isolated. In the middle of the morning Hirst looks out: 'the light . . . out there . . . is gloomy . . . hardly daylight at all. It is falling, rapidly. Distasteful. Let close the curtains. Put the lamps on. Ah. What relief. (*Pause*) How happy it is.'

But it isn't, his home is also his prison. When Briggs refuses to give him the bottle, he says: 'Refusal can lead to dismissal.' 'You can't dismiss mé.' 'Why not?' 'Because I won't go.' But he can usually keep his dignity. His household orders are obeyed, even though the thugs grumble at the housework. And they don't touch

Spooner, though one is expecting brutal trouble any minute. But Hirst's dignity crumbles sometimes. Briggs is slow bringing him a drink, so he demands what he is to do while waiting. *Biggs:* 'You'd crawl to the bottle and stuff it between your teeth.' *Hirst:* 'No. I drink with dignity.' Alas rarely. But often we are able to pretend not to be (I think it is) frightened of death.

When Spooner makes a long speech offering himself as secretary, he lapses into a kind of fustian prose and praise of the feudal relationship of vassal to master. He is probably romanticizing what he knows in reality must be a relationship of economic subservience. Anyway, almost anything may be better than the psychological bonds of complexity and loathing that appear to link Briggs and Foster. Foster sulkily refuses to drink champagne when it seems that Spooner is to stay.

> BRIGGS: 'The best time to drink champagne is before lunch, you cunt.'
>
> FOSTER: 'Don't call me a cunt.'
>
> HIRST: 'We three, never forget, are the oldest of friends.'
>
> BRIGGS: 'That's why I called him a cunt.'

Such is friendship in this new Pinter world, or is it ours too? But *No Man's Land* reveals a worrying and perhaps slightly false moral fixity and sameness about Pinter's characters, for all their unexpected comings, goings, sayings and not-sayings. 'I see it all about me continually', says Hirst, 'how the most cultivated and sensitive of men can so easily change, almost overnight, into the bully, the cutpurse, the brigand. In my day nobody changed. A man was. Only religion could alter him and that at least was a glorious misery.'

'At least'? Beware, Hirst speaks sententiously, and no character speaks for Pinter. Pinter really does let his characters speak their own thoughts in their own fictional right. But still, this is his gloomiest view of the world yet, and the only way to change— religion—that is even mentioned is, if historically obvious, plainly not for him.

There appears to be no other way of change in his world. Yes, indeed, one sympathizes with Pinter: all those earnest and silly folk who have not merely reproached him for being apolitical but have actually asked him for a social message. Like Wesker's, Trevor Griffith's, or even the early Osborne? Heavens forbid. Pinter is an artist, a dramatist and a poet, of extraordinary empathetic skill in following thoughts and language of others.

But is the world he paints a full one? A narrow one, admittedly, but done in such depth—is the usual received wisdom. But if this last play is a picture of the world, there is a shallowness in it. Much that is apparently superficial IS probably superficial, and even three or even seven ambiguities to a speech do not guarantee that any one of them is not shallow.

To be thoughtful, even if portraying thoughts of others, is not to follow any predetertained formula—even one's own. I am worried that *No Man's Land* is too much the mixture as before. The manner is marvellous, both in craft and in comic relief, but is repetitive: and therefore the matter, as if to avoid repetition, can only grow progressively and arbitrarily gloomier.

On such an a-rational view of man we can only turn, like Hirst, either to drink or religion. Harold Pinter's Noah's ark is stuck, albeit on a very high pinnacle (the Post Office Tower above Bolsover Street). But if he is going to move, it will, I suspect, either be away from the true drama of man in circumstances, plots and characters and back to the poetic non-dialogue of *Landscape* and *Silence,* or else—following the humane laughter that punctuates and somewhat contradicts the gloom—to explore sociability as well as dissociation: political dilemmas as well as existential dilemmas.

To put it bluntly, the existential dilemma of 'to be or not to be' can be hollow banality. If we do decide, as most of us do, to live until we have to or happen to die, the question then arises, how *should* we live. Don't tell us, Mr Pinter: that indeed is not the artist's job; but spare a thought for those difficult moral dilemmas as possible subject matters of drama. The existential dilemma is a bit simple, or rather repetitive, for all its apparent profundity. Some of us are getting a bit bored or irritated at the sweet narcissism of 'the identity crisis'. Individualism can go too far.

'Not surprised Harold got to Bolsover Street in the end. Persistent look about him. Told him he'd get stuck though, can't find his way out on his own. Going round and round the fucking tower in fucking circles. Perhaps he doesn't want to find his own way home. Perhaps he hasn't got a home. Perhaps he likes it on his own. Perhaps not. I don't know.'

Eighteen

Polly By Gaslight

From the *Times Higher Education Supplement,* 23 March, 1982.

'There is a young ingenious Quaker in this town who writes verses to his mistress ... It gave me a hint that a Quaker pastoral might succeed if our friend Gay could fancy it ... pray hear what he says ... Or what think you of a Newgate pastoral among the whores and thieves there?' (Swift to Pope, 1716).
'There is in it such a *labefactation* of all principles as may be injurious to morality' (Johnson, 1775.)
'I should be very sorry to have the *Beggar's Opera* suppressed; for there is in it so much of real London life.' (Boswell, 1775).
It was meet, right and proper that so many of the cast of the current 'smash hit' revival of *Guys and Dolls* should be transported from the Olivier into the Lilliputian Cottesloe for the *Beggar's Opera,* though by design as well as good fortune they neither guyed it nor dolled it. For Gay's *Beggar's Opera* is the mother of them all: ballad operas, music dramas, dramas with song and the modern musical. And until the work of Benjamin Britten, it was our truly national 'opera', both in the beauty and vitality of the folk melodies and in the satire of obsessive social class. Also, like the modern musical, it was highly speculative economically. Boswell records the Duke of Queensbury saying, when Gay showed him the text: 'This is a very odd thing, Gay; I am satisfied that it is either a very good thing or a very bad thing.' Congreve is supposed to have said: 'it will either take greatly or be damned confoundedly'; and Pope wrote to Swift (as close friends of Gay) that 'it will make a great noise, but whether of Claps or Hisses I know not'. Swift told Gay, perhaps with friendly exaggeration, that it was as great a satire on mankind as Gulliver.

Colley Cibber, the arbiter of fashion, refused it at Drury Lane, fearing that both its politics and its burlesque of Italian opera would offend the fashionable, but John Rich, a much more dour and down-to-earth character, a self-made businessman, took it for his Theatre Royal in Lincoln's Inn Fields. The first night was a great event, much of high society was present including Sir Robert Walpole, all gathered for the promise of novelty and the speculation as to whether the unsuccessful but promising Mr Gay could at last pull off what his great friends hoped. At first the audience was either quiet or restive, while Peachum and his wife mocked the manners of the age, or rather pursued the ironic line that the poor are just as corrupt as high society and the court; but then daughter Polly's first *chanson pathetique* brought the house down:

> O, ponder well! be not severe;
> So save a wretched Wife!
> For on the Rope that hangs my Dear
> Depends poor Polly's Life.

Gay's opera was repeated sixty-two times in that season, when a run of two weeks was counted a great success. It was soon said, with more wit than truth, that 'it made Gay rich and Rich gay'.

From then on hardly a year went by without it until late Victorian taste dismissed it as crude and dirty. Frederick Austin's famous revival of 1919, albeit a somewhat romantic version, puts it back on the road again. Brecht and Weill's plunder and rewrite job, *Die Dreigroschenoper,* at least restored the dark tones and the satire, and Britten's 'realization' of it (recently revived at Aldeburgh by the Kent Opera Company) was also dark in mood, though did not lose entirely the contrapuntal beauty of the folk melodies. These melodies vindicate a national common spirit against the cosmopolitan artificiality of the court (a common enough theme of those self-made men who practised the new profession of letters, and one that links Swift, Gay, Johnson and even Wilkes).

The text is more complex than many suppose, as the seeming simplicity and deadly punning of Polly's song well shows. It contains many themes and moods. There is satire against the court and the *beau monde*. Macheath sings to two of his gang that 'The modes of the Court so common are grown,/That a true friend can hardly be met', while he has risked his life to get them money; so honour does exist, but only among theives. And though Polly declares ' a Woman knows how to be mercenary, though she has never been in a Court or an Assembly', yet by reading literature, 'cursed Play-books' and 'romances', she has actually come to believe that she is *in love* with Macheath and, even more incredible and against 'the view of Interest' that has parents taught her, that he loves her and so should not be hanged 'by way of business'. Romantic love is satirized, Polly *is* silly; only that 'the view of

Interest' is satirized even more: Peachum and Lockit's utilitarian (and no holds barred) ethic is linked with that of Walpole's (any Prime Minister will do, it does outlive the topical gags and gibes), but it is utterly rejected: this is satire, not cynicism. So Polly comes across (should come across) as only seeming-knowing, silly but nobly innocent: in the true sense of the word, 'pathetic'. High life and high-flown sentiments are satirized, but virtue is not with the urban poor. The interest in povery and crime is partly prurient, though real; yet the plain melodies of the folk songs attest both to a satire on the town and to a rural popular spirit, spiritedness rather, not yet wholly crushed or urbanized. There is dark Swift-like misanthropy in it, but also great shafts of gaiety and light. The class war is there and the sex war too, not just the predatory Macheath—'I must have Women ... Money is not so strong a Cordial for the Time'—but also the brutally affable yet cruelly habitual tyranny of father over daughter.

All these themes and more are in *Beggar's Opera* and they must all be present in any production, but variations in pointing and proportion are infinite. If I ever go mad, as a scholar should go mad, the heading of the crazy manuscript in front of me will be 'Notes towards a definitive modern production of the *Beggar's Opera*'.

Richard Eyre's National Theatre production is neither definitive nor perfect, but it is very, very good: lively, vigorous and with actors full of joy and love for the play. I went out bouncing almost as if I had seen it in 1728 for the first time rather than in 1982 for the tenth. Such is the difference between a text and a production. Theatre must be theatre.

To start with, the director chose to have actors singing rather than singers acting. Now classical singing is not part of the training or acquired talents of most modern actors, so here is a crucial option: but even bad classical singing is closer to a beggar's opera than the horror of an over-orchestrated score and of trained singers trying to act low, as if in pantomime (the Scottish Opera Company did just a memorably awful version in 1981). Olivier once got the worst of both worlds in a film with real actors but dubbed singing voices, overall a view of a pretty eighteenth century as seen from a tea-shop window on Richmond Hill (the worst thing he ever did, bar *Hamlet*).

The stage of the Cottesloe was Peachum's lock or warehouse. Its wooden galleries and rafters blended into the side galleries of the theatre itself, a spendid unity of design. My fears arose that clever tricks were afoot when the beggars wandered in wearing late Victorian rags amid fog and dim gaslight; but when Peachum

began to sing, he put on a green velvet early eighteenth century
frock coat, just as Macheath appeared in scarlet above his
Victorian rags. Then all was well. The trick was vindicated. The
time change gave us a more familiar Mayhew world of poverty,
and these beggars then played their grand old opera: the first
thorough-going alienation effect. They even set up oil lamp
footlights (Peachum, Lockit or Robin of Bageshot, alias Black
Bob, must have had a quiet word with the GLC's safety officers).
And instead of the full-blown lush orchestration of the Edinburgh
Festival version, four good lads alone did everything that could be
done with clarinet, guitar, concertina, and violin, occasionally
picking up mandolin and psaltery. Loud and loving, in the
manner of the Albion Band, mainly the good simple folk melodies
with a sly touch of rock. But perhaps too simple, occasionally
coarsened.

The prevailing tone was dark. Never have I seen a production of
the *Beggar's Opera* in which the spoken dialogue and the words
and style of the songs were more of a piece. But perhaps too much
so: the irony was lost. For there is both light and darkness in the
text: if Eyre's version has an obvious fault, it is too uniformly Swift
and Brecht, not gay enough. The contrast of colourful and
ornamented singing, of mordant, silly cynical words with lovely
melodies, is part itself of the joke or satire. Intervals were
simplified and grace notes removed. Fair enough, to get a unity of
style; but that misreads and smooths over something deliberately
discordant. We do not merely have the original melodies, but in
the third edition of the text (the last in Gay's lifetime) the actual
setting of words to the notes: far more elaborate and—damn it—
lovely than used here. Gay while mocking the new fashion of
sentimentality, also adroitly indulges it through Polly; but Richard
Eyre ignores it.

This simplification may have been for unity of style or because
Polly, an unusually knowing, not an innocent Polly (Belinda
Sinclair) and Macheath (Paul Jones), marvellously played as a
handsome but vulgar Glaswegian street-seducer, simply couldn't
sing well enough. (Yes, I know it was *the* Paul Jones; but the former
rock star couldn't get the grace notes when folk melody satirizes
opera.) Lucy Lockit (Imelda Staunton) could, by God she could!—
a pocket volcano of anger, some comic effects but some pregnant
and real enough to create a shudder for ruined woman's lot: so
they left her all her songs and gave them full musical value, except
that the slanging match with Lucy (the satire of two divas going at
each other) had to be simplified. Polly even lost her most famous
'Oh, ponder well' and, even more astonishing, her duet with

Macheath, 'Oh what pain it is to part'. Inherently beautiful and touching, they had to go. And they got through possibly the loveliest love duet in the native repertory, 'Where I laid on Greenland's Coast/And in my arms embrac'd my Lass' as quickly as they could, flattening every note, just crooning to each other 'naturalistically'. Again, this misses the irony. Gay contrasts the natural and the artificial. The satire of 'Italian opera' of that period can surely extend to a type of opera of every period—and to an operatic view of life. It is not all lost even now. I'm philistine enough to be aware that much opera is, but for the great skill of the performers and the suspension of disbelief of the audiences, close to the edge of the ludicrous. And directors should 'ponder well' before cutting any song from the text: Gay is no Wagner, but my reading is that every song and its words are an integral part of a totally crafted mood or action.

Peachum (Harry Towb), since we cannot all laugh at Walpole any longer, adopted a thick Ulster accent in which he said the most terrible things about murder, death and betrayal with bland affablness. But Lockit (David Ryall) played the more traditional 'good old (nasty) cockney' role (complete with a timeless woolly waistc't) and sang with bold uproar as if in the Players Music Hall—absolutely right, just as Mrs Peachum (June Watson) both acted and sounded the part, a raucous thin-boned pseudo-gentility. Choruses went better, professional singers could hardly match the ugly oddity of the gang and the trio of Lockit, Peachum and Mrs Trapes were sublimely comic. Comic, yes, but as Irlin Hall sang the fat brothel keeper's last line, 'Lip to lip while we're young, then the Lip to the Glass', she shuddered with a Dr Johnson-like *momento mori*, old mortality crept in behind the gin fumes—that was a fine touch. The laughter of life and the fear of death are so close together in Gay's world. If Macheath and Polly were each well played as strong, palusible characters, the other main characters brought out better the light of song and the shade of words.

Yet it is a matter of stress and the vices of one producer can bring out unexpected virtues. The words of Macheath's 'dying' melodrama were wisely shared with two (somewhat more) musical off-stage voices of his gang. But I have never seen his final 'I tremble I droop!—See my courage is out' better acted as he 'turns up the empty bottle' (says the original stage direction, ignored by that toffee-nosed Edinburgh lot). For at the end the gallant Captain, brave and honourable with fellow men, utterly callous to any *individual* woman (if such a thing can be imagined), obsessed merely with 'the sex', can only face violent death brimmed up with

Dutch courage. It was a sobering moment. So 'Cry, a reprieve' is needed indeed if we are not to be frightened as well as shocked and amused at the inversion of social values. But on the other hand, I cannot tear myself away from this wonderful spectacle without commenting that, as usual, the ladies of the town were hideously overdone. Do producers think that Gay was a queer trying to put men off women? Excess breeds excess. Richard Eyre needs reminding that a single flash of an inch of gartered thigh is more erotic than constant exposure to (if gallantry did not forbid) two ageing drooping bosoms. I say this in the interests of proper prurience, not of public decency. Yet a score of subtle touches. We see Macheath go into the Marylebone gaming house to get money for his companions, as a stage within a stage; and when Lucy and Polly slang each other around the manacled Macheath, the other prison inmates and warders watch excitedly through the bars, like a theatre audience watching a beggar's opera.

The great satire certainly came out; that self interest should conquer natural feelings. When Filch admits to Mrs Peachum his fear of being cut off in the flower of his youth, she points her reply with a compassionate: 'I though, Boy, by this time, thou hast lost Fear as well as Shame'. And Lockit reproves his daughter: 'If you would not be look'd upon as a Fool, you should never do any thing but upon the Foot of Interest. Those that act otherwise are their own Bubbles.' So just a point of intellectual history to end this mildly critical celebration of a fine production of our great pre-Britten English opera. Lockit's remarks about 'interest' so far predate Adam Smith and utilitarianism that they show, as often, how much philosophy only systematizes (as it should) 'the thoughts of the age' or the *Zeitgeist.* But there is one author who preached utilitarianism before both Gay and Smith and, moreover, did it satirically—much like Gay: Bernard Mandeville in his *Fable of the Bees* (1714) or 'private vices, public benefits': private extravagance stimulates public industry and, on the other hand, public brothels preserve from assault the honour of respectable private women. I can find nothing in any of the books on Gay to suggest that he knew Mandeville. Yet they hunted in the same kind of territory: humane satire with mock harshness. Gay does not hate mankind, he would either change it—somewhat—or indulge it. And not by mocking the rich does he champion the poor: he speaks for 'the middling men' against both the mob and the aristocracy, a good bourgeois.

Nineteen

David Edgar Catches Peter Jenkins' Ear at the Barbican

From the *Times Higher Education Supplement,* 2 December, 1983.

I have tried hard to get away from this self-destructive infatuation, this obsessive love-hate relationship which stops me writing bold, original, serious and interesting things about institutionalised higher education. Next week I promise to turn to another institution, though one equally obsessive and easy to get lost in— North London Polytechnic. What draws me back to the Barbican is not just that David Edgar's huge new play *Maydays* raises fascinating issues concerning the nature of both theatre and politics, but also an extraordinary issue of responsibility in journalism.

The play has had an exceptionally mixed reception. Mixed both in that some critics have disliked it strongly and others admired it greatly, and in that some have reported a mixed reaction—not merely a 'good in parts' reaction but a puzzled, conditional reaction.

For once I am with the mixed economy men and the Social Democrats. I'm in the middle and I can't make up my mind. Go and see it, and make up your own mind; it is very, very good in parts—funny, noble even,with some dramatically effective scenes; and yet some strident, simple, cardboard cut-out and arse-achingly prolonged scenes.

In other words, it is a piece of epic theatre: it is very long (*two* intervals!), it has many different scenes and it portrays fictional individuals in real historical events in different countries over a long period, from 1945 to 1983 to be precise, from a flag-waving, mock heroic Communist Party victory demonstration to the women on Greenham Common.

It is a study of the extreme Left, or rather of extreme Left groups (the plural is very important, and was missed by some critics whose eyes were blinded by blood and rage). He attributes to them both nobility and folly. So many characters are involved that characterisations become humours, and there is little psychological depth; but recognising so many of the humours as typical, the roles that people have played in my political lifetime, I found some of the scenes both wildly funny and sadly terrible.

Yet one soft-centrist had no mixed response. The political editor of *The Guardian*, Peter Jenkins, 'devoted half a page (he has not used that sort of space since the Falklands War) to an extraordinary attack on David Edgar (October 26, 1983):

> *Maydays* with its cast of 50 occupies the vast acting space of the Barbican Theatre for three and a half hours. Lavishly staged there at some public expense by the subsidised Royal Shakespeare Company it is a play of declared political intent which, in its author David Edgar's words, seeks to provide a 'collective biography' of his generation.

Thus it began: a bad play, bad politics, bad thinking and an improper use of public money. That the last tolerant thought was not just an accidental splash of spume in Peter Jenkin's ill-tempered and imperceptive review was shown by *The Guardian's* front page lead-in: 'If David Edgar's lavish *Maydays* is a memo from the Left to the left, what is it doing on the Barbican stage of the Royal Shakespeare Company?' (Regular readers of *The Times* must believe me, this was Peter Jenkins of *The Guardian* and not Peterborough of *The Telegraph*).

As my mixed verdict admits, I must tolerate the plausibility (or else Crickpot just calls Jenkins-kettle black) of serious critics saying 'bad play, bad politics and bad thinking' though I disagree; but I find it intolerable to say that a subsidised theatre, the 'Royal Shakespeare Company' (I just say 'RSC'), should not spend the public money on such a play. That is their concern. Let us judge the merits of the play, and the public leave the seats empty if they don't like that kind of a thing. But I feel intolerant towards the intolerant. A very political political editor knows quite well that the RSC is currently under Treasury scrutiny and knows what kind of Government we have in power. The opinion grows in Government circles that subsidised theatres and broadcasting media should only pursue either non-political or strictly balanced themes. His polemic was intended to damage the RSC not to reason with the playwright.

So angry was Mr Jenkins with what he wittily calls the 'self-indulgent posturing and masturbatory impotence of revolutionary politics as practised by the Trots of the Seventies' (a vile phrase: are the poor Trots too impotent to masterbate, even?), that he doesn't seem to notice that David Edgar has, indeed, a very ambivalent attitude towards revolutionary enthusiasms.

Edgar has sense of their nobility of vision, but also of their folly, of the hardness and inhumanity of character they can create, and the ludicrous disproportion between what the broken-down, second-hand duplicator in the squat is churning out, and the sad squat itself.

All this is in the play: the mixture of good and bad. The sadness and humour of it seems to have escaped the bully in the china shop. There is, for instance, a scene of a 1970s party on (in?) Muswell Hill that to me was both hellish and nostalgic, wildly funny: I had met everyone there, and often before in different costumes 'Twenty Years After', as Dumas remarked, indeed.

Yet in such an epic form, scene interacts with scene, not character with character: the leading characters often talked *at each other*, unnaturally and with too long a wind. I winced during many a monologue, but then half an hour later delighted to spot the shifts, evasions and revisions in a character's next long monologue, a few years later.

David Edgar is a man of the Left, but as hard a man on his own camp was an Orwell. He had remarkable gifts of empathy. Mr Jenkins will not even grant him that. He says that his earlier play *Destiny* 'prefigured the coming of neo-Fascism in Britain'. Well, there was a little flourish like that in the last scene, but all the rest was an extraordinarily empathetic *study* of the interaction of different types of fascist, racialist and ultra-nationalist. I was astounded. The Left-winger entered into their minds, without rant and turned them to dramatic account; within their psychologically closed world we saw a Shakespearian clash of character with circumstances—just as in *Maydays* though, I think, less successful. The epic form of *Maydays* forced a pace and a simplification, more like his adaptation of *Nicholas Nickleby* than *Destiny*.

What I want to discuss publicly with Mr Edgar (at the ICA at lunchtime on December 8) is not whether the RSC should have staged his play, but what effect the sheer size and *grandeur* of that inflated stage had on how he wrote the play. I hope Peter Jenkins will come. The text *Maydays* is published by Methuen. Mr Jenkins writes in *The Guardian* on Wednesdays [now in *The Independent*]. The full Treasury reports on the finances of the RSC (which finds them to be both efficient and underfunded) will be published soon or sometime.

Twenty

Barrault at the Barbican

From the *Times Higher Education Supplement*, 4 November, 1983.

The lights dimmed into total darkness. Then a spot illuminated the great actor, black shirt and black trousers, miming walking up stairs, a routine mime-exercise done with mastery. There was huge applause for the 73-year-old cult hero both of the theatrical profession and all lovers of theatre. Then he began to speak, in French. The surprise should not have been too great, but as he went on and on, rustle and whispers spread as many waited for the performance to begin. But this was it. Now like most of the audience, I suspect, I certainly 'have to concentrate' and 'don't quite get every word', but he was going on and on, with beautiful gestures, eloquent face and hands part of the language, truly looking 20 years younger than we knew he was, so a good advertisement for part of what he was saying: 'By now I think I have contracted a religious fervour toward the human body. I don't mean the body limited to the skin and five senses but, let us call it, the integral, the magnetic, perhaps mystical body.'

I take this from a translated extract of a mere 150 words that appeared on a little leaflet on our seats, which was simply the first two minutes of a long lecture: 'And so I have wanted to compose a show that celebrates the language of the body by running in bird's eye view over the history of mime, of pantomime, both of breathed language and, more generally, of the "magnetic body".'

He used these exact words from the little leaflet. I make this point partly to convey something of the flavour but also, in view of what subsequently occurred, to make the point that there was a full script. Someone could have provided full programme notes as at a concert. Anyway, after about forty minutes of going on in a French philosophical way about mime being universal language of communication, punctuated or illustrated by two very brief mimes (that of the birds flying and of the man undressing on a stony beach and swimming) just as the paradox of talking about mime so fluently began to dawn on us and just as I was beginning

254

to tire a little—to be honest—at the effort of following a highly abstract discourse in a foreign language, though the sheer delight of watching him and of sharing in this great occasion left me very pleased and quite content, a voice cried out from the gods: ' I am very angry. I cannot understand this.' One of our *enfants du Paradis* stood up in the front row of the upper circle with arms outstretched in a mime of pleading. 'I want to understand you.'

Horror, shock, shame—speaking personally; could it be? No, it wasn't. Barrault stopped, looked half-annoyed, half-amused, gave a wry grin and said in English: 'they asked me to speak in French.' The young mime above continued: 'I forgive you, but I must understand.' Shouts of 'Sit down!' 'Go on', 'Please continue' to Barrault. But some counter-shouts of 'Translation! Translation!' and a bellow in what sounded like Franglais of *'Ce n'est pas un show!'*

He resumed his lecture with dignity and to a huge round of applause. But a drift began, more from the stalls than from the circles or galleries—my eyes were now more on the mob than on the stage. Who can measure crowd sizes on CND demonstrations, still less 'theatrical drift'? But I'd say it was of the order of two to five per cent. Quite enough to be disturbing. He was going on about the different forms of expression that could come from the cervical, thorasic and lumbar vertebrae, when either the volume of noise from little indignation meetings in the side-passages reached him, or another heckle in French (but this time it sounded English: *'Ce n'est pas mime, c'est paroles.'*) He stopped, the shouting and counter-shouting resumed. He walked off. 'Oh the shame of it!' cried the three girls in front of us. After a stunned pause, the overwhelming majority started applauding—a moment's fear that he could misinterpret the applause. But in less than a minute, he returned. I wonder what was said, or what he simply thought for himself? He had every excuse to walk out after being so insulted by an ignorant self-indulgent audience. All right, a misunderstanding about the nature of the occasion, but what lack of manners and respect if we couldn't suffer in silence for 90 minutes. Not merely did he return, but surprisingly dropped his lecture, with the small illustrations of mime, and plunged immediately into famous routines of his youth, the immensely technical and physical *Man Catching a Horse*, full of the symbolism of man's both loving and destroying nature, and the purely amusing, gentle *Fishing* (a mime of the kind of his pupil Marcel Marceau). Few words of explanation, he simply with extraordinary generosity of spirit entertained and calmed the audience: the old entertainer rather than the teacher mystic had us eating out of his hands. The septuagenarian stopped only when he was obviously exhausted.

Tremendous applause and three curtain calls, no encores of course. How can you give an encore in a lecture? A good man in the front shouted: 'I want to say for us all how ashamed we are at this insult to M. Barrault' (or did he actually say, 'national insult'?). But voices answered: 'The management's to blame', 'We didn't come for a lecture'.

I went into the King's Head to join Olly and found a buzzing swarm of angry mimes. They were collecting their ticket-stubs for one of them to write a letter of protest demanding their money back. For unemployed street-entertainers, as most of them were, to pay £9 for a ticket to not understand their hero, and to see but little miming until the uproar changed the evening's course, was sad. Most of them won't go near the Barbican again.

However many times they each had seen *Les Enfants du Paradis*, they evidently didn't know what the great cry from the turbulent gallery had meant: *'L'argent retour! l'argent retour!'* I wish I could have coached them in time. I felt sorry for them, and it so exposed our educational system. The few who 'could follow' were all drop-outs or dedicated artists from 'better schools', that was clear: the evening exposed the difficulties of the classless fraternity of mimes and poor young actors.

The RSC's advance booking forms and publicity said only 'Jean Louis Barrault', gave the date and a quote about him from the *Daily Telegraph*. They treated him like a cult figure, not a human being.

They brought this sad, comic but shameful and revealing episode on themselves. But it was total theatre all right.

Index